The Dynamics of Bureaucracy in the U.S. Government

How Congress and Federal Agencies Process Information and Solve Problems

This book develops a new theoretical perspective on bureaucratic influence and congressional agenda setting based on limited attention and government information processing. Using a comprehensive new dataset on regulatory policy making across the entire federal bureaucracy, Samuel Workman develops the theory of the dual dynamics of congressional agenda setting and bureaucratic problem solving as a way to understand how the U.S. government generates information about and addresses important policy problems. Key to the perspective is a communications framework for understanding the nature of information and signaling between the bureaucracy and Congress concerning the nature of policy problems. Workman finds that congressional influence is innate to the processes of issue shuffling, issue bundling, and the fostering of bureaucratic competition. In turn, bureaucracy influences the congressional agenda through problem monitoring, problem definition, and the provision of information that serves as important feedback in the development of an agenda.

Samuel Workman is an assistant professor of political science at the University of Oklahoma. He has held the positions of J. J. "Jake" Pickle Research Fellow and assistant professor at the University of Texas at Austin. He is affiliated with the Center for Intelligence and National Security and the Center for Risk and Crisis Management, both at the University of Oklahoma. He also serves as the bureaucracy and regulatory policy expert at the Policy Agendas Project at the University of Texas. His work has appeared in *Policy Studies Journal* and the *Journal of Public Administration Research and Theory*.

The Dynamics of Bureaucracy in the U.S. Government

How Congress and Federal Agencies Process Information and Solve Problems

SAMUEL WORKMAN
University of Oklahoma

CAMBRIDGE
UNIVERSITY PRESS

CAMBRIDGE
UNIVERSITY PRESS

32 Avenue of the Americas, New York, NY 10013-2473, USA

Cambridge University Press is part of the University of Cambridge.

It furthers the University's mission by disseminating knowledge in the pursuit of education, learning, and research at the highest international levels of excellence.

www.cambridge.org
Information on this title: www.cambridge.org/9781107061101

First published 2015

A catalog record for this publication is available from the British Library.

Library of Congress Cataloging in Publication Data
Workman, Samuel, 1979–
The dynamics of bureaucracy in the U.S. government : how Congress and federal agencies process information and solve problems / Samuel Workman.
    pages   cm
Includes bibliographical references and index.
ISBN 978-1-107-06110-1 (hardback)
1. United States. Congress – History.   2. Bureaucracy – United States – History.   I. Title.
JK1021.W67   2015
352.3'80973–dc23   2014043079

ISBN 978-1-107-06110-1 Hardback

Contents

List of Illustrations

List of Tables

Acknowledgments

In developing the idea that was to become this book, I have left a trail of intellectual debt in my wake. Bryan Jones was a major source of encouragement, sometimes over coffee, sometimes over a cold beer. Always as kind as he was sharp and encouraging, our conversations about bureaucracies, the nature of human decision making, and organizations have given life to the central theme of this book and his criticism sharpened my argument considerably. I also owe an enormous debt to Peter May. Much of our time together was spent in the middle of the water trying to win "Goosepumps" races in the frigid waters of Lake Union with an amateur crew. Our conversations about regulatory politics formed the empirical foundation for the argument presented here and, more importantly, my thinking about how bureaucracies go about making policy. As engaging scholars, mentors, and friends, I could never thank them enough.

Several scholars offered thoughtful criticism of my ideas and approach, and they deserve mention. Frank Baumgartner is chief among these. Frank has been as persistent in forcing me to hone my argument as he has been encouraging. Frank provided advice at critical moments in the development of the ideas presented here. Jeff Worsham at West Virginia University first sparked my interest in the study of bureaucracy and deserves credit for pushing me to think differently about it. I would also like to thank Andy Whitford, David Lewis, and Susan Yackee, all of whom were kind enough to read a portion of the argument or sit down to discuss the project with me at various conferences.

Many colleagues and friends offered valuable thoughts on the work and my approach. Among these, Christian Breunig, Josh Sapotichne, Graeme Boushey, and John Ahlquist deserve mention. It is a valuable thing in life to have friends who will look you in the eye and tell you that an idea or approach is bad.

Collecting and coding every item on the regulatory agenda of the federal bureaucracy is not something that can be accomplished without resources. To that end, I am grateful for a National Science Foundation dissertation award that supported this project at its earliest stages. In particular, I thank Brian Humes at NSF's political science program. Along with the support of the NSF, David Pritzker and John Thomas at the Regulatory Information Service (RIS) were instrumental in helping me to gather the needed files to accomplish such a large project. David in particular was never too busy to discuss the project in person or on the phone.

Many of the folks at Cambridge deserve thanks for seeing this argument to fruition and guiding me along the way from submission to production. I owe the greatest debt to Lew Bateman for his consistent patience and support of this research. Anyone who has talked with Lew understands his amazing grasp of a large number of fields. Lew saw the value in my argument very early and pushed me to speak to citizens and not just scholars. Shaun Vigil also played a major role in moving the work through the various stages of the process. He was never too tired to field an email or answer a question from a first-time author twice.

In closing, I would like to thank my family. William, Vivian, Michael, Abby, and Jason have been an inextinguishable source of support, encouragement, and belief. Conversations over hot tea and coffee before dawn with my father and grandfather on a small farm ignited much of my interest in politics and public policy. Finally, I would like to thank Sheri for her love and support in the final mile of the project, providing a respite from bureaucracies, signaling, and models.

I

Bureaucracy and Problem Solving

"In fact, organizations can be remarkably effective devices for working out difficult public problems.... Formal authority travels from top to bottom in organizations, but the informal authority that derives from expertise, skill, and proximity to the essential tasks that an organization performs travels in the opposite direction...this means that formal authority, in the form of policy statements, is heavily dependent upon specialized problem-solving capabilities further down the chain of authority."

– Richard F. Elmore (1979, p. 606)

1.1 WHAT IS THIS BOOK ABOUT?

This book develops a theory of dual dynamics within the administrative state in the United States. Agenda setting in the administrative state is characterized by the dual dynamics of information provision and communication by the bureaucracy and simultaneous "tuning" of this information supply by Congress. Bureaucratic problem solving generates a flow of information to Congress as bureaucracies monitor the agenda for potential problems, define these problems for action at higher levels of government, and transmit information pursuant to these definitions. The information supply generated by bureaucracy both influences and informs congressional problem prioritization such as efforts to shape that supply through issue shuffling, issue bundling, and congressional manipulation of bureaucratic competition in the provision of information.

By developing and extending systems and communications frameworks to the study of bureaucracy, I lay out an explanation of agenda setting in the United States as a product of a communications system characterized by feedback and the competitive provision of information in steering problem definitions. It subsumes classical top-down, preference-driven approaches in a more complete explanation of agenda setting in the administrative state.

The empirical foundation of the book is a dataset comprising the policy-making agenda of the entire federal bureaucracy over a quarter-century. The dataset is enormous, containing 226,710 regulations issued by all bureaucracies in the federal government since the early 1980s. In addition, this dataset is unique, having no peer in academia, the public sector, or elsewhere: it is the first and only of its kind. Collecting, organizing, and coding the data represented an enormous outlay of time and effort.

The development of the dual dynamics of the administrative state required a dataset that was not only issue sensitive but also comparable to data gathered by other institutions of government. Using the Policy Agendas Project coding scheme, I gave each regulation an issue code, making it comparable to similar data for Congress. The coding of the regulations by issue was an interactive process between specialist and machine. I personally hand-coded 40,000 regulations and used them as a training database for the coding of the remaining regulations. Using an iterative coding process, I trained an automated text-coding machine to recognize and code (i.e., "learn to code") the remaining regulations, with routine samples drawn for reliability. The empirical strategy used here represents a useful template for how large-scale, nonsurvey, archival research may be accomplished through the interaction of specialist and machine in the social sciences generally (typically these types of projects are completely computer-based).

This book focuses on the influence of the federal bureaucracy in setting the issue agenda in the United States. Which issues become prioritized for government attention is strongly influenced by information provided by the bureaucracy on various policy problems. The bureaucracy expands the capacity of the governing system to address important problems by detecting their emergence, defining them for government action, and providing information about them to elected officials. I use the issue agenda of the federal bureaucracy over the past quarter-century to examine how and when issue attention in the bureaucracy influences the prioritization of problems in Congress.

What I call the *dual dynamics* of agenda setting characterize the environment in which bureaucratic influence occurs. From above, the bureaucracy influences the process of policy making within the strictures of democratic politics and the rule of law (Bertelli and Lynn, 2006), which subordinate the bureaucracy to the elected branches of government. From below, the bureaucracy monitors potential problems, including their severity, and generates information that forms the basis for policy and political calculations at higher reaches of government. What is true of Elmore's (1979) organizations described in the epigraph is true of government generally. The elected branches of government must influence the bureaucracy, yet setting an agenda for action and, in fact, taking action require bureaucratic expertise emanating from proximity to various policy problems. The information generated by bureaucratic proximity to problems is influence.

From the perspective of the dual dynamics characterizing agenda setting, a vastly different view of federal bureaucracies comes into focus. Accompanying this view is the realization that the "front end" of the policy process is more important in understanding the place of bureaucracy in the policy process than scholars have previously recognized. Problem definition and agenda setting, both central ideas in the study of the policy process generally (Cobb and Elder, 1972; Dery, 1984; Kingdon, 1984; Dodd and Schott, 1986; Rochefort and Cobb, 1994), are immensely important in understanding the influence of bureaucracy in the policy process.

Given the emphasis on the way in which bureaucracies detect potential problems, aid in defining them, and generate a supply of information about them, a different view of how bureaucracies present themselves in the policy process is necessary. If the supply of information yields bureaucratic influence, then bureaucracies must be willing to be attention-seeking and attention-attracting organizations, rather than the backroom dealers of subsystem lore. The dual dynamics of agenda setting engender a more open system of interaction and influence based on communicating information about policy problems. In this context, understanding how bureaucracies help set the agenda and define problems is of importance, even to preference-based theories of bureaucratic oversight.

Bringing the dual dynamics of agenda setting into focus requires a major departure from the standard approach to understanding bureaucratic-congressional interactions, which is centered on information as a privately held good (Alchian and Demsetz, 1972; Mitnick, 1975; McCubbins, 1985; Epstein and O'Halloran, 1999; Gailmard and Patty, 2012). Under this standard approach, uncertainty plagues the decision making of policy makers and stems from information asymmetry: bureaucrats have it, whereas elected officials do not. Instead, the dual dynamics approach of agenda setting takes the perspective that uncertainty is rooted in the difficulty of defining policy problems and results from competition among bureaucracies over the generation and supply of information about these problems. The core problem relating to information in policy making is not its paucity, but that it is attended by noise. Given these principles, this book sets out to understand the role of bureaucracy in agenda setting and adopts a perspective grounded in a communications framework.

Bureaucracy may foster or hinder the adaptability of government to the set of problems on the agenda, depending on the nature of information gathering and processing in the system. The central questions as related to the quality of governance then become: how and when does bureaucracy expand the ability of government to address problems important to elected officials and citizens alike? Further, under what conditions does bureaucracy facilitate government's ability to process information about policy problems and incorporate it into policy making, hence, enhancing governmental responsiveness? What do reforms aimed at the bureaucracy or its relationship with political overseers imply for the ability of government to address important policy problems?

1.2 WHY THIS BOOK? WHY NOW?

Understanding how and when bureaucracy enables government to address important and pressing policy problems is particularly important because elected officials face looming decisions about the size and scope of the federal government in the coming years. The changes wrought by these decisions could have drastic consequences for the numbers and types of problems that government may be expected to address and solve.

These decisions are much more basic than what government will do and how big the bureaucracy will be. The decisions of policy makers and citizens alike are largely influenced by information generated by the government itself, most especially by bureaucracies. For citizens, housing decisions based on crime rates, interest rates, and available services; retirement questions based on the fiscal health of corporations; public health decisions based on information concerning likely epidemics; and information concerning extreme weather or natural disasters are all examples of the day-to-day decisions profoundly affected by the ability of the government to generate information concerning these problems. For policy makers, decisions concerning such weighty issues as climate change, homeland security, and economic growth require a steady stream of information generated by governing institutions. Most of this information is undersupplied in the private sector or is inadequate in the context of competitive pressures. As a consequence, a key question for the governing system concerns how to reform the system and make policy with an eye toward preserving the supply of information and analysis necessary for many of these day-to-day decisions, regardless of preferences for governmental intervention or the private sector provision of public services (see Williams, 1998).

In modern American politics, the importance of policy making in the bureaucracy is heightened by the persistence of features of politics such as divided government, polarization (Theriault, 2008), and the interdependency and complexity of problems that span the boundaries of traditional issues (May et al., 2009a, 2011). In this context, administrative policy making is a mode of governing and politics. Its centrality to the U.S. system is borne out in the way that members of Congress and presidents have chosen to spend their time and go about making policy over the past thirty years. For instance, Congress spends an increasing amount of time in oversight as compared to other activities. Hearings that are primarily geared toward oversight of federal agencies and programs have exceeded 90 percent of activity in recent years,[1] and their importance has been strengthened by passage of the Congressional Review Act

---

[1] For data concerning hearing activity, see www.policyagendas.org.

(CRS, 2008).[2] As a result, members of Congress and their staff now spend less time crafting and passing legislation (Aberbach, 1990). Lest this is assumed to be strictly a congressional phenomenon in an age of presidential government, the president now also spends a tremendous amount of energy and capital on what scholars have termed the "administrative presidency" or an "administrative strategy" (Moe, 1989; Golden, 2000; Lewis, 2003; Rudavelige, 2005; Lewis, 2008). This is government by delegation and oversight.

Furthermore, the centrality of administrative policy making is not confined to the day-to-day activities and strategies of the president and members of Congress. Interbranch conflict, from Reagan through Obama, has come to center on the nature and activities of the federal bureaucracy. This conflict has been further reflected in popular political rhetoric of the past thirty years. Our major political debates have come to center both on how much government should do and how it should act – the how pertaining most strictly to the bureaucracy. The ability to steer bureaucracy directly influences how government intersects, or interfaces, with its citizens. Because citizens primarily interact with government through bureaucrats or at least come to "know" government through experiencing regulations and programs administered by bureaucrats, both party and institutional conflict necessarily come to rest on influencing the nature and prevalence of these interactions.

An understanding of bureaucratic influence in the policy process also goes a long way toward the formulation of criteria for the evaluation of governance. Major decisions in the coming quarter-century regarding the size and power of the federal bureaucracy must be made with a firm understanding of the precise part played by bureaucracy in the policy process and, further, of what is to be gained and lost from reforming or adapting this process. Bureaucracies must balance responsiveness to politics and the general direction of policy suggested by larger macro-political dynamics with problem solving and addressing problems important to citizens and policy makers.

For instance, there exists a need to understand regulatory failure in the context of the politics of the dual dynamics of agenda setting. Potential reforms pursuant to regulatory or service provision disasters such as Enron, Katrina, and the Deepwater Horizon oil rig explosion (and the accompanying environmental fallout) must be made with an eye toward the particular politics that characterize the dual dynamics within which federal agencies operate. Bureaucracies sit at the hub of the dual dynamics engendered by authority relations and expertise.

Finally, political scientists have debated for some time the distinction between responsive and neutral competence (Aberbach and Rockman, 1988; Moe, 1989; Lewis, 2003; Aberbach and Rockman, 2005; Huber, 2007) and the connection of each type of competence to effective governmental performance (Lewis, 2008). To some degree, this debate fails to separate what is

[2] 5 U.S.C. §801–808; P.L. 104–121.

from what should be. The position of the bureaucracy in the American policy process embodies the best and worst features of each perspective – and this is perhaps the most fundamental truth or fault line in the policy process in the United States, a truth that neither bureaucrats nor elected officials can escape. Bureaucrats must monitor the agenda for problems, yet the way in which they search, even the problems that they are able to identify, and the way they become defined are strongly colored by the broader political forces that influence which issues get prioritized in Congress. On the one hand, members of Congress desire, indeed need, to be able to influence bureaucrats and interject when necessary. Yet, on the other hand, their interjecting has the potential to either increase the quantity and quality of information from the bureaucracy or hinder its production. Elected officials must hold the reins of influence, but not too tightly.

1.3 DUAL DYNAMICS, OR "ELMORE'S PROBLEM"

I begin with the assertion that Elmore's observation concerning authority and expertise in organizations holds for government generally. In the American political system, democratic authority and legitimacy flow downward from elected officials to bureaucrats, whereas the information deriving from expertise on which collective decisions are based flows upward from the bureaucracy to elected institutions. The tension created by democratic authority and bureaucratic expertise forms what I call the *dual dynamics* of agenda setting. These dual dynamics create a tension in the policy process because elected officials must influence the bureaucracy, setting out a general direction for policy, yet the bureaucracy supplies the information on which many policy decisions and political calculations are based.

I further assert that the primary function of government is to address policy problems, if not solve them. Though "problem responsiveness" varies with political institutions and even across countries, political institutions and governments in general attempt to address problems important to citizens (Jones and Baumgartner, 2005; Jones et al., 2009; Soroka and Wlezien, 2009). The government is bombarded, almost continually with issues and problems that demand attention. The set of problems confronting government and citizens alike constitute the agenda (Kingdon, 1984). There are many reasons, both political and practical, for taking this problem-centered agenda as a major point of departure. The adaptability of government is critically linked to its ability to define and incorporate new and changed issues in policy making as necessary or as demanded by citizens. For example, much of the earlier discussion around the development of an approach to what is now homeland security revolved around ascertaining the general contours of the problem itself, what relevant issues were involved, and how to understand a problem that spanned the boundaries of several existing issues on the agenda. To understand the politics underlying the dual dynamics of agenda setting, it is necessary to recognize that these dynamics and the tension they engender occur in a governing system whose primary focus is addressing and processing information about problems.

1.3.1 Leveraging Studies of the Policy Process

Attention to the policy process and research based on the policy process provide a useful lens for coming to grips with the tension created by the dual dynamics of agenda setting. Dual dynamics govern a system whose primary concern is addressing policy problems by detecting, defining, and processing information about real and potential policy problems. Research in the policy process has long focused on the processes of problem definition, agenda setting, and how organizations and government generally deal with the vagaries of limited attention when attempting to process information about emergent issues and problems.

From this vantage point, several implications are important. First, research in the policy process has always understood delegation to bureaucrats and accompanying discretion as the norm in American politics. That delegation is the norm is borne out in the immense amount of attention given to control and influence after the fact by policy makers and scholars alike. However, studies of the policy process usually relegate depictions of the role of the bureaucracy in the policy process to policy implementation or studies of enforcement. In contrast, the argument put here makes bureaucracy central to understanding agenda-setting dynamics and the front end of the policy process in which issues are prioritized and laws are developed.

Second, Congress delegates to the bureaucracy for the purposes of detecting emergent policy problems and generating usable information about these problems, and not simply for purposes of program implementation. Bureaucracies are the main analytical units of government. They are charged with generating a supply of information for decisions and, even more importantly, with informing elected officials about the amount of uncertainty faced by policy makers: bureaucracies inform the system of what is not known.

For example, the U.S. Senate Committee on Agriculture, Nutrition, and Forestry met on February 14, 2013, to discuss the effects of severe weather on the agricultural economy. The hearing is instructive first because the bureaucrats asked to testify were not cabinet-level bureaucrats or under-secretaries, as would be the case when committees are intent on uncovering the preferences and stance of the president in regard to oversight. Instead, the chief economist of the U.S. Department of Agriculture and the director of the National Integrated Drought Information System (of the National Oceanic and Atmospheric Administration) were called to discuss the uncertainty surrounding the abnormally severe weather of the previous year and its likely impact on agricultural production and markets. This is an indication of the committee's demand for policy-relevant information, rather than for the positioning information usually yielded by calling bureaucrats closer to the president. Second, the two bureaucrats' testimonies centered on the information generated and the forecasts for weather, agricultural production, and market values for these goods. In other words, there was very little oversight in the traditional sense. The hearing served to set the state of knowledge, of what is known, about the particular problem. The final point worth noting in the hearing is that, apart from delivering information on the state of the problem, the testimonies conveyed what is *not known*: they conveyed the uncertainty facing bureaucrats and policy makers alike.

Pursuant to this stance, bureaucrats are influential and derive their autonomy in part from problem expertise. Understanding what constitutes a problem, and thereafter how to understand the problem, is as important as and, in fact, is a prerequisite to, developing and implementing a solution. Moreover, this type of attention-driven problem expertise generates an alternative foundation for the sources of bureaucratic autonomy. Finally, authoritative decisions from political overseers have a strong bearing on the information that the system will be able to produce and the problems it will be able to detect and define in the future. From these implications, one may begin to see the connections between the dual dynamics of political authority and legitimacy and bureaucratic expertise.

1.3.2 Bottom-Up Problem Detection and Definition

To address the array of problems or issues confronting government, two conditions must be met. First, the institutions of government have to be aware that there is in fact a problem. Alongside other notables in an American system defined by pluralist governing arrangements, bureaucracies play a vital role in the policy process in identifying existing and emergent policy problems. Quite simply, bureaucrats are paying attention when problems and concerns have left the halls of Congress and are far from the mind of the average citizen. Bureaucratic influence in the policy process depends on being attentive to problems that bureaucrats monitor at the behest of elected officials.

Once detected, problems must also be defined in such a way that makes government action possible (Dery, 1984; Rochefort and Cobb, 1994). This is an important process because it is integral not only to formulating solutions to the problems (i.e., public policies) but it also allows for the understanding of the problem in terms of simpler dimensions such as preferences and ideologies (Simon, 1947; Poole and Rosenthal, 1997; Jones, 2001). Studies of the policy process have demonstrated sometimes drastic shifts in attention to substantive issues (Baumgartner and Jones, 1993). Whereas preferences over solutions (e.g., market mechanisms versus regulation) are fairly stable, preferences over problems are not (e.g., risk-accepting financial institutions versus consumer credit).

Finally, how bureaucrats come to understand problems influences the quantity and types of information generated in the policy process. Bureaucracies generate information concerning problems detected and identified and pass this information along to Congress. This information, which itself is derived from how bureaucrats define the problem or issue, becomes part of the basis for congressional decision making. Although ultimately unable to influence congressional decisions to a large degree, bureaucrats often determine the parameters of choice.

1.3.3 Top-Down Prioritization, Synthesis, and Feedback

For Congress, the problem becomes one of prioritizing problems (Jones and Baumgartner, 2005), synthesizing the information generated by the bureaucracy's problem monitoring, and coordinating government activity to address the problems. Even in an institution as robust as the U.S. Congress, attention is limited and zero-sum: attention allocated to one issue necessarily means less attention to other issues or problems. The nature of attention in Congress, indeed in all political institutions, means that Congress is presented with tradeoffs among issues. Prioritizing among these issues is perhaps the most important function of elected officials (and rightfully so in a representative democracy).

In addition to making difficult decisions about the prioritization of the various issues that are on the agenda, members of Congress must synthesize the vast amount of sometimes conflicting information presented about the relative importance and severity of problems. Whereas bureaucracies often operate within issue spaces that are comparatively neatly defined, members of Congress operate in an entropic environment in which issues are often interdependent. Boundary-spanning policy problems such as homeland security, climate change, energy, and food security place tremendous demands on the ability of members of the system to forge a working definition of these problems. This demands the synthesizing of vast amounts of disparate information generated from the bottom of the policy process where bureaucracies monitor existing and emergent problems.

Finally, Congress must coordinate the government's response to the issues that become prioritized. These decisions have far-reaching implications for the performance of the system in regard to future problems, including what information will form the basis of future policy decisions through delegation to particular bureaucracies. Authoritative decisions in Congress favor some problem definitions over others; they also structure the kind of information that bureaucracies will generate in the future and even what types of problems will be detected by government. Put straightforwardly, congressional decision making strongly influences the types of problems and information that members of Congress will receive in the future from federal agencies.

1.4 MY APPROACH

I begin from the perspective that the administrative state constitutes a system whose primary concern is addressing policy problems by detecting, defining, and processing information about these problems. This concern with addressing policy problems generates the dual dynamics of agenda setting, for which the fundamental principle is the limited attention of all organizations. The bureaucracy generates information on policy problems, fueling political calculations and policy decisions at higher reaches of government. In turn, elected officials adjust the system of problem monitoring pursuant to the information generated by bureaucracy, much like tuning an antenna for better reception and a clearer signal. The theoretical and empirical focus of this research is on the dynamics of bureaucratic signaling about policy problems and how this signaling influences policy making at higher levels of government.

My approach offers a unique perspective on three fronts. First, bureaucratic influence stems primarily from the attention limits of political institutions as opposed to expertise or agenda control. The federal bureaucracy economizes on these attention limits. By paying attention to problems not currently on the institutional agenda of the elected branches of government, the bureaucracy allows the governing system to address many more issues than would otherwise be possible, potentially fostering adaptability and flexibility under a changing agenda.

Second, existing literature based on control or, at least, influence necessarily emphasizes the preferences of bureaucrats and elected officials with regard to policy solutions rather than policy problems. The most typical line of questioning proceeds by asking whether bureaucratic activities and behaviors are reducible (or not) to incentive systems designed by political overseers, because their preferences are stand-ins for citizen preferences. The "problem" is generated from the presumption that bureaucratic activity should be reducible altogether or in great part to popular political will for democracy to function and flourish. I argue instead that there is an important and more dynamic interaction between the bureaucracy and Congress that layers over the development and maintenance of these systems for control and influence. This process – the dual dynamics of political authority and bureaucratic expertise – pertains primarily to setting the agenda for government. Yet, this transmission of information by the bureaucracy and steering of the process by Congress set the stage for a more complete understanding of the development and implementation of solutions and a more complete view of bureaucracy in the policy process.

The theory of dual dynamics draws attention to the ways in which federal agencies signal the dimensions of policy problems relevant to choice at higher levels of government, rather than examining particular preferences with regard to solutions. From this vantage point, bureaucracies play an important part in U.S. policy making because of their expertise and proximity to problems, rather than to solutions.

In place of an emphasis on preferences and control, the theory of dual dynamics offered here analytically severs the problem space and the solution space of issues.[3] Bureaucracies detect and identify problems contained in the policy environment. The attributes of problems that bureaucracies choose to transmit to Congress help form the working definition of the problems that are detected and identified. The distinction between the problem space and solution (or alternative) space of issues dates to Newell and Simon's (1972) path-breaking theory of problem solving, in which they argue that issues can be broken down into their component problem and solution spaces. They claim that problem solving requires first the construction of a representation or definition of the problem at hand and then the choice of alternatives pursuant to a particular representation of the problem. Put simply, problem spaces are the set of attributes or dimensions relevant for choice. Thus, agenda setting and problem definition are precursors to the application of preferences in choosing public policies.

Consequently, the empirical focus of this research is on policy agendas in the federal bureaucracy, rather than on program implementation and regulatory enforcements prevalent in most studies of the federal bureaucracy. This strategy moves beyond the examination of agency enforcement actions and other downstream agency outputs, which are themselves products of substantive decisions made at an earlier point in time, and turns attention to substantive agency agendas and how they influence and are influenced by politics at higher levels of government. Thus, this book examines the front end of the policy process, which is a point of departure from most studies of bureaucracy, which tend to focus on bureaucratic drift in policy implementation.

Third, dual dynamics in the system are fostered by a feedback mechanism from the bureaucracy to Congress. The essence of this feedback mechanism is the capacity of the federal bureaucracy to monitor problems and provide information on these problems. The system is cumulative in the sense that each delegation to the bureaucracy feeds back into policy making via the agenda-setting activities of the federal bureaucracy, further layering policy change on delegation on policy change and so forth, as the process of adjustment to changes in the policy environment iterates over time. Congress and the bureaucracy interact to produce approximate solutions to problems on an ever-changing agenda, allowing for an adaptable, real-time adjustment to the agenda. This iterative process subsumes the traditional view of the process as hierarchically structured. Existing studies of bureaucracy take a largely top-down view of the administrative system and fail to consider bureaucracy's

---

[3] There are some issues for which problem spaces are nearly inseparable from attendant solutions such that the set of solutions defines the problem (Jones, 2001, p. 66).

considerable influence as these top-down delegations feed back into decision making at higher levels of government.

In terms of both theory and empirical focus, any analysis of the policy process necessarily highlights some characteristics of the system and places less weight on others. My approach aims to shed light on the general dynamics that drive information processing between bureaucracy and Congress as each institution addresses policy problems. This approach necessarily means that less attention is paid to the institutional structure of Congress or given federal agencies. The same is true of preferences – whether of individual policy makers or the revealed preferences embodied in the collective decisions of political institutions. Although these are important considerations, they are often empirically peculiar to the particular actor or policy area that is the focus of research. Thus, research on the bureaucracy often proceeds in piecemeal fashion and is often not cumulative. I eschew the focus on particular federal agencies at particular points in time in favor of the goal of identifying the broad processes that characterize agenda setting in the administrative state. This focus means that other prominent institutions such as the president, courts, the media, and interest groups will remain in the background.

I have constructed a large archival dataset of federal rulemaking activity to assess the operation of dual dynamics in agenda setting between the bureaucracy and Congress. Analyzing the interplay of bureaucracy and Congress in addressing policy problems requires developing a research strategy that allows for the comparison of attention to the same issues among the different institutions of government and how this attention changes over time. To accomplish this objective, I use the topic coding scheme developed at the Policy Agendas Project (see Appendix A) to code the dataset on agenda setting in the federal bureaucracy; use of this coding scheme makes these data both reliable over time and directly comparable to attention to the same issues in the other institutions of government. The collection and coding of this large, comprehensive dataset form a strong empirical foundation for the findings and theoretical contribution of the research.

1.5 PLAN OF THE BOOK

The following chapters develop a theory of bureaucratic influence nestled within the dual dynamics of agenda setting in the United States. Throughout the book, the focus is on the interaction of the federal bureaucracy and the U.S. Congress in addressing the issues confronting government. The American system of government embodies a fundamental tension – "Elmore's problem" – between successful governmental problem solving and democratic responsiveness that lies at the core of concerns about the place of bureaucracy in the policy process.

Chapter 2 begins by considering what elected officials "see" and "hear" when they look out across the expanse of the federal bureaucracy. The chapter develops the logic underlying the dual dynamics of agenda setting and problem solving, focusing on bureaucratic influence in the American political system. In addressing the agenda, bureaucrats and members of Congress communicate about policy problems in a medium filled with the noise of everyday issue politicking. The key animating force of these dual dynamics is the notion that bureaucracies expand the carrying capacity of the governmental agenda by economizing on the attention limits of Congress.

Bureaucracies monitor policy problems and the potential for emergent problems. The argument centers on the nature of communication between the federal bureaucracy and Congress about these real and potential problems. The organization of elected and administrative institutions relative to one another influences their communication and how this communication shapes the response of the system to policy issues over time. The dual dynamics generated by bureaucratic influence and governmental problem solving reflect different positions in the constitutional order of the American system of governance and determine the broad patterns of adjustment and adaption to the agenda over time.

The argument is orthogonal to many existing conceptions of bureaucracy in the American political system because it highlights bureaucracies as attention-seeking and attention-directing institutions vital to the system of problem monitoring, rather than as smoky-room policy makers. Bureaucracies institutionalize problems just as they institutionalize solutions to them (see Dery, 1984, p. 35). Bureaucracies generate information about policy problems, alerting Congress to important issues as they emerge on the agenda and leaving their own institutional trace on this information as it is passed up the ladder of government. Because of this institutional trace, Congress receives signals or clues about the nature and content of the agenda confronting government.

Chapter 3 begins with a detailed discussion of the history and process of regulatory policy making as laid out in the Administrative Procedures Act of 1946.[4] This discussion offers three insights on the process of regulatory policy making and its importance to understanding the broader governing system. First, it highlights the fact that the process of regulatory policy making resembles legislative policy making much more than presidential policy-making processes, despite the bureaucracy's location in the executive branch. Second, the depiction of regulatory policy making also reveals how the development of regulations leads to the generation of both policy-relevant and politics-relevant information. Third, and finally, the discussion demonstrates the relevance of regulatory policy making for the ability of the governing system to adapt in the face of a dynamic issue agenda.

Chapter 4 argues for the importance of thinking about and coming to grips with the agenda of the federal bureaucracy in light of key conflicts and debates concerning the relationship between the executive and legislative branches of

---

[4] P.L. 79-404; 5 U.S.C. §500 et seq.

government. Conflict among the elected branches of government, and indeed between the two mass political parties, has been fueled by debate on the nature, scope, and control of the bureaucratic levers of government. Political rhetoric on both sides of the aisle over the last thirty years testifies to the centrality of bureaucracy (or debates thereabout) in American policy making. Indeed, the chapter demonstrates a rise over the last thirty years in administrative policy making and oversight as a mode of governance.

Given the increasing centrality of bureaucracy to American politics, Chapter 4 introduces a comprehensive new dataset on agenda setting in the federal bureaucracy and develops the measures used to assess the bottom-up influence of bureaucracy as one side of the dual dynamics governing agenda setting. Borrowing from communications frameworks, it develops, conceptually and empirically, signal-to-noise ratios and signal amplitudes to begin to relate bureaucratic policy agendas to those in Congress. Chapter 4 demonstrates the importance of institutional organization for the content and dynamics of communication from the bureaucracy.

It also highlights the importance of the partisan and structural features of American politics in structuring bureaucratic problem monitoring. The dual dynamics of agenda setting occur in relation to not only an ever-changing set of issues confronting government but also changing partisan and institutional configurations of American politics through time. Given these two features, Chapter 4 demonstrates that the popular notion of slothful, inertial federal bureaucracy is inaccurate. The federal bureaucracy resides at the hub, along with Congress, of a dynamic system of communication, information processing, and agenda change.

Chapter 5 begins by assessing congressional problem prioritization and how these processes influence information generation and problem solving in the bureaucracy. Perhaps the greatest determinant of how Congress steers the system of information processing is party control of Congress. Using differential party control of Congress, Chapter 5 examines how the problem monitoring and the generation of information in the bureaucracy change as Congress engages in issue shuffling and issue bundling and alters bureaucratic competition in the monitoring of policy problems.

Equally important, the chapter demonstrates that the dual dynamics are a product of issue attention and attempts by each institution and its members to process the information about policy problems. This response to problems is not solely a function of lawmaking and structural hierarchy. Congress need not write statutes to direct bureaucratic attention, and bureaucracies need not rely on technical expertise to influence the congressional agenda. The emerging theory subsumes traditional principal-agent approaches to the interaction of bureaucracy and Congress. Congressional agenda dynamics foster a context in which control of and influence on bureaucracy are innate to the system of addressing problems. At its base, incentive structures are not absolutely necessary, because influence stems from issue prioritization and information about policy problems.

This is an important finding, because it speaks to the dynamic adaptability of the system even in the presence of divided government, polarization, and difficulty issuing policies from the elected branches of government. Government responsiveness and democratic direction of public policy are possible even under the strictures of many of these features of politics. Each institution struggles to address and adapt to the changing agenda confronting government. This interaction produces a dynamic adjustment and adaptation to various issues over time. Understanding this interaction yields important implications for attempts to reform the policy process in the United States.

Chapter 6 assesses the bottom-up influence of bureaucracy on the problems monitored in the system, the development of problem definitions at higher levels of government, and the provision of feedback about the issue agenda. The chapter finds that the carrying capacity of the system in terms of issues is heavily dependent on problem monitoring in the bureaucracy. In particular, the bureaucratic agenda serves to concentrate or disperse the issue agenda in Congress, functioning as a potent signal about the range of problems. The chapter also examines problem definition in policies in energy and public lands & water, finding that particular bureaucracies vary over time in their influence and ability to affect problem definitions in Congress. The chapter concludes by demonstrating substantial feedback between policy agendas in the bureaucracy and those in Congress for most major issues in American politics.

In Chapter 7, I discuss the relevance of this approach to how we view the place of bureaucracy in the policy process in the United States. The key question relating to bureaucratic influence is whether the bureaucracy enhances or hinders the government's ability to address problems important to the broader public: I offer this as a new criterion for judging the quality of democracy. I also discuss the relevance of the central argument for the size of government, especially where privatization and contracting are concerned. This discussion highlights the "hidden" costs of deregulation in an era that has witnessed deregulation in large swathes of society and the economy. The perspective offered here brings these tradeoffs into sharper focus. These hidden costs present an administrative or organizational problem for elected officials and citizens. The set of choices surrounding bureaucracy, especially in agenda setting, largely determine the ability of government to address problems important to us as citizens.

The Dual Dynamics of the Administrative State

The primary business of government is understanding and responding to problems. Democratic systems must address important and salient policy problems facing citizens, groups, and policy makers. This simple assumption is relevant to understanding not only the part played by bureaucracy in policy making but also democracy itself in a system in which citizens rely on elected officials and bureaucrats alike to address and solve problems they deem important. Put another way, democratic control of the federal administrative apparatus is meaningless if elected officials do not muster bureaucratic might in an effort to address policy problems important to attentive citizens. The quality of democracy depends in part on whether important problems make their way to elected officials for consideration and decision.

What Is the Administrative State?

Dual dynamics characterize the relationship between the bureaucracy and Congress and govern policymaking in what Dodd and Schott (1986) famously termed the administrative state. By "administrative state," I mean the set of administrative and elected institutions that make policy on a day-to-day basis on various issues. The most significant bureaucracies and congressional institutions, especially committees, are those involved in monitoring and making policy in various issue areas. The administrative state also includes actors less visible in the process such as committee staff. In the terms of a much older literature, the administrative state is the collection of subsystems governing policy making in more or less defined issue areas.

What Is a Problem?

Given that government is geared toward processing information about policy problems, it is worth defining what constitutes a policy problem. The

institutions of government must be able to detect problems, generate information about them, and formulate a definition of them that allows the generation of solutions or alternatives. Simon (1979, p. 147) likens the defining of policy problems to a maze (also see Dery, 1984, p. 25). Whereas
most scholarship addresses the choice among alternatives (i.e., different paths
through the maze), problem definition involves the construction of the maze
itself.

Policy problems have their roots in two types of changes that occur within
and across issues on the agenda. The first is a discrepancy between something
observed and what is expected. When policies do not yield the expected outcomes, this results in the identification of a problem. However, problems need
not have a basis in existing public policies or involve a mismatch between policy and real-world conditions. Problems also arise as a result of disturbances
within issues monitored by bureaucrats and policy makers alike. Whereas discrepancies often have to do with gauging the performance of the system on a
problem, disturbances refer to emergent policy problems with which government has not before dealt. The most publicized disturbances in recent times
have been associated with terrorism and climate change. In each instance, public policy had to be adapted to address issues that differed from past experience
in traditional issue areas such as the environment, energy, civil defense, and
public risks. Both discrepancies and disturbances may lead to the detection
and identification of a problem worthy of consideration by bureaucrats and
policymakers.

Closely related to discrepancies and disturbances is Dery's (1984, pp. 24–27)
notion of problems as either bridgeable discrepancies or problems as opportunities. Both of these notions relate the recognition of problems to potential
action in the form of public policy. In the case of problems as bridgeable gaps or
discrepancies, policy makers and bureaucrats must envision some solution that
would bridge the gap between what is and what can reasonably be expected.
In this situation, policy makers are able to construct a problem in such a way
that it can be "made better" with public policy.

The notion that problems represent opportunities attaches particular definitions and potential solutions to problems. How a problem is defined and how
solutions or alternatives are generated depends on who is paying attention
to the problem. The U.S. Department of Agriculture (USDA) defines climate
change much differently than the Environmental Protection Agency (EPA).
For the USDA, the definition of climate change centers on its ramifications
for the food supply and commodities markets. Given this definition, climate
change may very well represent an opportunity for the USDA. In fact, it did
so when the USDA appeared alongside the EPA to argue for policies regarding carbon sequestration (farmers would receive subsidies to re-forest certain
acreage). Problems represent opportunities when bureaucracies are able to
build influence in steering policy pursuant to the problem. In the case of generating information for use in policy making, problems represent opportunities

for bureaucracies to maneuver into more prominent positions as purveyors of information to elected officials.

To sum up, problems represent discrepancies between public policies, on the one hand, and observable conditions, on the other. In terms of governmental problem solving, problems must represent bridgeable gaps; that is, those monitoring and detecting the problem must envision a public policy solution. Alternatively, problems may be identified as resulting from disturbances, which produce a fundamental change in the issues confronting government. Bureaucracies, and policy makers more broadly, may view these disturbances as opportunities to craft particular problem definitions and to maneuver into prominent positions as suppliers of information about the problem. In turn, the definition of problems allows the generation of alternatives or solutions such that policy makers can choose among alternatives. The identification and definition of problems therefore are of prime importance in understanding information processing in government specifically and policy change generally.

The Processing of Policy Problems

The concept of dual dynamics describes the confluence of bureaucratic problem solving and congressional problem prioritization in the course of addressing policy problems. The remainder of this chapter fully develops the theoretical foundation and logic of the dual dynamics of agenda setting in the administrative state from the perspective of bureaucrats and members of Congress. I argue that the capacity of government to address issues on the agenda is greatly expanded by the information processing fostered by this system of dual dynamics. All governing institutions, elected and administrative, respond to the influx of problems as they barge onto the agenda.

From this discussion, a view of the bureaucracy's place in the policy process emerges that is vastly different from that of classical depictions. Some of these classic depictions of bureaucracy suggest that it is hidden beneath the veil of subsystem and interest group politics. Others hold that the bureaucracy is embroiled in a near constant battle with political overseers over whose preferences are realized in the implementation of policies. The following discussion sheds light on how these standard notions leave us with an inadequate understanding of how bureaucracies make policy within the system. The drastically different view of bureaucracy presented here starts with the notion that the bureaucracy is an influential policy maker at the beginning of the policy process when problems are defined and the agenda is set.

In making and implementing public policy, bureaucracies contribute to what Dodd and Schott (1986, p. 2) call the "refining of congressional intent."[1] In

---

[1] Note that Lowi (1969) also saw the need for refinement of these policies, but preferred that this function be carried out in the judiciary; hence, his advocacy of "juridical democracy."

this sense, they ensure the workableness of public policies in specific contexts. Bureaucracies also serve as political "pressure valves," allowing policy to change marginally in response to partisan and ideological shifts over time. A law passed by Congress and signed by the president is necessarily politically rigid and/or substantively vague. Successful legislation at best represents a compromise among the factions supporting the legislation and often is an outright rejection of the losing coalition's arguments. Shepsle (1992) has noted that there are many congressional "intents" encoded in bills rather than any single notion of the purpose of legislation. Bureaucracy is not only the key to the ongoing representation of the losing and compromised interests in legislative policy making but is also integral in the crafting of public policy for adaptivity to the changing policy environment. The role played by bureaucracy in policy refinement presumes that bureaucracies will not merely implement public policies but will also *make* or *legislate* policy in specific contexts.

Bureaucracy's part in the policy process hinges on the generation and transmission of information about problems to higher levels of government. This means bureaucracies are attention-attracting and directing organizations rather than the clandestine agents of subsystem lore. To understand bureaucratic influence in the policy process, I offer a theory of bureaucratic signaling based not on the classic notion found in economic models of politics, but rather on the notion of signaling from the field of communications.

In developing the theory of the dual dynamics of the administrative state, I first examine two traditions in the study of bureaucracy: overhead democracy and classic public administration. Perhaps no two literatures have taught us more about the interaction of elected officials and bureaucrats. Each tradition has also at times been mired in questions of influence or management and been unable to address larger concerns about the part played by bureaucracy within the broader policy process. Each tradition looks almost exclusively at top-down control of the bureaucracy or at the bottom-up rationality of public management, largely without understanding the connections between the two. Research on the policy process is useful for beginning to understand these connections and offers some building blocks for a discussion of the dual dynamics of agenda setting. After fully developing the components of the system of dual dynamics, I offer up the logic of each dynamic from the perspective of the actors and of the system as geared toward attending and responding to policy problems.

This perspective hearkens to the 1960s when scholars offered depictions of the federal bureaucracy often at odds with then current understanding of the federal bureaucracy in the American system and its role in democratic government. In the early days of bureaucracy studies, scholars such as Rourke (1965), Mosher (1968), Redford (1969), Lowi (1969), and Dodd and Schott (1986) grappled with the question of reconciling modern democracy's need for a large, robust federal bureaucracy with the precepts of democratic and representative government. Whereas Rourke and Lowi worried about the excesses of bureaucratic power and the insular nature of subsystem politics, Redford saw the system as much more open to democratic influences and to policy change. Dodd and Schott went even further, arguing that bureaucracy was very influential in helping define and "refine" congressional intent, as noted earlier. Although these scholars held different conceptions of the administrative state and prescriptions for reform, they all sought to understand the set of relations that comprise the democratic system in the presence of robust bureaucracy in the American setting.

The two traditions in the study of bureaucracy discussed in the next section began with an overarching concern for the political-administrative system and the bureaucracy's place in this system. For the tradition of overhead democracy, the concern was how to ensure democratic accountability and responsive competence, whereas classic public administration was concerned with how bureaucrats could faithfully implement public policy by handling outputs and politics through the sound science of management. However, each tradition quickly abandoned the systemic questions of this older literature on bureaucracies within the system of government. Where political influence on the bureaucracy or, alternatively, bureaucratic behavior in the face of political and organizational constraints was concerned, these traditions were very relevant. But the larger question of the place of bureaucratic policy making and influence in the system remained, and given changes in the system since the discipline last addressed this question, it is as important as ever.

2.1 DUELING TRADITIONS OF BUREAUCRACY

Scholarly attention to bureaucracy can be boiled down to two fundamental traditions. The first tradition is the study of "overhead democracy," whose animating question is how to reconcile the necessary existence of an unelected, technocratic, and meritorious bureaucracy with the precepts of representative democracy and government by popular will. Within this framework, the concept of control linkage is important because, if elected officials do not direct bureaucracy, then citizens cannot judge the worth of officials' policies. Thus, citizens cannot make informed choices about their elected representatives. Overhead democracy evolved in parallel with the classic public administration perspective whose central tenets hold that expertise is vital to executing (if not helping determine) the public will. Classic public administration further holds that politics and administration constitute separate spheres. Although this separation is unrealistic in practice because bureaucracies owe their existence to politics and are fundamentally political institutions, this tradition nevertheless embraced the potential for public good embodied in a robust, modern, and scientific bureaucracy.

The traditions of overhead democracy and classic public administration have offered a very different set of assumptions about bureaucrats and about the part played by bureaucracy in policy making. These differences stretch from the micro-foundations underpinning research to particular orientations toward bureaucrats and the nature of their work. From these micro-foundations, the two traditions offer different notions of bureaucratic autonomy and tend to focus on different stages of the policy process. As with any theoretical endeavor, different starting points lead to pursuit of some types of questions while ignoring others. Each tradition has offered a wealth of understanding on the fundamental nature, behavior, and purpose of bureaucracy that is not found – in fact, not pursued – in the other tradition. When pieced together, these traditions lead to different conceptions of what is and should be the role of bureaucracy in the policy-making process.

2.1.1 Overhead Democracy and Responsive Competence

Overhead democracy begins from the premise that it is paramount that citizens or their elected representatives be able to control or influence the vast unelected bureaucracy. Democracy is preserved in a system that operates from the top down. From this concern, this tradition then turns to the study of when, how, and to what effect elected officials are able to exert control or influence over the bureaucracy. All else equal, elected officials want a bureaucracy that is competent. Nevertheless, overhead democracy puts a premium on a responsive bureaucracy. This emphasis on responsive competency reflects as much the realities of politics rife with partisan and institutional conflict as it is a belief about the place of bureaucracy in democratic government (Aberbach and Rockman, 1988; Moe, 1989; West and Durant, 2000; Aberbach and Rockman, 2005; West, 2005b).

Given this orientation, hierarchy is central to understanding the relationship between the bureaucracy and Congress. This hierarchy embodies a principal-agent problem in which bureaucrats and elected officials have divergent preferences and the design and implementation of incentive systems become the objects of analysis. Bureaucratic autonomy and discretion in this tradition flow from information asymmetry and agenda control. Work on the sources of bureaucratic power point toward expertise, agenda control, and reputation among issue networks as key to bureaucratic autonomy (Kaufman, 1960; Niskanen, 1971; Carpenter, 2001). Bureaucrats hold information relevant to policy making that must be induced because it is rarely offered. Further, bureaucrats, by virtue of their position are able to control or set the agenda for elected officials. Again, this power flows from an information asymmetry: bureaucrats know the true nature and severity of problems "out there" and elected officials do not.

Based on the economics of the firm, scholarship addressing democratic control and accountability of the bureaucracy made great strides in formulating one of the central problems of bureaucracy and representative government: understanding the pathways by which elected officials controlled or at least influenced an unelected bureaucracy (Niskanen, 1971; Mitnick, 1975). Research making use of principal-agent theory has generated a wealth of information on how elected officials are able to influence the federal bureaucracy. This research has shown that both Congress (McCubbins, 1985; McCubbins et al., 1987; Balla, 1998; Balla and Wright, 2001) and the president (Moe, 1989; Wood and Waterman, 1994; Golden, 2000; Rudavelige, 2005; Lewis, 2003; Whitford and Yates, 2009) have their say in bureaucratic affairs through various avenues of monitoring the bureaucracy and designing incentives that conform bureaucratic behavior to the preferences of elected officials. The political control research associated with rational choice and principal-agent models concerns how political institutions design incentive structures such that control of federal agencies is attained and democratic accountability secured (Gormley, 1989; Huber et al., 2001; see Miller, 2005, for an alternative perspective).

Given the full development of the administrative presidency and the vast increase in congressional oversight, this research reflects American political reality. Research in overhead democracy has demonstrated the importance of the preferences and priorities of elected officials and of understanding the mechanisms by which these are transferred to the federal bureaucracy. Yet, the overhead democracy tradition, and even its realization in American political institutions, downplays some fundamental truths concerning the importance of bureaucracy and the nature of delegation and influence in American politics.

2.1.2 Classic Public Administration and Neutral Competence

Despite scholarly and popular interest in the ways in which elected officials influence the federal bureaucracy, delegation to bureaucracy is the norm in the policy process. According to the classic public administration tradition, bureaucracy has a more robust role or part to play in the policy process than envisioned in the overhead democracy literature. With this more robust view of the role of bureaucracy, the classic public administration tradition eschews the premise that bureaucrats do or should occupy themselves solely with making the policy preferences of elected officials come to fruition. Bureaucrats are competent, even at the expense of responsiveness to elected officials. They are statespeople, or managers, whose professional norms and allegiances make them somewhat "above" politics. This view of the policy process decidedly takes a bottom-up perspective on policy making, in which bureaucrats lend dispassionate expertise to the policy process.

Scholars working with bounded rational models of human decision making have also reached different conclusions from overhead democracy about the nature of bureaucratic behavior and influence on the policy process (Simon, 1947; March and Simon, 1958; Lindblom, 1959; Wildavsky, 1964; Lipsky,

1980; March and Olsen, 1989; Wilson, 1989; Jones, 2001).[2] Collectively, these works take a more benign view of bureaucratic influence and point to the difficulty of decision making in complex policy environments, taking into account individual cognitive limitations and public settings in which bureaucrats are governed by considerations other than consequences (e.g., "appropriateness," tasks, or rule-bound behavior). Since the dawn of the science of administration in the early 1900s, scholars have pointed to the "inner" controls (e.g., sense of obligation, professionalism, self-interest, group loyalty, etc.) as well as the constraints placed on bureaucrats by their organizational settings as important in checking bureaucratic excesses (see Wilson, 1887; Simon, 1947; Finer, 1972; Friedrich, 1972; Lipsky, 1980; Miller, 1992; Brehm and Gates, 1999).

Some recent scholarship has even debated the merits of having a politically responsive bureaucracy in all cases (see West, 2005b). For example, Lewis (2008) examines the politics of presidential appointments to the bureaucracy and finds that political appointees often contribute to the poor performance of executive branch agencies. Moreover, the potential for a corrupt or otherwise misguided principal (in the principal-agent framework) presents a major challenge to the fundamental assumption that elected officials are a direct link to the popular will of citizens (Miller, 2005). If elected officials misrepresent or skirt the public will, the democratic linkage between citizens and their bureaucrats is severed, and the question of whether politicians can control or influence bureaucrats becomes much less meaningful.

2.1.3 Reviving Tradition

By the mid-1990s, both of the foundational approaches to understanding bureaucracy had lost influence because they were asking and answering questions of increasingly limited significance for understanding the process of policy making. These questions were increasingly irrelevant to the broader institutional and partisan conflict that was structuring the relationship between bureaucrats and elected officials.

For overhead democracy, this meant a turn to contract theory and transaction costs. Contract theory and analysis of transaction costs have taught us much about the bureaucratic response to elected officials' efforts to enact and implement their chosen policies generally and to influence bureaucratic behavior specifically. Yet, the finely delineated focus on the design of incentive structures and measurement of bureaucratic response failed to be attentive to larger questions, including the sources of bureaucratic autonomy, the rise of the administrative presidency, and the nature of bureaucratic policy making.

---

[2] Also see Brehm and Gates (1999) who use an "enhanced" principal-agent model and find that street-level bureaucrats, by and large, work rather than shirk. At the federal level, Golden (2000) suggests that officials from the EPA carried out the general direction of policy preferred by the Reagan administration, even though it ran counter to the mission and preferences of the agency.

The work also failed to appreciate the strong force of the rule of law, institutional conflict, and constitutional order in setting the stage for the interaction of bureaucrats and elected officials (Huber et al., 2001; Bertelli and Lynn, 2006).

More to the point, a literature that was born of efforts to understand or reconcile the existence of bureaucracy with the precepts of democratic government failed to relate many of its conclusions about incentives, congressional and presidential control, and bureaucratic response to the broader concern that spurred the original work. The work failed to heed Moe's (1984) exhortation concerning attentiveness to the political and decision-making context within which bureaucracy was embedded.

Classic public administration fared no better, at once denying the overall approach and assumptions of overhead democracy while embracing much of its language. Classic public administration was rooted in a concern for the broader role played by bureaucracy in both implementing public policy and providing valuable and reliable information that ensured that democratic or majority choices were *informed* choices. Bureaucrats therefore became "public managers." The concern for public management (or new public management) focused on how various organizational resources and settings and, more to the point, the management of these resources influenced implementation and policy outcomes. Public managers could be expected to mechanistically transform resources into predictable policy outcomes or at least policy outputs that were measurable. These functions were closely related to the typical processes governing private sector organizations with some accounting for the public nature of bureaucracy. Here again, the larger question of the role of bureaucracy in democratic government that animated the field was forgotten as the work grew more concerned with the nuts and bolts and less with the machine of government.

The overhead democracy perspective was the first to be revived, with the realization that no theory of control or influence could be complete without a theory of delegation (Epstein and O'Halloran, 1999; Huber and Shipan, 2002; Shipan, 2004). One cannot fully understand why, when, or how elected officials may begin to influence bureaucrats without first understanding why and when delegation to the bureaucracy would occur in the first place. In addition to the fact that delegation is theoretically and logically prior to the choice of incentive structure and methods of control, delegation to some degree is the norm in the administrative state.

Public administration experienced a similar revival with a renewed focus on the meso-level political context in which bureaucracies operate. This approach is exemplified in the research addressing shared and network governance (Durant, 2000; Durant and Warber, 2001; Lubell and Scholz, 2001; Schneider et al., 2003; Lubell, 2007). Much like the older research concerning the operation and maintenance of policy subsystems, shared governance and networked governance approaches emphasize the cooperation of private sector groups and interests with elected and administrative institutions in successful policy making.

In a separate line of research, scholars are also beginning to demonstrate that bureaucratic structure need not contribute to inertia (Robinson, 2004; Robinson et al., 2007). The classic public administration tradition has returned to its earlier concerns with the statesman-like neutrality and the proper place and function of bureaucrats. The new emphasis on this old concept embraces the finding of overhead democracy that "strategic neutrality" (Huber, 2007) in policy implementation is a prudent political strategy for bureaucracy and one that conforms to its traditional historic role in the policy process.

2.2 FINDING TAILS AND FORGETTING BUREAUCRACY

The questions animating the study of the policy process over the last three decades offer a way to step back from the dueling traditions and bring the larger process of policy making in the administrative state into view. In doing so, we lose some details, which have been so powerful in theories based in overhead democracy and public administration, but the general features and processes that govern the system come into sharper focus. The study of the policy process offers the building blocks for the dual dynamics of congressional problem prioritization and bureaucratic problem solving that give life to the administrative state.

A byproduct of fruitful lines of questioning in any scholarly field is that competent scholarship bores ever deeper into the subject matter and causal linkages among phenomena until the questions that animated the line of research at the outset are forgotten. It is very much like holding an object in one's line of sight and drawing the object ever closer. In doing so, details of the object come into focus, while the object, its general nature, and contours are lost. This has been the course of scholarship on the bureaucracy until very recently. Bureaucracy does not operate today on the basis of many of the concerns that spurred the original thinking in the overhead democracy and public administration traditions. Vast changes that have swept American politics over the past thirty years – the rise of the administrative (some say imperial) presidency, legislative oversight, party polarization, and the rise of privatization as a mode of government – make understanding this new context ever more pressing for both scholars and reformers.

Research on the policy process conducted as early as the mid-1980s has been cognizant of the inadequacy and limitations of each specific tradition in understanding what part bureaucracy plays in policy making and change. This frustration was summed up well by Sabatier (1986) in discussing the limitations of thinking about bottom-up versus top-down approaches to policy implementation. Notwithstanding the strictures placed on bureaucrats by elected officials or, alternatively, a reluctance by bureaucrats to engage in politics, policy scholars have noted the central part played by, indeed the omnipresence of, bureaucrats in the policy and political process (Miller, 2005).

Yet, lest we think too highly of scholars of the policy process (of which this author is one), there have been no serious and systematic efforts to study the part played by the bureaucracy in the policy process outside implementation studies or policy subsystems, in which bureaucrats are implicit actors (Sabatier, 1986; McCool, 1990, 1998). In the major theories in the field, bureaucracy is background noise and rarely connected theoretically or empirically to the policy change that is the target of these lines of inquiry (Baumgartner and Jones, 1993; Sabatier and Jenkins-Smith, 1993). This is in contrast to the important and visible position that bureaucracies occupy in the American political system (Kaufman, 2001; Miller, 2007). These theories further undervalue the importance of bureaucratic policy making in the course of addressing the government's agenda.

The undervaluing of bureaucracy's role in the policy process stems from a shift in scholarly attention away from incrementalism and toward theories of rapid, large-scale policy change. Scholars, of course, do not usually identify bureaucracies as a major contributor to or locus of this type of policy change. Nevertheless, subsystem policy making, of which bureaucracy is the centerpiece, is the norm in American politics. Large-scale policy change need not happen only in the elected branches of government. Bureaucracies sometimes are part and parcel of large dramatic changes in public policy.

2.3 DUAL DYNAMICS

The dual dynamics of the administrative state hinge on information processing between the bureaucracy and the congressional committee system. The first dynamic involves bureaucratic problem solving and bottom-up influence. Bureaucracies are the first line of receptors for information in the system, as they monitor issues for changes and potential problems. They then formulate a representation of the problem, defining it for use at higher levels of government. They finally transmit problem definitions and information to higher levels of government for consideration. The second dynamic involves congressional steering of information processing through processes of problem prioritization and agenda setting. By shuffling the prominence of issues on the agenda, Congress is able to alter the flow of information from bureaucracies coming into the legislative branch. Further, Congress may bundle issues together, melding multiple problem definitions and streams of information from the bureaucracy to form "custom" understandings of complicated issues that span the boundaries of traditional issues (e.g., climate change, which involves energy, environment, agriculture, science & technology, and public lands & water). Finally, Congress is able to ensure reliable streams of information from the bureaucracy about policy problems by fostering or mitigating competition among bureaucracies for supplying that information.

Bureaucracy enables democratic systems of government to better address the policy agenda by influencing decisions at higher levels of government and by allowing the government to address more issues. The capacity of the governing system to address important policy problems depends in part on the ability of the bureaucracy to influence agendas at higher levels of government. Delegation occurs, in part, to allow elected officials to move on to other issues, confident that someone is paying attention. This stands in contrast to the theory of overhead democracy, which contends that influence should flow from political institutions to the bureaucracy. It also differs from the classic public administration perspective on bureaucracy. Bureaucrats have influence beyond providing unbiased assessments of policy problems and competently carrying out the implementation of congressional policies. Bureaucracies influence what elected officials attend to, linking important and salient policy problems appearing in the policy environment they monitor to elected officials and functioning as a bridge from the public or policy agenda to the government's institutional agenda (Kingdon, 1984).

Bureaucracies also expand the carrying capacity of the governmental agenda. They pay attention to issues long after they leave the halls of Congress and the confines of the Oval Office. Especially with regard to low-salience issues, bureaucracy serves a representative function as a substitute, or backstop, for a lack of attention in the elected institutions of government. Where do issues go when attention at higher levels of government fades into the background? In all likelihood, these issues are addressed by a government bureaucracy. By attending to issues not currently on the agenda at higher levels of government, the bureaucracy increases the carrying capacity of the governmental agenda.

As the bureaucracy attends to issues that cannot be ignored yet may not be salient, it follows that this frees agenda space for the elected institutions of government to focus on particularly salient issues with obvious political benefits. Note that this sort of relationship is omnipresent in U.S. politics. It occurs between the committee system and the floor in Congress, between policy subsystems and the macro political system generally, and between bureaucracies and elected officials. This configuration allows the processing of both high- and low-salience issues simultaneously and offers heightened public responsiveness to the most salient issues. Both by alerting the elected institutions of government to pressing policy problems and emergent issues and serving a substitution and issue maintenance function, bureaucracies greatly increase the ability of government to address problems arising on the agenda. In doing so, they have the potential to render the governing system both more adaptive and more responsive.

Given that the governing system must attempt to process information concerning various policy problems, the key question then becomes how bureaucracy aids or hinders the ability of elected institutions to first understand and then act on various problems as they emerge on the government's agenda. In the dual dynamics perspective, bureaucracy is viewed in terms of the overall ability of government to generate and process information about problems. Note that bureaucratic problem solving amounts to an issue representation criterion for the quality of democracy. Understanding bureaucracy's place in the democratic system in terms of the information processing framework[3] developed here represents an effort to renew discussion of the system of relations that comprise what Emmette Redford (1969, p. 4) and Dodd and Schott (1986) labeled the "administrative state" and moves toward an examination of how bureaucracy fits into the broader governing system.

Addressing issues on the policy agenda requires that the federal bureaucracy conduct discretionary surveillance of the policy environment. That is, federal agencies must be free to monitor the policy environment for potential problems and to transmit them to higher levels of government. Bureaucratic problem solving is central to democratic responsiveness, because government must address important and salient problems. To the degree bureaucracy enables this type of issue responsiveness or allows for government to address more issues, it is a net good to democracy. It should further be noted that elections are not sufficient to produce this type of issue responsiveness. Democratic responsiveness of the type argued here is based on an understanding of the relationship between bureaucrats and elected officials that is dynamic, issue dependent, and characterized by feedback in the process of addressing and solving policy problems.

The dual dynamics argument offered here takes Elmore's organizational tension as a given in government. Understanding agenda setting, which problems government addresses, how it understands them, and ultimately how government acts on them depends in part on the dual dynamics developed here. Agenda change in the administrative state is a result of bureaucratic problem solving from below and congressional problem prioritization from above. From below bureaucracies monitor problems, aid in defining them for government action, and generate information that is passed on to elected officials. From above, Congress synthesizes this vast amount of information, faces tradeoffs among which issues to attend to, and coordinates action on policy problems. Each of these dynamics is vital to understanding how the policy-making system addresses and adjusts to the problems confronting it, and hence to the question of the quality of government raised earlier.

Before discussing the mechanics of each of the dual dynamics of agenda setting, it is important to understand two fundamental properties of the system. First, the dual dynamics of agenda setting demand a different view of the sources of bureaucratic autonomy and its implications. Second, the system (like many systems) is characterized by two types of feedback between bureaucrats and elected officials as they each attempt to address the problems on the agenda.

---

[3] I aim here to avoid debates about the difference between frameworks and theories (a debate very prominent in scholarship on the policy processes, see Sabatier and Jenkins-Smith 1999). Suffice it to say that the information processing perspective or framework turns our attention to a few concepts important for explaining policy change; yet it leaves room for a number of different theories all rooted in the notion that the key role of political institutions lies in processing the issues comprising the policy agenda.

2.3.1 The Delegation of Attention and Bureaucratic Autonomy

The system of dual dynamics is fundamentally dependent on how organizations cope with limited attention or, more specifically, on how attention is delegated. In turn, delegation of attention within the administrative state defines bureaucratic autonomy. Bureaucracies are influential in the policy process because they are paying attention.

Scholars of federal bureaucracies have long attributed these bureaucracies' autonomy to several factors: the cultivation of their reputation within issue networks (Carpenter, 2001), the impact of professionalism within their organizations (Kaufman, 1960), their expertise within given task environments (Wilson, 1989; Krause, 1994), and even their ability to distribute the costs and benefits of policy (Krause, 1996, 1999; Sheingate, 2001). Turning the focus to how government addresses the flow of policy problems brings the sources of bureaucratic autonomy into sharp relief. All of these aforementioned sources of autonomy, at their base, assume or require the delegation of attention from elected officials to bureaucrats. Bureaucratic autonomy hinges most directly on the attention limits of elected institutions and on the organization of government itself, especially the lines of delegation that characterize the system.

Research in mainstream U.S. politics has begun to underscore the importance of what exactly is delegated (see Spence, 1997a, 1997b; Epstein and O'Halloran, 1999; Huber and Shipan, 2002), rather than skipping to the political control of bureaucracy pursuant to delegation that was studied at an earlier point in time. Overhead democracy has its central locus in the interbranch conflict that characterizes institutions holding different preferences and facing disparate incentive structures. What is notable of this work is that it tends to ignore the *organizational* tensions of the system that form the backdrop of much of this conflict. Even in instances such as employment contracts in the private sector, the organizational tensions of these relationships set the contours of the resulting institutional dynamics (see Miller, 1992). Managers must respond to information that they only glean from employees; otherwise goal- and preference-oriented control and influence are impossible. Although political influence and control have been much studied in the tradition of overhead democracy the influence of delegation and bureaucratic discretion pursuant to various organizational influences are actually the norm.

In addition, scarcity of attention is a persistent feature of the system. Fundamentally, bureaucratic autonomy and influence derive from the scarcity of attention via delegation by the elected institutions of government. Whether a bureaucracy is making, implementing, or adjudicating policy, it has been delegated the responsibility to attend to policy problems that may or may not be on the agenda of Congress, the president, or the judiciary. Note that this delegation occurs not only inter-institutionally (e.g., between Congress and the bureaucracy) but also intra-institutionally (e.g., between a chamber floor and the committee system in Congress or between high-level offices within departments and line bureaus). One could argue that the *delegation of attention* is the trademark of the organization of political institutions of all types[4] and is the foundation of the modern administrative state.

Bureaucracies require a measure of autonomy both in order to monitor for policy problems and to lend credibility to information generated and transmitted to elected institutions. Without autonomy, the expertise accumulated in both elected and administrative institutions and subunits lies dormant in the face of change and, ultimately, atrophies like an unused appendage. In other words, expertise must be used or it will not be generated – usage is an incentive to generate and transmit valuable information concerning both the politics of the issue and the policy (see Gailmard and Patty, 2012, for an incentive-based system of information generation). Note that whereas overhead democracy is concerned with the extent of bureaucratic autonomy and discretion, the dual dynamics perspective on the system asks whether bureaucracies have the autonomy and discretion necessary to ensure that elected institutions are supplied with useful information about problems.

Where the monitoring of the policy environment is concerned, a lack of autonomy at lower levels of the system means that important problems will go unnoticed. As a direct consequence, the system will fail to respond and adjust to potentially important changes. More broadly, a lack of autonomy constrains the adaptability of the institutions to issues on the agenda. Even if granted the ability to freely monitor for potential problems arising in the policy environment, bureaucrats must fundamentally believe that the information they generate pursuant to these problems will be credible both in the eyes of peers and elected overseers. Where federal agencies have little faith that their monitoring and information-generating activities will be taken seriously, they have little incentive to generate information about the problems they observe.[5] Worse, the information processing perspective offered here suggests that federal agencies may fail to monitor the policy environment for problems at all.

Elected institutions, especially Congress, need not always heed the information generated by bureaucracies, but bureaucrats must at least reasonably believe their efforts will be taken seriously – and I argue shortly that there is good reason to believe that this is often the case. Stated plainly, elected and administrative institutions must believe in the efficacy of these inter-institutional efforts to detect, define, and communicate information about policy problems.

This general belief is never more important than where the administrative institutions of the system are concerned. Federal bureaucracies are constitutionally sublimated to the elected branches of government and have long required

---

[4] Perhaps it defines all organizations both public and private. CEOs are delegated the responsibility of monitoring corporations (and profit margins) for the board and ultimately shareholders.

[5] Patty (2009) has shown formally that the information generated by bureaucrats can be heavily influenced (and biased in some instances) by the views and preferences of their political overseers.

justification in a system of democracy going back to the republic's founding (Hamilton, 1788). Given the constitutionally subordinate position of the federal bureaucracy, bureaucratic autonomy, where it is useful to the governing system, is much more fragile and fleeting than for the elected branches of government, and understanding its sources of autonomy explains a great deal about bureaucracy's role in the policy process.

The role of federal agencies is then to act as the "antennae" of the elected branches of government. They monitor for and detect potential problems, participate in the process of defining these problems for government action, and generate information about these problems that is transmitted to elected officials for consideration and decision. Arrow (1974) notes that one of the many functions of organization is to channel information. Not only does an organization channel information within and across institutions but I argue that the institutional structure channels attention and prioritizes information (see May et al., 2008). In this sense, bureaucracies economize on the scarce attention of the elected institutions of government, serving as harbinger of emergent policy problems. They do so because the elected institutions simply cannot attend to every problem facing government and must prioritize. The delegation of attention thus allows bureaucracy to play an essential role in the policy process in American politics. Furthermore, it provides a role for bureaucracy that is premised on their influence in agenda setting and the front end of the policy process, rather than serving merely as implementers.

2.3.2 System Feedback

Not only is the delegation of attention the foundation of the system of dual dynamics but it also creates a second key feature of the system: feedback. Feedback is a characteristic of systems theories of politics in general (Easton, 1965; Deutsch, 1966; Jervis, 1997; Miller and Page, 2007). In the administrative state the policy process is characterized by bureaucratic problem solving from below and congressional problem prioritization from above. Policy making at the level of subsystems merges these two forces, which results in feedback.

Congress delegates the responsibility of paying attention to policy problems to various federal bureaucracies by passing enacting and reauthorization legislation outlining general bureaucratic missions and goals in more or less distinct issue or policy areas. Thereafter, bureaucracies implement policies and programs pursuant to this and to all previous legislation. This means that legislation and policy making in the bureaucracy do not occur in real time, allowing for much more policy adaptability in the system (see Chapters 3 and 4 for more on this topic). But bureaucracies do more than just engage in implementation. They attempt to detect potential problems within their substantive spheres. They define these problems for elected officials and generate useful information pursuant to these problem definitions. This information then forms the basis for the ongoing prioritization and addressing of policy problems within the various subsystems and in the halls of Congress. Bureaucratic problem solving feeds into congressional problem prioritization.

For example, the U.S. Senate Committee on Governmental Affairs held a hearing titled "Agroterrorism: The Threat to America's Breadbasket" on November 19, 2003. At the hearing, officials from the Department of Homeland Security (DHS), the Food and Drug Administration (FDA), and the U.S. Department of Agriculture (USDA) delivered testimony on the potential risk of terrorist adulteration of the food supply. In testimony to the committee, each bureaucracy crafted a definition of this risk centered on its particular take on food security. Taken together, the public risk posed by threats to the food supply was crafted from three very different approaches to the issue. This hearing is instructive in both the competition over the definition of agroterrorism among bureaucracies and the committee's efforts to use these diverse perspectives to inform policy making on the issue.

Difficult decisions about problem prioritization and tradeoffs in Congress structure the way bureaucracies monitor for problems and the information they are able to generate in the future. Members of Congress choose not only among the problems put forth by bureaucrats and other actors in the process but also among particular definitions and blends of definitions of these problems. The hearing on agroterrorism illustrates that members of Congress are not only able to promote competition and to choose among problem definitions but also may choose to foster a "blend" of information in crafting an understanding of the problem. Bureaucracies then alter future monitoring of problems and definitions based on these congressional choices. For instance, that Congress defines agroterrorism in terms of dimensions related both to food production and supply (USDA) and those related to contaminants (FDA) and monitoring at points of entry (DHS) means that these bureaucracies will move to gather information more closely related to the cross-cutting risk of agroterrorism. They are likely to do so simply because they want to influence policy on the issue. Congressional problem prioritization feeds into bureaucratic problem solving through these difficult decisions about what aspects of a problem are important. This example also highlights the fact that decisions made about issue prioritization and problem definitions in Congress affect the quantity, quality, and even types of information about future problems that members of Congress can expect to glean from the bureaucracy. This occurs because congressional problem prioritization and agenda setting fundamentally alter the future information processing of bureaucracies.

In the course of addressing policy problems that emerge on the agenda, two types of feedback are possible as bureaucrats and politicians interact to address problems. One type of feedback is an equilibrating force on the dynamics of agenda change in the policy process, whereas the other is a destabilizing force.[6]

---

[6] Here I use the notion of equilibrium loosely to simply imply a degree of stasis or at most incremental change across time. Equilibrium in this sense is not the same as in classical economics

The dual dynamics of agenda setting foster both negative and positive feedback depending on the salience and severity of problems and the partisan and structural features of American politics (i.e., the political context surrounding the problem).

That there is the potential for both negative and positive feedback in the course of policy making and the relationship of each to stasis and change are key insights of research on the policy process (Kingdon, 1984; Baumgartner and Jones, 1993; Sabatier and Jenkins-Smith, 1993); these insights have long figured into descriptions and theorizing about the nature of the administrative state, especially about its subsystems (Lowi, 1969; Redford, 1969; Dodd and Schott, 1986; McCool, 1990; Worsham, 1997). Feedback and its relationship to system equilibrium are also evident in classical studies of pluralism, political parties, and issue expansion (Schattschneider, 1960; Downs, 1972). Where bureaucratic problem solving and congressional problem prioritization are concerned, two types of negative feedback are possible. Although each form has a different basis, both comport with the classical notion of negative feedback in that they foster the marginal adjustment of policy to the set of problems facing government.

From below, bureaucratic problem solving incrementally adjusts the system through problem monitoring, definition, and the information transmitted to elected officials and helps define and refine the goals of elected officials via administrative policy making. From above, elected officials periodically effect large-scale change in the prioritization of problems by shuffling the prominence of issues on the agenda. These decisions reorient bureaucratic problem solving to different issues or types of information.

Through the delegation of attention, bureaucracies monitor real problems in real time. If elected officials act to restrict this flow of information when it should be expanded, then the system is likely to be maladaptive. This maladaptation will mean that important issues and policy problems fail to make their way to policy makers for consideration and decision. In this scenario, vital issues go unaddressed and important questions go unanswered. Likewise, if the flow of information is expanded in a way that is unnecessary given the problems on the agenda, then the system is also maladaptive. In this alternative scenario, the administrative state suffers from an excess of potentially frivolous or trivial problems as bureaucrats and elected officials search for something to address. This state of affairs severely taxes the ability of the elected institutions of government to make sure that potentially dire problems are prioritized in the system. And with so many problems identified, attention limitations become more acute.

Bureaucracy serves as a backstop for attention to problems that are not currently on the agenda of Congress. In this instance, bureaucracy and Congress

---

when concerned with the solution to a game. It is much more analogous to the equilibrating forces of supply and demand.

work like a set of balance scales on which Congress delegates the responsibility of paying attention to certain issues to the bureaucracy, while turning its attention elsewhere.

Conversely, bureaucratic problem solving and congressional problem prioritization may also work to redefine existing problems, come to grips with unique or new problems, and generally feed on one another – producing sizable shifts in policy making more in line with classical systems' notions of positive feedback. To understand how the facets of bureaucratic problem solving contribute to these types of positive feedback, it is necessary to examine more closely the component processes of problem monitoring and problem definition and how bureaucracy generates information in the course of problem solving.

2.3.3 Bureaucratic Problem Solving

At the beginning of this chapter, I argued for the importance of thinking of the government as addressing policy problems as they arise on the agenda. Understanding how government responds to the flow of problems requires a recognition of the fundamental tension in all governments between those with expertise and those with authority. The dual dynamics of agenda setting represent the confluence of bureaucratic problem solving and congressional problem prioritization.

First, bureaucracies are monitors of the set of social, economic, and environmental conditions that give rise to various problems that end up on the governmental agenda. In addition to engaging in this proactive stance on emergent policy problems, bureaucracies also monitor the set of policies and programs enacted by Congress and signed into law by the president. These are not emergent problems, but constitute a major source of issues that from time to time reappear on the agenda. From their vantage point on the frontlines of government and their close connections with organized interests, bureaucracies are the primary institutions for detecting existing and emergent problems.

Second, bureaucracies help define policy problems for government action. This is a vital aspect of bureaucratic policy making. Just because many actors in the policy process recognize that there exists some condition or a problem with an existing policy does not mean that the problem is ripe for or warrants a government response. That recognition is just the first stage in a three-stage process in which the governing system, the bureaucracy being among the first institutions, comes to view the problem as warranting government action. In the second stage, the problem must be defined in such a way as to allow a government response.

Third, bureaucracies generate information about policy problems that is then transmitted to elected officials. The importance of bureaucratic problem definition becomes apparent in this third stage of the process. The way in which a policy problem is defined governs the types and quantity of information that is collected or generated and transmitted to elected officials for consideration.

The three components of bureaucratic problem solving are important because they form in part the parameters of choice at higher levels of government. Bureaucratic problem monitoring, problem definition, and generation of information define bottom-up influence in the administrative state. In the following sections, I address each of these in turn.

Problem Monitoring

The administrative state is a system that must respond to new or emergent policy problems and must also be prepared to adjust based on the past performance of the system in relation to the programs, regulations, and incentive structures already in force. Like all systems, the administrative state must gather information about exogenous events and processes that influence both the system and its past performance. Bureaucracies form the first line of "receptors" (Easton, 1965, p. 420) in detecting emergent policy problems (also see Deutsch, 1966, p.182) and changes in the general nature of existing problems.

Problem monitoring is the first stage in the process of adjusting both means and goals to the realities of an evolving set of problems. It involves two subprocesses: *detection* and *identification*. Detection lies at the heart of the problem-solving system. Plainly stated, the system must be able to detect changes in problems it confronts. One of the central problems of detection is numerical sufficiency. There must be enough bureaucracies to adequately monitor for changes in the issues on the agenda, and the set of bureaucracies must be adjusted through time to approximate the issues on the agenda.

Whereas detection depends on the size and capacity of the bureaucracy, identification involves the quality of the bureaucracies as receptors. Bureaucracies must be able not only to detect that something has changed but also to identify these changes as having consequences for policymaking. When problem monitoring, bureaucracies are attentive to two general types of information. The first type is information about the issue that relates to public policy, such as whether a policy change is warranted or whether a given solution is good policy. The second type of information pertains to politics: which actors in the issue area care or do not care about changes or potential policies. This information goes to the core of how constituencies within these issue areas are affected by policy change. Issues addressed by the bureaucracy change all the time, but this does not mean that all changes have consequences for policy making or for decision making at higher levels of government. Bureaucracies must be able to distinguish changes that warrant action from those that have no implications for policy making. The ability to make these distinctions lies at the heart of identification.

Bureaucratic autonomy is absolutely critical to problem monitoring. Of the three processes that define bureaucratic influence in the policy process – problem monitoring, problem definition, and generation of information – problem monitoring requires the most autonomy. Bureaucracies must be free to detect potential problems across the range of issues that are monitored and to identify problems that may warrant consideration in policy making. It is then up to policy makers in the elected branches of government to prioritize the problems detected and identified by bureaucracy. Without bureaucratic auton-omy in problem monitoring, however, the administrative state wanders blind through the emergent and evolving issues confronting government. Like an advance guard, bureaucracy offers elected officials an information-rich pre-view of the the issues on the agenda.

Although expertise in a given policy area is often cited as the proximate cause of bureaucratic influence in policy making, it is the delegation of attention, and the problem monitoring that this fosters, that is the ultimate source of influence. After all, expertise is not usually gained without long hours spent attending to problems and to problem solving in given policy areas. It is therefore useful to distinguish between expertise geared toward policy solutions and implemen-tation versus expertise geared toward agenda setting and problem monitor-ing. Bureaucratic expertise in service of policy solutions, particularly policy implementation, is well known. Having implemented various policies over the course of time, bureaucracies are a bastion of information on which policy tools, designs, incentives, regulatory instruments, particular service delivery mechanisms, and so on are likely to work in given policy areas and on partic-ular policy targets. But bureaucracies possess a much more fundamental type of expertise associated with recognizing and even anticipating changes in the policy environments they monitor. Problem expertise fuels problem detection and identification.

In monitoring the policy environment, bureaucracies become sensitive to changes in the nature of the problems they face and become adept at antici-pating problems that are likely to arise pursuant to these changes. This type of expertise pertains most directly to defining the policy problems that are to com-prise the agenda of government. Unlike expertise pertaining to policy solutions and their implementation in stable and established contexts, problem expertise highlights adjustment to change in the problems confronting government; thus, it pertains directly to the ability of the system to adapt over time to a changing agenda.

Arguably, the problem expertise gained by bureaucracies by performing their monitoring or "fire alarm" (McCubbins and Schwartz, 1984) function is much more fundamental to the functioning of government, and certainly to bureaucratic influence, than solution expertise. Bureaucracies alert politicians to problems as they arise, yielding benefits to politicians in terms of policy and political strategy. This view differs from the traditional perspective that bureaucrats are influential because of their expertise in matters of policy imple-mentation in particular areas. Instead, the bureaucracy is influential in part because it is delegated the responsibility of attending to the policy environ-ment, detecting disturbances in this environment, and generating information about these policy problems (see also Katzmann, 1989; Feldman and March, 1981; Rose, 1989).

Problem Definition

Once a problem has been detected and identified as having consequences for policy making, it must be defined in such a way as to facilitate government action. It should be noted that not every problem can be defined in a way that allows government to act. Poverty is an example of a widely recognized problem that has been notoriously hard to define.

Problem definition involves the linking of causes and consequences (Dery, 1984) and embodies a direction for addressing the problem. As such the process of problem definition highlights certain causes and consequences and downplays others. For instance, a problem in the economy might be viewed as stemming either from inflation or from unemployment and would warrant monetary or fiscal policy, respectively, depending on the causal explanation for the problem. Some problems, however, such as the stagflation of the 1970s, are difficult to define in terms of existing policy and bureaucracies, making policy solutions more difficult to generate.

Problem definition is no trivial matter because the basis of policy making is the development of a "problem representation." Although many problems are definable in terms of their solutions, others are not. For those latter problems, generating a problem definition is a prerequisite of choice, especially in policy-making environments rife with uncertainty and participants who are risk averse and self-interested. A working problem definition is then based on assumptions that favor some policy alternatives and preclude others.

Due to the delegation of attention, bureaucracies are in a position to influence problem definition by setting the parameters of policy choice for elected officials at higher levels of government. Bureaucracies can signal the emergence of new or redefined issue attributes for consideration that pertain to the structure of the problem. They may also highlight some dimensions or attributes and downplay others. In this way, bureaucracies influence how elected officials weight the different dimensions or attributes of a given issue. This is not to say that politicians adopt policy solutions preferred by the agency carte blanche; nevertheless, the dimensions of choice – the issue attributes that are relevant for policy making and the relative weighting of different attributes in the context of choice – are influenced by problem definitions constructed in part by bureaucracy.

Bureaucratic leverage in defining problems stems first from its problem monitoring function. The information concerning any problem that Congress is able to harvest from the bureaucracy depends on which and how many bureaucracies are paying attention to the problem. If a certain sector of the economy is monitored closely by the Department of Labor, then the problem definitions that result will be oriented toward a labor force perspective on the issue; note that the definition would differ greatly if the problem was monitored by the Department of Commerce. In the course of monitoring the economy, the Department of Labor would be likely to detect and identify perturbations in the unemployment rate more readily than perturbations in the inflation rate. The reverse would likely hold true for Treasury or the Federal Reserve.

Problem definitions also vary because bureaucracies are created to address specific problems. To some degree, bureaucracies can be seen as the institution-alization of the demands made on government by organized interests, social movements, and the mass public to address certain problems in certain ways. For example, the Environmental Protection Agency represents the institution-alization of the concerns of the environmental movement that began in the late 1960s. In addition, enacting legislation imbues bureaucracies with mis-sions within more or less defined areas of policy making. These missions imply causes, consequences, and particular theories linking those causes and conse-quences. These missions broadly structure the types of problem definitions that bureaucracy will generate.

This initial proclivity for certain problem definitions is reinforced by the internal organization of bureaucracies. Bureaucracies are organized to address specific problems using particular offices, personnel, and even tools of imple-mentation. In addition to organizational structure and staffing, standard oper-ating procedures and other organizational processes specify both how to label given problems as they arise and how to understand (or define) these prob-lems. Often, these organizational processes go so far as to automatically con-nect certain changes with certain responses. Problem definition is important in part because it begins to imply some solutions and preclude others. In these cases, the problem definition is structured such as to trigger immedi-ate and automatic solutions. Finally, the affinity for certain problem defini-tions is influenced by the professional norms of the individuals staffing any bureaucracy.

The theory of dual dynamics offered here analytically severs the problem space and the solution space of issues. The attributes of problems that bureau-cracies choose to transmit to Congress help form the working definition of the problems that are detected and identified.

For example, the issue of agriculture was once defined almost entirely in terms of production and price supports. However, since the early 1970s with the emergence of the environmental movement, environmental quality became part of the discussion around agriculture (especially where pesticides and runoff from fertilizer are concerned). This redefinition is even reflected in the orga-nizational makeup of the USDA in that one of its most influential and visi-ble organizational subunits is the powerful Natural Resources Conservation Service (NRCS). The environmental dimension represents a wholly different attribute on which to judge agricultural policy alternatives. The problem of run off further brought the agricultural subsystem into conflict with both com-mercial and sport fishing interests because the resulting pollution depleted fish-eries (Heilprin, 2006; Fish Need Food, 2008). Bureaucratic influence results from its signaling just such intrusions on conventional understandings of issues.[7] Key to the theory of dual dynamics and the provision of information is that this signaling occurs in the context of competition (e.g., between USDA and EPA over how agriculture affects the environment).

The key assumption of standard theories of bureaucracy in U.S. politics is that the preferences of elected politicians diverge from those of the bureaucrats whom they oversee. Although it is true that both politicians and bureaucrats may prefer different policy solutions (e.g., market mechanisms versus regulation or preferences for certain types of regulation), it is less clear that they hold different preferences regarding particular policy problems (e.g., regulation of derivatives versus the independence of accountants in the case of securities regulation). Whereas agency theory and other economic approaches to the study of bureaucracy understand preferences as determinative as they interact with incentive structures and institutional constraints, the theory of dual dynamics developed here suggests that limits of attention constrain the operation of preferences. That is, preferences for particular solutions matter only after one's attention is directed to a given problem and a particular definition of that problem.[8]

Problem definitions specify causes, consequences, and theories connecting these two and implying a strategy for government redress of the problem. These problem definitions shape both the information that bureaucracies generate for use internally and that is ultimately passed on to elected policy makers. Problem definitions favor not only certain types and quantities of information but also certain types of analysis of this information. With the construction of a problem definition or the understanding of a problem, the stage is set for its transmission to higher levels of government for consideration and decision.

Information Generation

The end result of problem monitoring and definition is a particular perspective or conceptual understanding of the problem useful for generating and evaluating alternative solutions. Dodd and Schott (1986, p. 2) attribute the centrality of bureaucracy to its "refining of congressional intent." The influence of bureaucracy in public policy goes to the core of helping define not only the means but also the goals of government. When the notion that bureaucracy

---

[7] With the poor harvests of Russian grain harvests in the early to mid-1970s, agriculture further became a matter of foreign policy and national security. Agriculture has in recent times again become important in matters of foreign policy (Kilpatrick, 1972; Egan, 1973; Kraft, 1973; Agricultural Export Controls, 1984; A Worsening Food Crisis, 2008) because of heightened attention to concerns surrounding energy independence and alternative fuels such as ethanol. The foreign policy dimensions will likely weigh heavy in future foreign policy, trade, and national security debates because a global food crisis seems all but certain in the coming years (Bourne, 2009).

[8] Simon (1996, p. 108) suggests that the search for solutions can take place only after one has formed a problem representation.

helps refine the intent or goals of Congress is combined with what I label the "Elmore problem," it is clear that bureaucratic influence stems most fundamentally from the provision of information concerning the problems on the agenda. This information is garnered from problem expertise developed by bureaucracy through proximity to the problem, on the one hand, and through congressional prioritization and steering, on the other.

Goal adjustment is an important feature of the dual dynamics of the system and depends on feedback (Deutsch, 1966). As the receptors in the administrative state, bureaucracies acquire and transmit information on emergent and evolving issues as well as the current performance of the system with regard to existing issues. Again, even the control envisioned by overhead democracy requires this information in order to assess how to steer the bureaucracy. This information forms the building blocks for the adjustment of policy through time and across different issues. Goal adjustment is made possible as problem monitoring and definition build toward information generation, which ultimately feeds back into the system through the authoritative decisions of elected officials. This feedback adjusts not only the goals of policy making but also, through congressional prioritization, sets the bounds of problem monitoring and definition into the future. Chapter 4 discusses the increasing importance of this feedback in the system of policy making over time.

Information has many meanings in political science and public policy. To understand the place and importance of the bureaucratic provision of information, it is important to understand both the features of bureaucracy that bear on the information and those features of the information that are valuable to elected officials.

Information generation is the final stage involved in the bottom-up dynamic of bureaucratic problem solving. Though I label this process information generation, it really comprises two related activities by bureaucracy. First, the bureaucracy must generate information concerning the issues or problems confronting government. Second, it must provide or communicate this information to elected officials for their consideration. The generation of information is heavily dependent on the earlier processes of problem monitoring and definition. In turn, the communication of this information to elected officials is heavily dependent on the interaction of bureaucrats and elected officials within the context of policy subsystems.

Issues, and especially working definitions of problems within given issues, presuppose certain types and quantities of information. For instance, the generation of information in the issue of agriculture is predisposed toward economic types of information involving food production and markets for commodities. In contrast, though the issue of the environment bears heavily on business productivity and the economy, information types in this area tend toward the scientific and legal. The nature of the information generated depends in part on the problem or issue at hand.

Moving from the problem to the organization, bureaucracies represent the greatest diversity of institutional organization in the entire political system in the United States. The bureaucracy contains many organizational forms such as cabinet departments, independent regulatory commissions and boards, and government corporations, to name a few. The organizational form influences not only the types of information provided but also the quantity and dynamics of its generation. For instance, the Department of Interior is home to the Bureau of Land Management, Minerals Management Service, U.S. Fish and Wildlife Service, and the National Park Service. These very different organizations and the different types of problems they are expected to monitor lead to diverse definitions of the central problems facing Interior and, hence, the types and quantity of information that it generates. More generally, independent regulatory commissions are often thought to be more nimble organizations than their departmental counterparts, responding more quickly to problems that arise in the policy-making environment. Cabinet departments are more adept at dealing with a diverse policy agenda, processing vastly different issues simultaneously.

The type of activities that bureaucracies choose to carry out in pursuing their policy goals and those of elected officials is another influence on information generation. In general, there are four avenues through which bureaucracies pursue policy goals: substantive rulemaking (the bureaucratic equivalent of lawmaking or legislation), regulatory enforcement, legal proceedings, and subsystem politicking. Most bureaucracies utilize all four of these mechanisms, but some use one more than the others. For example, the USDA spends a great deal of time in substantive rulemaking, refining the guidelines for its various programs geared to agricultural production. In contrast, many independent boards and commissions favor legal proceedings and enforcement actions (e.g., National Labor Relations Board).

Delving deeper into bureaucratic organization, the internal controls so prevalent in the older public administration literature influence the generation of information. Some bureaucracies are staffed by individuals with professional allegiances beyond the confines of the gray, marble building they occupy in Washington, D.C. Economists, lawyers, scientists, engineers, sociologists, and public policy experts are only a few of the professional disciplines represented in the bureaucracy. These and other professions demand a certain allegiance to the tools and craft of their trades or disciplines. Other internal influences on information generation include the political allegiances of bureaucrats (Clinton and Lewis, 2008) and bureaucrats' beliefs and values concerning their careers and work (Downs, 1967).

Bureaucracies must choose which information that they have generated to transmit to elected officials and the broader subsystem. At that point it is important to understand what is valuable to elected officials. The degree of influence of the information provided by bureaucracies hinges on two aspects of bureaucratic problem solving and what elected officials might glean from these features.

The first aspect of the information is its political relevance. Who cares about the problem and why? Though scholars and schools of public policy often stress the politics–administration dichotomy, bureaucratic problem solving carries with it both explicit and implicit information about the state of politics surrounding the problem for elected officials. Information generation is not neutral, even when geared to solving policy problems that are real and detrimental to the broader system and general public. It favors some citizens' claims and demands on government and not others, and some organized interests and not others. It privileges some political stances and arguments over others. When bureaucracies issue regulation, carry out enforcement activities, and administer programs, their efforts offer a wealth of information relevant to the political strategies of elected officials and other members of the subsystem.

The second aspect of information is its policy relevance. Political science has created more than three decades of work whose goal has been to understand how democracy is served when bureaucrats' preferences diverge from those of elected officials. What still lingers in the background is that these preferences often diverge because bureaucrats have well-intentioned, well-informed preferences for what they consider proper or good public policy.[9]

The bureaucracy, along with congressional and some presidential staff, is the institutional memory of government. Bureaucracies contain a wealth of information on the likely consequences of given courses of public policy, including the likelihood of failure and success, the difficulties associated with implementation using given policy tools or mechanisms, and their differential effects on specific policy targets. Whether or not elected officials agree with these assessments, ignoring this information often puts the policy objectives of elected officials at great peril. These considerations motivate the logic of bureaucratic influence from both the bureaucratic and congressional perspective.

In the course of generating and transmitting information to elected officials, bureaucratic competition in the provision of information comes into play. Bureaucracies do not operate in issue or policy vacuums where their information is the only information available. This understanding stands in contrast to work in overhead democracy, which usually depicts single-source information in theories and models. The theory of dual dynamics offered here engenders competition-based, rather than incentive-based, provision of information. Jurisdictional competition and overlap define both politics and policy making in the administrative state. This is as true for bureaucracies as

---

[9] Miller (2005) has argued that bureaucrats, and not elected officials, are potential guardians of the public will and welfare under conditions of "corruption" of the principal. The argument centers on whether bureaucrats should be beholden to elected officials when elected officials do not have the public interest at heart or when elected officials do not understand the problem with sufficient detail.

for congressional committees, which are the anchors of policy subsystems, and hence the administrative state (see King, 1997).

Bureaucracies compete in the communication or transmission of information to elected officials. The effect of this overlap and competition is easily understood by contemplating what legislators or committees might glean from the chorus of bureaucracies transmitting information about various policy problems. For instance, if the problem or issue at hand concerns pesticide regulation, three bureaucracies are immediately relevant: the Department of Agriculture, the department of the Interior's National Oceanographic and Atmospheric Administration (NOAA, which regulates commercial fishing), and the Environmental Protection Agency. Obviously, these three institutions will often be at loggerheads over the proper course of public policy or even the nature of the problem (or if there is a problem at all). Members of Congress are savvy at promoting or restricting this competition. For this reason, the dual dynamics of bureaucratic problem solving and congressional prioritization subsume much of the logic of information provision in overhead democracy.

Consider an alternative scenario. What if the three organizations listed earlier transmit information concerning the problem that tends to dovetail toward very similar conclusions for the course of public policy? If these diverse bureaucracies are essentially "saying" the same thing about the problem, this is a powerful signal to policymakers that the problem is not only of great importance, politically and policy-wise, but also that the information they provide is highly reliable and not likely biased by politicking peculiar to those bureaucracies or subsystems. Barring information external to the system, the extent of the diversity of perspectives is a good indicator of the proper course to take and greatly reduces both the political and policy uncertainty associated with the decision making of elected officials.[10]

This discussion of bureaucratic competition and jurisdictional overlap raises a final point that is important for understanding the theory of dual dynamics. When bureaucracies transmit information to Congress based on problem monitoring and definition, they do so amidst the din of other bureaucracies and political actors in the process. It is therefore useful to think of bureaucracies as "signaling" information to elected officials, rather than simply turning it over or trading it. That is, the information they transmit is attended by noise and uncertainty, but this uncertainty arises from competition rather than from information being privately held. Bureaucracies transmit a plethora of information to elected officials, and this information from multiple bureaucracies must be prioritized by Congress and given meaning so it can steer the course of public policy.

---

[10] This would be a straight forward implication of the theory of congressional decision making promulgated by Kingdon (1981).

2.3.4 Congressional Prioritization

The counterpart to bottom-up bureaucratic problem solving is congressional prioritization at the upper echelons of the administrative state. Congressional influence on the policy process is pervasive at every point in the process. The mere act of congressional prioritization of issues changes the way bureaucracies generate information and define problems. Like the bureaucracy, congressional influence stems in part from the limits of attention of the institution. Much scholarly work on the policy process has centered on issue dynamics and attention in Congress (Jones, 1994, 2001; Jones and Baumgartner, 2005).

Attention, at some level of aggregation, is limited for institutions and organizations in much the same way that it is limited for individuals. Further, delegation to bureaucracy is in part a product of this limited capacity for attention to various issues in Congress or, more generally, in elected institutions in governing systems of all types. Given this state of affairs, the way in which Congress prioritizes issues and the policy problems associated with these issues over time becomes incredibly important in the dual dynamics of the administrative state. This importance can be traced to two broad sources in the course of congressional policy making: the constitutional, authoritative position of Congress within the governing system and issue dynamics in Congress.

The influence of congressional prioritization begins with the creation and authorization of bureaucracies. Bureaucracies are created and imbued with missions in broad but defined areas of public policy that roughly match the issues on the governmental agenda. Bureaucracies also extend the substantive delegation that begins with the congressional committee system. It is no coincidence that both congressional committees and bureaucracies substantively resemble the set of subsystems that make policy day to day in American politics.

Bureaucratic problem solving is structured by these mission statements and the goals of public policy that give life to these missions. Around this core set of ideas and goals, regulations and programs are developed that are meant to accomplish the goals and mission of the given bureaucracy. This mission, set of goals, and implementing programs, regulations, and other activities amount to what is a "first draft," or at least the structure of, congressional intent. This intent is then refined through the information generated in bureaucratic problem solving.

This top-down, authoritative influence of congressional prioritization is direct and may occur without reference to bureaucratic maneuvering or politicking. The influence of congressional prioritization that stems from agenda-setting dynamics in Congress is at once less direct and much more pervasive, and it involves efforts by the bureaucracy to gain the attention of Congress. For various reasons identified in the literature on congressional agenda setting, issues rise and fall in prominence on the congressional agenda. For Example, in the months following the terrorist attacks on the World Trade

Center in New York City, the issue of terrorism and responses to the attacks dominated the congressional agenda. In the wake of the attacks, many issues came to be framed and understood in terms of their relationship to terrorism. For example, the Public Health Security and Bioterrorism Preparedness and Response Act,[11] reframed the goals and missions of bureaucracies in areas of food safety and agriculture in such a way as to benefit from overwhelming congressional attention to terrorism. This is one of many instances in which political actors in other issues highlighted or reframed the aspects of their issue area relevant to terrorism and homeland security (May et al., 2009a, 2009b).

Note that both types of influence of congressional prioritization stem from the limits of congressional attention. The top-down influence provided by authoritative policy pronouncements proceeds from the need to delegate the responsibility of problem monitoring and problem solving generally to bureaucracy. Beyond this top-down, authoritative influence, congressional prioritization of issues in the course of agenda setting structures bureaucratic problem solving and provision of information by providing the impetus for bureaucratic issue politicking. This bureaucratic issue politicking moves the bureaucratic agenda more in line with the issues and problems most salient to elected officials.

Both of these types of prioritization are important for understanding congressional influence within the dual dynamics of the administrative state. The agenda-setting dynamics of Congress structure bureaucratic problem solving in absence of the top-down intervention that many scholars and pundits cite as the source of congressional influence or control of bureaucracy. In addition to the influence of prioritization offered by top-down, authoritative policy making and the more organic influence offered in congressional agenda-setting dynamics, Congress structures bureaucratic problem solving more specifically by also synthesizing the vast array of information provided by bureaucracies and making tradeoffs among the myriad issues whose constituents clamber for attention and congressional agenda space.

Synthesis of Information
Members of Congress are faced with a vast expanse of information emanating not only from bureaucracies charged with problem solving but also from organized interests and the general public. This information comes to elected officials for the most part already imbued with a particular problem definition and a sense that the issue or problem is in some way important for policy makers. This is not to say that elected officials always agree with these definitions and sense of importance. Further, elected policy makers sometimes have a high degree of uncertainty about both the meaning of the information and its purported consequences.

---

[11] P.L. 107–188.

Problem definitions often do not come to Congress "whole." This notion partly underlies Kingdon's (1984) claim that problems and solutions are often not connected in any rational fashion – that problems "search" for solutions and solutions "search" for problems for which to attach themselves. Often problem definitions carry only the information that something is wrong or, even, that something *may* be wrong in the policy environment.

Elected officials have a different vantage point than that of bureaucracies. Bureaucracies are purposefully delegated the responsibility of attention in more or less distinct areas of policy. Elected officials, however, must interpret a vast array of information, which is often incomplete and spread across disparate issues. Information supplied from the bureaucracy and other actors must be given meaning, interpreted and synthesized into public policy. With this synthesis, Congress privileges some information, groups, and bureaucracies over others. It also privileges some problem definitions over others with a resulting future influence on the information supply.

The information must be interpreted in light of prevailing governing arrangements and prevailing politics. This presents the central tension of congressional policy making, if not of democracies of all types: responsive versus problem-solving government. If being responsive to the general public and organized interests in a pluralist system coincides with solving the policy problem at hand, all is well and good. However, being democratically responsive and accountable often comes at the expense of solving or at least addressing sometimes severe policy problems. This predicament is made more acute by the relationship between issues and their supporting publics in American politics.

Tradeoffs among Issues

Congressional problem prioritization is vital in understanding the administrative state because of the nature of the issues on the governmental agenda. Specifically, members of Congress are faced with tradeoffs among issues because of two circumstances of congressional decision making. First, Congress faces limits of attention and, hence, a finite capacity for the institutional agenda. Second, the nature of the issues themselves presents Congress with inevitable tradeoffs.

Limits to congressional attention and the resultant consequences for the information and problem definitions generated by bureaucracy have already been discussed. Equally important, however, is the fact that issues are often interdependent or even boundary-spanning, which poses severe problems for attaining policy goals simultaneously across the array of issues. For instance, performing well on the environmental goals of public policy often necessarily entails performing less well on policy goals related to agriculture or energy. This interdependency means that the collection of goals are zero-sum ventures: progress on one goal often means regression on another.

The interdependent nature of issues fosters tradeoffs that affect bureaucratic problem definition and generation of information in ways related to the limits of congressional attention. Problem definitions are affected as the bureaucracies and other political actors struggle to redefine the linkages among issues in a more favorable light that obscures, if not remedies, the tradeoffs. This is easily seen with recent arguments concerning "green" jobs creation, which try to link performing well on environmental goals to creating a strong labor market. Although issue tradeoffs faced by elected officials position some bureaucracies and publics in an advantaged position, bureaucracies and publics not in the spotlight are forever adjusting their definitions and supply of information to fit with prevailing issue attention in Congress.

Coordination, Competition, and Policy Pronouncements

Elected officials must make policy and coordinate action among the different bureaucracies populating each issue area on the governmental agenda. Further, policy makers must do so in the face of issue tradeoffs and incommensurate, even incomplete, information and problem definitions generated by bureaucracies.

The bureaucratic arm of the administrative state is designed along functional and topical lines of specialization. Functional and topical specialization is the essence of modern bureaucracy going back to its origins in the 1930s. This specialization and the separability it fosters cultivate expertise in specific policy areas. At the level of Congress with its committee system, elected officials are tasked with synthesis of this vast array of information on issues that present tradeoffs. Bureaucratic functional and topical specialization places high demands on the ability of members of Congress to coordinate the levers of government in making and implementing public policy.

Both coordination among bureaucracies and competition among bureaucracies benefit members of Congress. Both are useful for understanding how the administrative state goes about addressing the issues on its agenda. Members of Congress collectively or particular congressional committees may choose to foster either coordination or competition by mandate or through the prioritization of issues. Attempts at fostering coordination are well known in the study of policy implementation, but perhaps less so in the generation of information that feeds into policy making. For example, the bureaucracies charged with the disparate aspects of what we now label homeland security were faced with demands to coordinate their activity in preventing and responding to terrorist attacks. The issue of prime importance in these debates about homeland security involved the generation, synthesis, and use of information about various aspects of the boundary-spanning problem. Competition among different bureaucracies shows up in research more as a particular management strategy within organizations (e.g., the competitive management style of FDR) than as a phenomenon related to the government's ability to address issues on the agenda.

Despite an organizational and institutional bias toward stasis, congressional prioritization may foster coordination and competition absent any need to issue a formal mandate from the floor. By considering issues in bundles, elected officials can decrease those issues' separability, thereby decreasing the separability of the bureaucracies charged with problem solving in these issues and fostering their coordination.

Although coordination has probably received more fanfare in scholarly attention to bureaucracy, competition plays an especially important role in the dual dynamics of bureaucratic problem solving and congressional prioritization. Where elected officials are able to foster competition, the diversity of problem definitions and the quality of the information generated in bureaucratic problem solving likely reduce the uncertainty faced by Congress in charting a course for public policy.

Finally, the fostering of competition within broad issue areas means that thare are multiple bureaucracies monitoring for emergent policy problems. This decreases the likelihood that elected officials are caught off-guard when a major problem comes to the fore. Bureaucratic problem solving and its relationship to agenda setting are very different from policy implementation and especially regulatory enforcement. This problem solving also stands in contrast to complaints of regulatory uncertainty when bureaucratic jurisdictions overlap. In the dual dynamics model of bureaucracy, bureaucratic overlap is a tool of problem monitoring. If one bureaucracy fails to transmit relevant information to Congress, another will assuredly do so, gaining advantage in resultant efforts to formulate public policy. A focus on the dual dynamics of agenda setting in the administrative state leads to some different assumptions and logic undergirding the relationship between bureaucrats and elected officials than found in overhead democracy or public management.

2.4 LOGIC OF DUAL DYNAMICS

The dual dynamics of bureaucratic problem solving and congressional prioritization presuppose an alternative way of looking at the micro-interactions that occur between bureaucrats and elected officials. At the core of the existing framework for understanding bureaucracy in American politics is the assumption that bureaucracies hold private information that must be induced through incentive structures. The dual dynamics theory does not dispute the importance of incentive structures, but offers an alternative way to view their operation in light of agenda setting in the administrative state.

In addition, most work on the bureaucracy and on subsystems more generally proceeds from the assumption that information generated by bureaucracies is biased in some way, either because of self-interest or political affiliation. The dual dynamics of agenda setting takes the view that bias is ultimately an empirical question. It further rests on the notion that elected officials are able to garner useful information from bureaucratic problem solving, even in the presence of bias, through the processes associated with congressional prioritization of problems. It is the provision of information that yields influence in agenda setting, and not its withholding, and this influence requires gaining the attention of policy makers. This assertion follows from the presence of competition among bureaucracies and other actors in the provision of information for steering policy change.

The assumption undergirding the logic of dual dynamics is that Mayhew's (1974) view of politics holds for elected officials and to some degree for bureaucrats. Elected officials and bureaucrats want to preserve their positions and extend their influence. The argument offered here also assumes that, in addition to more base political considerations, both bureaucrats and elected officials on some level care about public policy and want to influence its course.

In terms of decision making pertaining to the course of public policy, the dual dynamics of agenda setting take as a given that the most fundamental concern for policy makers is uncertainty and its mitigation, particularly regarding what problems are relevant and how to understand them. These notions lead straightforwardly to the view that bureaucrats and the bureaucracies they inhabit are *attention-seeking* where agenda setting is concerned. In contrast to existing theories, which view bureaucrats as preferring policy making outside the spotlight of congressional politics, bureaucratic problem solving requires that bureaucracies are able to get the attention of elected officials.

2.4.1 The Logic of Bureaucratic Problem Solving

The suggestion that bureaucracies seek attention from political overseers stands in contrast to the logic underlying the theory of overhead democracy. Research in American politics, with its emphasis on political control and subsystem depictions, suggests that bureaucracies prefer to make policy in the dark alleys of government, shielded from the peering eyes of the elected officials as well as the broader public.

In agency theory, the central animating feature of political–administrative relations is the notion that bureaucracies possess private information on their performance and the true nature of policy problems that must be induced via the design of incentive structures (Niskanen, 1971; Mitnick, 1975; Moe, 1984; McCubbins, 1985; Moe, 1985; Banks and Weingast, 1992; Bawn, 1997).[12] Specifically, politicians face both adverse selection (where they do not have information concerning which agency would be best for the job) and moral hazard (where there is difficulty observing performance pursuant to delegations that have already occurred). Particularly where problems of moral hazard are involved, bureaucracies are believed to both covet and foster the inability of

---

[12] Agency theory is social scientific terminology for the contractual paradigm in economics. At the center of the contractual paradigm is the notion of transaction costs, or the costs of doing business. Analysis of transaction costs has shed much light on the behavior and interaction of firms, and it is from the contractual paradigm that principal-agent models are formulated. Moe (1984) cautions against the straightforward application of the model to politics.

politicians to observe behavior and performance, because doing so increases bureaucratic power vis-à-vis political principals.

Likewise, theories of subsystem politics depict bureaucracy as part of a triumvirate of actors (along with organized interests and congressional committees) that make policy within specific issue areas whose boundaries are defined by non-interference pacts among the "subgovernments" (Lowi, 1969; McCool, 1990; Worsham, 1997).[13] Freedom to make and implement policy within these arrangements requires not only that non-interference pacts be stable among subsystems but also that the subsystem is free from interference from above by the elected institutions of government and the federal judiciary.[14]

Key to both overhead democracy and the notion of subsystem politics is the underlying view that bureaucracies avoid attention and are most successful in the making and implementing of public policies when they are screened from democratic forces. Yet, neither of these theories fares well in explaining why bureaucrats are so prominent in policy debates (Miller, 2007), even when the issue represents a political hot button. For example, the financial crisis of fall 2008 witnessed then Secretary of the Treasury Hank Paulson, Chairman of the Securities and Exchange Commission (SEC) Christopher Cox, and Federal Reserve Chairman Benjamin Bernanke take center stage in the crafting and implementation of a bailout for large financial institutions. Their role was striking given that the regulatory failures of theses agencies, with congressional complicity, were in large part the cause of the financial collapse.

More recently, Timothy Geithner, Paulson's successor as secretary of the treasury; Sheila Bair, chief of the Federal Deposit Insurance Corporation; and head of the SEC Mary Shapiro were locked in a very public debate about restructuring the financial regulatory system in the United States (Appelbaum and Goldfarb, 2009). In fact, economic crises in general are notable for the degree to which they propel bureaucracies to center stage. Especially in situations of crisis involving the most salient political issues, bureaucrats are prominent players in the policy debate about both the nature of problems and the formulation of solutions (May et al., 2009b).

Naturally, bureaucrats gain attention for an assortment of reasons, not all of which are desirable from the perspective of the bureaucrat. Then-head of the

---

[13] Variations on the notion of subsystem government are almost infinite in the study of policy processes, which has led to considerable confusion and debate about what constitutes a subsystem (see Burstein, 1991; McCool, 1998; Sabatier and Jenkins-Smith, 1993) and about the influence of subsystems on policy change and government (Baumgartner and Jones, 1993; Worsham, 1998; Howlett and Ramesh, 1998; May et al., 2006). Similar notions of non-interference in institutional arrangements have also animated the study of congressional organization (Shepsle, 1978, 1979; Shepsle and Weingast, 1987).

[14] Note that institutional and policy process scholars have found maintaining these pacts and avoiding attention from above to be difficult, especially over extended periods (Baumgartner and Jones, 1993; King, 1997). See Melnick (1983) on the interference of the courts in subsystem affairs, especially regulation.

Federal Emergency Management Agency (FEMA) Michael Brown, "Brownie," probably would have preferred a little less attention in the wake of the disastrous government response to Hurricane Katrina in 2005. The same could be said for officials at the Minerals Management Service after the Deepwater Horizon oil rig disaster in April 2010. Despite those circumstances in which bureaucracies cannot avoid attention from the broader political system, there is a clear logic to attention-attracting and directing behavior by the federal bureaucracy. Influencing public policy requires getting the attention of elected officials and even the broader public. The dual dynamics of agenda setting highlight the role of this attention-seeking and attention-directing behavior.

The proclivity for federal bureaucracies to both attract attention from elected institutions and to attempt to direct or channel this attention arises from a concern for both policy and organizational maintenance and survival. Bureaucracies have an interest in the issues they monitor, and they hold opinions about the appropriate course of action given particular problems or configurations of issues in the policy environment. As I noted earlier, this interest precisely explains why bureaucracies develop *problem expertise* associated with the monitoring of the policy environment, along with the more traditional *solution expertise* associated with policy implementation.

This concern for issues manifests itself in how bureaucrats define given policy problems as they arise. For example, an economic disruption might be viewed by the Treasury Department as a consumer credit problem and simultaneously by the Federal Deposit Insurance Corporation as a problem of predatory lending by banks (this closely mirrors the situation in early fall 2008). These varying views occur both because the two agencies have problem expertise that tends to color their response to disturbances they observe and because they are staffed by professionals with different orientations toward the economy stemming from their respective professions. Agencies are often "out in front," demanding attention because their affiliations and experience lead them to care about policy making in given areas or about particular policy problems. Even more so, bureaucracies care about how given disturbances in the policy environment are interpreted by the public at large and by political overseers in particular.

The constitutional position of bureaucracy in the U.S. system of government means that bureaucracies are often not legally or materially equipped to solve the problems they observe and define. Under such circumstances, problem solving requires appealing to the elected institutions for authority and resources to both monitor problems in the policy environment and engage in problem solving. Bureaucracies need to attract the attention of political overseers who have the power to grant such authority and channel resources to given bureaucracies or can prioritize issues associated with particular sets of bureaucracies. Put differently, bureaucracies must sometimes engage in classic conflict expansion to perform their monitoring and information-generating function within the system and, more fundamentally, to influence policy. In terms of the dual dynamics of agenda setting, bureaucratic problem solving relies on congressional problem prioritization not only for direction but also for policy making discretion and resources.

Of course, bureaucracies' interests in issues and policymaking are not always so benign or benevolent. Bureaucracies also care about policy because prescribing the contours of debate on given issues serves to foster their control of the issue and ability to steer the policy debate. Both Aberbach (1990) and King (1997) note the importance of controlling problem definitions for steering resultant policy debates and, ultimately, policy change. Although these scholars were primarily interested in congressional committee jurisdictions, their insights' relevance to bureaucracy cannot be denied. Bureaucracies compete with one another for influence on policy issues, and this competition saturates the entire administrative system. The USDA struggles with the EPA for control of issues relating to pesticide use and runoff. The FDIC competes for influence with the SEC, Federal Reserve, and Department of Treasury for influence in banking regulation. The SEC wrestles with the Commodity Futures Trading Commission over securities regulation, and so on. Bureaucratic jurisdictions are no less competitive than their congressional committee counterparts: this is a fundamentally underappreciated feature of the administrative state.

In practice, this competition means that important information that may affect a policy debate will not be withheld, because competitors will likely supply this information. The EPA may not be able to transmit information on the details of agricultural policy, but if this information is withheld by the USDA, then the EPA can certainly render an environmental definition of the policy problem with attendant information. This competition is a key factor in studies of subsystems and overhead democracy. The duplicative, overlapping nature of both congressional committee jurisdictions and those of their administrative counterparts fuels the tug of war among multiple principals and agents (Whitford, 2005).

The battle for influence among institutions in the system suggests that steering the policy debate in one's favor requires speaking up and drawing the attention of the elected institutions. Although this motivation is more self-interested than statesman-like, steering the policy debate also requires conflict expansion in an attempt to influence inter-institutional politics. Often, the outcome of this battle for problem definition will determine the very jurisdictions that define the boundaries of bureaucratic problem monitoring. Sometimes losing these battles means losing the ability to attend the issue at all. Influencing the parameters of the policy debate and the general direction of policy making implies that bureaucracy must seek out attention and channel this attention to its benefit – whether out of policy interest or more base self-interest. In the institutionally fragmented U.S. system, influencing policy dynamics means influencing other elected and bureaucratic institutions.

The propensity of bureaucracies to attract and attempt to direct attention is also rooted in a more nuanced understanding of how federal agencies, or even institutions generally, view risk. Studies of bureaucracy assume (sometimes explicitly and other times implicitly) that the subservient position of bureaucracy in the governing system means that agencies are risk averse. These studies further imply that this risk aversion means bureaucracies will keep a low profile and act behind the scenes in both responding to political principals and in advocating openly for their own objectives. The dual dynamics of agenda setting implies a more nuanced conception of bureaucratic risk aversion. For bureaucracies operating within a system based on problem monitoring and information generation, risk aversion does not always equate to a reluctance to garner attention.

Perhaps the biggest enemy of policy makers (or decision makers generally) of all types is uncertainty. For a federal bureaucracy charged with monitoring the policy environment for potential problems, it does not pay to allow unexpected problems to blindside elected officials. Further, to the degree these disturbances in the system represent real policy problems and not just political problems, such surprises will bring the bureaucracy not only political but also public condemnation. In addition, assigning blame to a federal agency becomes harder if the agency has fully communicated the nature and severity of the potential policy problem to elected officials. In this case, information on policy problems generated by the bureaucracy serves as a mechanism for blame avoidance for federal agencies.[15]

Moreover, recent research has shown that agencies are going to greater lengths than ever to communicate their activities to the broader public and to play a role in cultivating their own public perceptions, perhaps for the very reasons outlined here (Graber, 2003). Simple blame avoidance (Mayhew, 1974) requires the garnering of attention to potential policy problems (and thus to the agency sending the signal), as well as attempting to direct the attention of elected officials to policy problems. Here, risk aversion requires attention-seeking and attention-directing behavior by the bureaucracy. The same holds true for efforts to claim credit. Bureaucratic credit claiming requires attention-seeking behavior in much the same way as for election motivated politicians. For these reasons, risk aversion in the administrative state for the bureaucracy demands a proactive stance toward monitoring for policy problems and directing attention to real and potential policy problems.

Still, bureaucracies do not signal and press for influence in a vacuum. The political-administrative system is home to an array of powerful interests and institutions. Chief among these are organized interests. Understanding bureaucratic influence requires a clear understanding of the context in which bureaucracies interact and influence policy dynamics in the administrative state. Yet, bureaucracies are still central to the ability of government to address its policy

---

[15] For more on blame avoidance and its effects on policy, see Mortensen (2013).

agenda because they possess distinct informational advantages vis-à-vis their private sector counterparts. Furthermore, the relationship between organized interests and the bureaucracy is a two-way street of influence, as bureaucracies structure interest group participation and integrate it with the machinery of government. For these reasons, the federal bureaucracy remains an important influence on policy dynamics even in the presence of other powerful actors populating the administrative state.

2.4.2 The Congressional Logic of Bureaucratic Influence

Congressional attentiveness to bureaucratic signaling cannot be explained solely by the standard perspective that Congress lacks the time, resources, and expertise to write detailed legislation.[16] Although bureaucratic policy making discretion certainly involves these sorts of calculations, politicians are loathe to choke off the supply of information feeding political and policy calculations. Detailed legislation, by its nature, necessarily restricts the spectrum of the policy environment that a given bureaucracy might monitor. This reluctance to restrict the sphere that the bureaucracy could monitor increases as politicians face uncertainty. The type of uncertainty I am suggesting here is not the type associated with the ideal points of relevant members of Congress and bureaucrats, but rather uncertainty concerning the nature of the problem confronted by elected and bureaucratic institutions alike.[17] The congressional logic of bureaucratic influence is fundamentally about the problems faced by government at any point in time and the emergent problems that members of Congress might reasonably expect to face. The congressional logic of bureaucratic influence also extends to the uncertainty that pervades the process of congressional problem prioritization.

Kingdon (1981) argues that members of Congress make decisions by searching for consensus among groups of people who serve as important cues to the politically prudent choice. These groups included fellow members of Congress, constituencies, interest groups, and even bureaucrats. Kingdon's theory of congressional voting decisions is a general one. For Kingdon, the goal of the process of decision making is to reduce uncertainty in the political environment of members of Congress. Most importantly, Kingdon (1981, p. xv) notes that this decision-making process has "implications for the *patterns of information flow* in the legislature" [emphasis added]. Building on the notion that elected officials look to the larger political environment to reduce the uncertainty that

---

[16] I recognize, of course, that this is often true (see Huber et al., 2001; Huber and Shipan, 2002).

[17] Nevertheless, scholars of American politics rightly observe that politicians are uncertain about the preferences of both other political actors and administrative officials and that this uncertainty in part drives interactions in the administrative state (see Moe, 1989; Epstein and O'Halloran, 1999; Lewis, 2003).

plagues decision making in complex policy environments, one can start to see the general contours of the congressional logic of bureaucratic problem solving and influence. Bureaucracies become key purveyors of information, even in the presence of organized interests and other actors in the process. Further, this process of decision making, which allows bureaucratic signaling to be influential, has tremendous consequences for how information flows up and down the ladders of the administrative state.

This propensity to reduce uncertainty pertains not only to making decisions on public policy but also has straightforward implications for political strategy. As noted earlier, attention in politics is a scarce resource. The delegation of attention allows the elected institutions of government not only to increase their capacity to pay attention to many issues simultaneously but also to engage in issue politicking. The promotion of pluralistic information flows has political payoffs. Just as Franklin Roosevelt promoted competition among the members of his "Brain Trust" for the purpose of hearing all relevant information concerning particular policy problems, so too promoting additional flows of information has its political benefits.

Multiple streams of information allow a politically motivated policy maker to more fully gauge the nature of both the policy and political environment. Remember that policy makers need to understand not only the pros and cons of a policy but also who cares and who is apathetic about the issue. Moreover, pluralistic arrangements for the flow of information contribute to the provision of information: if one unit or group refuses to supply the information relevant to the decision, others will likely do so in an effort to steer the discussion or debate.[18]

A cursory review of congressional hearings and even of legislation signed into law reveals that much of what bureaucracy is directed to do relates to the generation of information: issue reports, coordinate with others, and generally monitor the policy environment.[19] It would be an oddity if elected officials delegated to bureaucracies the responsibility to monitor policy environments and then took no note of the information feedback pursuant to these grants

---

[18] Of course, pluralistic arrangements for information provision also have their drawbacks. These drawbacks are rightly noted by scholars examining how policy subsystems or subgovernments limit access in an effort to control problem definitions and limit the role of outside interests (Lowi, 1969; Aberbach, 1990; Worsham, 1997). These same scholars, however, show that it is simply not possible in the long run to completely restrict and control the flow of information in a given policy area, especially under the strain of shifting attention at the congressional level (Baumgartner and Jones, 1993; King, 1997).

[19] Nevertheless, this could be viewed as paperwork in the service of political accountability and control, and this is certainly part of the story. Even in the instances where these directives to generate information are in service of political influence, elected officials could not very effectively maintain that influence without attending to this information. Put simply, political control of the bureaucracy requires attention to the information flows generated by the federal bureaucracy, whether oriented toward control of the bureaucracy or to discretion and delegation.

of responsibility. When elected officials ignore that information, they fuel a tendency of the system toward maladaptation and contribute to the inefficiency of the problem-solving process.

Of course, information generated by the federal bureaucracy pursuant to disturbances in the policy environment need not be objective. Bureaucratic preferences are no longer the stuff of assumption in formal models, but are real and measurable (Clinton and Lewis, 2008). Here again, the pluralistic and competitive jurisdictional configuration of the bureaucracy, along with the institutionalized and regularized relationships that are the hallmark of policy subsystems, foster the generation and provision of useful (if not entirely "accurate") information, because policy makers are able to triangulate among multiple biased sources of information.

In general, systems can be characterized by either efficiency or reliability: efficient systems are not usually reliable systems and vice versa. Landau (1969) and Bendor (1985) have argued that system redundancy is of prime importance where reliability is vital.[20] Long a source of contempt by popular observers and some politicians, bureaucratic redundancy serves to make the system more reliable. A bureaucracy not providing objective information on the policy environment risks losing sway with policy makers to a competitor. Because bureaucratic redundancy, overlap, and even duplicity aid the system in the generation and provision of useful information concerning policy problems, redundancy, far from indicating wasteful government, can be helpful in the processing of the policy agenda. This is true whether the problem is a failure to generate objective information or the more benign error in the system of monitoring.

Bureaucracies are also embedded within policy subsystems, long a focus of research on the administrative state. Subsystems are notorious for sheltering participants from democratic influences and ensuring that the powerful receive the benefits of policy making (see Lowi, 1969).[21] However, these "cozy" relationships between organized interests, congressional committees, and federal bureaucracies possibly salvage the best of what many view as a bad situation.[22] These relationships are regularized and institutionalized in the system of legislative oversight and sustained over long periods of time (especially where career bureaucrats and staffers of congressional committees are concerned). The result is that bureaucracies are likely rewarded for consistency in the generation and provision of information. Further, even in cases where the information is not entirely objective, the nature of the relationships over time ensures that politicians are likely to be able to adjust their estimates of the information and come

---

[20] A sample of the research on redundant systems also includes: Felsenthal (1980), Heimann (1993, 1995), Rowan and Lerner (1995), and Ting (2003).

[21] More recently, scholars have shown that subsystems are not impregnable and that their collapse may be just around the corner (Baumgartner and Jones, 1993; Worsham, 1997, 1998).

[22] For a view on the role of policy subsystems in fostering *coherent* policy making, see May et al. (2006).

very close to an accurate representation of the problem.[23] So long as these conditions hold, even information that is not objective in the truest sense is useful for policy and political calculations. Given increased congressional attention to government via oversight, one might even say that bureaucratic bias has become easier to assess, and hence even more useful.

From the vantage point of these theories of congressional decision making, the relative influence of bureaucrats and organized interests in the policy process is dependent on how Congress searches for information under uncertainty and on the distinct facets of information that are valued by risk-averse politicians. The federal bureaucracy holds some distinct advantages in comparison to organized interests in the provision of information to politicians plagued by uncertainty. These advantages are primarily due to the political economy of interest group supply and organization.

Patterns of interest mobilization and participation in policy making are influenced by the cross-pressures of congressional decision making and by the political economy of interest organizations from below. From the vantage point of Congress, organized interests populating any given policy area face market-like pressures on their survival as some groups fade away and others rise to prominence in the competition to represent latent interests. Although the organized groups populating the interest system face competitive pressures for survival, they must also confront the ever-present internal tensions deriving from the politics of collective action that threaten to destroy or dissolve given organizations. Olson (1965) noted that interest groups face the problems of collective action, especially free riders, in their formation, whereas Salisbury (1969) later argued that group maintenance is dependent on an exchange between the originators of the group and the rank-and-file membership. Although the nature of congressional decision making and institutional organization brackets mobilization from above, these market-like forces for interest representation influence group mobilization and maintenance from the supply side. These factors combine to produce an interest system that is more volatile in its supply of information for policy making than that of the bureaucracy.

Three characteristics of information are key for the reduction of uncertainty in the decision calculus of policy makers: accuracy, reliability, and consistency. Information must be accurate – in other words, factual or truthful, or at least close enough to allow the accurate weighting of the information for biases. Information must also be reliable. Put simply, information must not only be

---

[23] This might be easier understood in terms of the characteristics of statistical estimators. Statistically speaking, a mean that diverges slightly from the true mean, but has reliability and consistency (small variance), is much more easily weighted and incorporated into the decision calculus than information that is objective on average (or "right") yet highly inconsistent and unreliable (large variance). This holds so long as it is possible to generate a measure of the "bias" or inaccuracy in the more reliable indicator. In this case, members of Congress are not known for being in the dark with regard to the preferences of other actors in the process, especially those they deal with often.

"right" on average but must also have low variance. A provider of information that takes a given stance at one time and a completely different stance at another destabilizes decision making. This happens because an unreliable supplier of information prevents the type of weighting for biases that allows even inaccurate information (if reliable) to be weighted and used in the decision calculus. Put simply, small variance outperforms accuracy where accuracy is plagued by a large variance.

Policy makers require a consistent supply of information to inform their policy and political calculations. Volatility in the supply of information destabilizes congressional information gathering and, ultimately, policy change. These central characteristics of information supply and the cross-pressures discussed earlier highly favor the federal bureaucracy as a primary supplier of information in U.S. politics generally, and especially in the political-administrative system. This dynamic of bureaucratic provision of information is a topic lost in both the literature on political control and in interest group research, which focuses on interest group primacy.

Federal agencies have advantages vis-à-vis organized interests in the provision of information to Congress. Bureaucracies in general have longer shelf-lives than the vast majority of groups populating the interest system. This longevity is due to the nature of competition these groups face in the interest marketplace. Comparatively short life-spans plague the overall supply of groups as well as the make-up of the population. Even as organized interests proliferate, the life-span of any given group is necessarily short. The competition in the interest system compromises the consistency and reliability of information from these groups within any given issue area. Federal agencies, in contrast, do not face similar competition in the public sector.[24] Federal agencies are imbued with missions by federal statute and populated by professionals beholden to the norms of both their profession and to the general orientation of the organization. These features promote the type of stability, for better or worse, that increases the consistency and reliability of information from the federal bureaucracy. This is not to say that bureaucrats are less self-interested than organized interests, but simply that they do not face the same economic pressures (both external and internal) that private sector groups face.

Research on the relationship between bureaucracy and the democratic system has long noted that bureaucrats have the upper hand on policy makers because they hold private information and generally exert agenda control (Niskanen, 1971; Alchian and Demsetz, 1972; Mitnick, 1975). That is, bureaucrats are free to bias information in favor of expanding budgets and increased agenda control. This tendency for biased information is in part mitigated by two factors. First, bureaucrats, by virtue of longevity, are engaged in repeated

---

[24] However, scholars have yet to fully come to grips with the effects of the recent explosion in government contracting, which may introduce a degree of market-like pressure in the public sector.

interactions with Congress in an effort to define policy problems (Aberbach, 1990; Baumgartner and Jones, 1993; King, 1997). What this means is that, although bureaucrats may very well bias their provision of information to policy makers, policy makers are likely aware of the biases (detected over decades of interaction) and are able to weight these biases more accurately (compared to those of interest groups) in their decision calculus. Even if the information provided is biased, repeated relationships allow for the systematic adjustment of the congressional stance based on even biased information. Sometimes smaller variance trumps pinpoint accuracy, especially where this accuracy often comes at the cost of some very bad misses. Second, it has recently been suggested that the economics of information do not work in the way that classical theorists envisioned (Stigler, 1961). That is, the provision of information is pluralistic in a democracy such as the U.S. system of government (Workman and Shafran, 2015). Information not provided by one entity will assuredly be supplied by another as organized interests, federal bureaucracies, and policy makers engage in the struggle to define the contours of debate (Workman et al., 2009). Information that might be held private is revealed in the competition for ideas. Thus, there is the general expectation that bureaucrats will be influential in the generation of information, processes of congressional search, and, most consequentially, in problem definition.

Still, any serious student of the policy process is well aware of the fact that both bureaucrats and organized interests permeate the policy process. The debate over whether bureaucracy or interest groups are more influential obfuscates points of synergy between administrative institutions and those whom they regulate and to whom they distribute policy benefits. If we grant that interest groups hold the power in the relationship with the macro-political institutions of government, then how do we explain the ubiquity of bureaucracy? Even granting the influence of organized interests, it is likely that bureaucracies do much more than distribute policy benefits. Do bureaucracies serve to validate or lend legitimacy to interest group signals in the policy process? It is also quite possible that bureaucracies lend organizational capacity to interest mobilization that might otherwise peter out. The bureaucratic influence on interest mobilization is a question largely, if not wholly, ignored in research on the administrative state. The logic of bureaucratic influence offered here generates some testable hypotheses concerning interest group participation relative to the bureaucracy in policy making.

It is worth bearing in mind that the proclivity of elected officials to be attentive to the information generated by bureaucracy does not require the assumption that they are interested in good policy. Given the finite nature of attention, attention to one issue represents an opportunity cost in another area. By delegating attention to federal agencies, elected officials are free to pursue other politically beneficial ends. But as a consequence, elected officials must attend to bureaucratic signals to know when to claim credit, avoid blame, or otherwise intervene in the process of administrative policy making (see Mayhew, 1974). Of all the charges that one might level on modern-day politicians, inattentiveness to the political environment in which they operate surely is not one of them. This delegation of attention comes with the realization that credit claiming and blame avoidance for election-minded politicians come at the expense of having to respond to, among other things, information generated by the bureaucracy.

As the antennae of the elected branches of government, agencies serve as a pipeline of information about both public policies (especially where problem spaces are concerned) and politically prudent courses of action. Bureaucracies, after all, institutionalize various latent interests in the political system. As much as they are the targets of the "fire-alarm" system (McCubbins and Schwartz, 1984), bureaucracies themselves also serve a fire-alarm function for elected officials in both the political and policy spheres of action.

Bureaucracy is situated at the core of the central nervous system of the government alongside congressional committees and organized interests; it serves as the major artery linking the public with their governing institutions. Moreover, the bureaucracy sits at the hub of inter-institutional conflict over the direction of public policy. This conflict testifies to the centrality and importance of bureaucracy's position and influence in the policy process. In this position, bureaucracy as an attention-attracting institution holds sway over the standard depictions of federal agencies as reluctant to bask in the bright lights of politics. Further, the logic of this attention-seeking behavior is related both to the self-motivated objectives of bureaucrats and to their role in the communications system from the administrative vantage point – peering both outward at sister administrative institutions and upward at powerful political overseers.

2.5 THE NEW HISTORY OF THE "PUBLIC" BUREAUCRACY

In U.S. politics and society, there is a view of bureaucracy that depicts it as resistant, hidden, and incapable of initiating change. Yet, there is good reason to rewrite the history of the bureaucracy. Bureaucrats are in general incredibly visible players in the political system. Bureaucratic influence in the policy process is often premised on their ability to garner the attention of elected and democratically accountable officials.

The dual dynamics of the administrative state offers a view of bureaucracies as attention-seeking institutions influential in the early stages of the policy process, including agenda setting. Further, the major changes occurring in the relationship between bureaucracies and elected institutions over the last thirty years have buttressed the depiction of the public bureaucracy, as institutional reforms have fostered growth in the visibility of bureaucratic policy making and behavior. Some of this public orientation has been mandated by Congress or the president, but much of it results from the ability of bureaucracies to influence the course of public policy through their visibility and their provision of policy and politically relevant information.

The nature of subsystem politics has also changed over the past thirty years. Bureaucracies are rewarded politically and with policy influence for attracting attention to important policy problems and helping define them. The dual dynamics theory offers a perspective on policy making in the administrative state derived from the attention limits of governing institutions and bureaucratic influence in agenda-setting processes.

In the major academic disciplines concerned with the making of public policy, it has become out of fashion to discuss the importance of bureaucracy to policy making. Today's scholars both in the United States and elsewhere prefer to study and discuss the virtues of voluntary regulation, networks, clubs, market mechanisms, and other forms of "governance" or "steering." Yet, the presumed demise of traditional forms of bureaucracy belies the centrality and visibility of bureaucrats in policy making and their ability to influence how government addresses problems.

Today's forms of governing are much like yesterday's forms of governing. Bureaucracy is indeed leaner in modern times, but policy making still occurs in subsystems governed by the dual dynamics of agenda setting. Further, the dual dynamics of bureaucratic problem solving and congressional prioritization have given rise to modes of government that are even now changing the way government makes policy and the institutions of government interact. The dual dynamics of the administrative state, with bureaucracy a permanent and potent player, are giving birth to a new type of policy making centered on administration and oversight.

3

The Regulatory Process as an Attention Mechanism

Herbert Simon (1971, pp. 40–41) noted more than forty years ago that information "consumes the attention of its recipients." The policy-making process generates massive amounts of information, and given the scarce nature of attention, knowing which bits of information to attend to is vitally important for decision making. The regulatory process functions as an attention mechanism, channeling eyes, ears, and resources to important and salient problems. This view of the process is consistent with its creation as a legislative process and its subsequent legislative development. Its value in regard to information processing is also a consistent theme in empirical research on the process of rulemaking.

The legislative development of the regulatory process shows that it was, at its inception, intended to be legislative in nature (Rosenbloom, 2001). This intent shows up in both the substance and procedure of bureaucratic policy making, as well as in the organizational relationship between agencies and units within Congress. In their specialization and functional differentiation, agencies roughly mirror the substantive structure of the committee system. Members of Congress envisioned the regulatory process as an extension of legislative power, and Congress's modifications of the process have both deepened and broadened its influence. In addition to the legislative development of the regulatory process, Congress has steered the institutional development of its own bureaucracies, such as the GAO, in such a way as to heighten the informational value of the regulatory process. Empirical research suggests the value of the process in generating information about politics and policy, functioning as a signal to policy makers, and enhancing congressional prominence in steering the course of regulatory policy.

3.1 LEGISLATIVE DEVELOPMENT

Table 3.1 shows the major pieces of legislation affecting how bureaucracies make public policy. Taken together, these laws mold the regulatory process as legislative in nature, address oversight by Congress, and facilitate the creation of information in the process. The regulatory process was built to mirror or mimic similar processes in Congress for the development of legislation. This can be seen in legislation structuring how regulatory agendas are set, how regulations are developed after their proposal, and how these modifications are monitored after coming into effect.

The bureaucracy's regulatory agenda is influenced by a variety of factors. Bureaucracies develop regulations in response to recognized policy problems, presidential and congressional policy priorities, and, likely, the prodding of interest and citizens groups. The regulatory agenda is structured, first and foremost, by the procedures for proposing and developing regulations laid out in the Administrative Procedures Act (APA). The APA molds the regulatory process in the image of the legislative process in Congress by ensuring responsiveness and the ability of the public and interest groups to have input; it focuses on the development of the final version of the regulation as a result of building consensus among the bureaucracy, political overseers, citizens, and interest groups. Looking at Table 3.1, the historical trajectory of the regulatory agenda is one in which Congress has moved from shaping a process in its image to becoming more directly involved in substantive agenda setting over time. Legislation such as the Government Performance and Results Act in 1993, which stipulates that agencies must develop their policy objectives in consultation with Congress, suggests a legislative branch that not only shapes the regulatory *process* as a legislative process but also aims to exert influence on the substantive *content* of regulatory agendas.

Several of the laws in Table 3.1 also make it easier for citizens and interest groups to monitor the process and provide input. The Freedom of Information Act (FOIA; 1966) and the Federal Advisory Committee Act (1972) are prominent examples of legislation meant to make the regulatory process more transparent. The FOIA provides an avenue for citizens and groups to avail themselves of information on government policies and activities, mostly after the fact. Alternatively, the Federal Advisory Committee Act provides a conduit for direct interest and citizen participation in the development of the agenda beforehand. The ability to influence regulatory agendas in their earliest stages was extended to the general public initially by the APA, but was strengthened by the Government in the Sunshine Act (1976), which requires public meetings and advance notice of them so that citizens have ample time to become acquainted with the regulatory issue and form an opinion or strategy for influence. These pieces of legislation enhance the ability of the public, citizens' groups, and organized interests to participate at the earliest stages of the

TABLE 3.1 *Legislative Development of the Regulatory Process*

Legislation[a]	Major Implication
Administrative Procedures Act (1946)	Structured the regulatory process as a legislative process built on responsiveness, public input, and consensus building
Legislative Reorganization Act (1946)	Reorganized committee structure to follow federal administrative structure along substantive lines
Federal Tort Claims Act (1946)	Allowed agencies to settle claims, alleviating the need for members of Congress to introduce private bills
General Bridge Act (1946)	Granted authority to instigate bridge construction to the Army Corps of Engineers
Freedom of Information Act (1966)	Increased transparency of agency actions and policies
Congressional Research Service (1970)	Upgrade the Legislative Reference Service
Federal Advisory Committee Act (1972)	Makes advisory committees transparent and representative
Government in the Sunshine Act (1976)	Requires public meetings and advance notice of them
Inspector General Act (1978)	Inspector Generals conduct audits for efficiency in programs and departments and to provide information to Congress about problems in administration
Regulatory Flexibility Act (1980)	Requires review of regulation having significant economic impact
Paperwork Reduction Act (1980)	Requires assessment of the costs of paperwork on small businesses
Negotiated Rule Making Act (1990)	Establishes a process whereby agencies may choose to negotiate the language of a rule with representatives from organized interests, citizens' groups, and other affected parties
Government Performance & Results Act (1993)	Requires agencies to develop objectives in consultation with Congress
Congressional Review Act (1996)	Requires formal congressional review of major regulations prior to their issuance, with specific emphasis on congruence with *legislative* intent
E-Government Act (2002)	Creates the position of Federal Chief Information Officer within the OMB and establishes measures requiring the use of internet-based technology for the delivery of government information and services
REINS Act (2013)	Did not become law, but attempted to make major regulations contingent on majority approval in Congress

[a] The sample of legislation comprises Rosenbloom's (2001) summary of legislation pertaining to congressional influence on the regulatory process, as supplemented by more recent legislation. The list of legislation contained in the table is not exhaustive.

regulatory process. In addition, they provide the bureaucracy with ample time to adjust policies and respond to public input.

Going beyond agenda setting, Congress has sought to strengthen its ability to monitor the regulatory process through time. This effort began, as Rosenbloom (2001) notes, with alleviating themselves of having to make some burdensome and time-consuming decisions. Congress first transferred decisions about tort claims and bridge construction to federal agencies in the Federal Tort Claims Act and the General Bridge Act, both passed in 1946. After that, the most significant change in Congress's ability to monitor bureaucratic policy making has come through the strengthening of congressional expertise in various policy areas. The first law to address this was the Legislative Reorganization Act (LRA; 1946), which reorganized the congressional committee structure to roughly mirror the federal administrative structure along substantive lines (e.g., the Agriculture Committees in both houses oversee the Department of Agriculture). The Inspector General Act of 1978 placed Inspector Generals within federal agencies and charged them with conducting audits for efficiency in programs and policy and providing Congress with general information about ongoing problems in policy implementation. Finally, Congress greatly strengthened the regulatory process as an extension of its legislative function by developing and extending the power of its own set of bureaucracies.

3.2 CONGRESSIONAL BUREAUCRACY AND INSTITUTIONAL DEVELOPMENT

When we think of bureaucracy, we usually think of the executive branch of government. However, Congress has a set of powerful bureaucracies whose sole purpose is to generate information and analysis pertaining to federal regulations and programs. The institutional development of this set of bureaucracies is key to understanding the broadening of congressional influence in regulatory policy as a legislative process. This effort to delegate the generation of information and oversight began in 1970 with the creation of the Congressional Research Service (CRS), which was an enhancement of the older Legislative Research Service. The CRS sits within the Library of Congress and provides members of Congress of both parties with research on various policy topics, including both domestic and foreign policy. The research is supposed to be nonpartisan, unbiased, and confidential, if so requested by the member. The CRS provides members with reporting, expert testimony, briefings, and even workshops on various policy topics. Many CRS reports focus on major areas of regulation, such as financial regulation, transportation, the environment, science, and technology.

After strengthening the CRS as a source of information for the legislative process, Congress created the Office of Technology Assessment (OTA) in 1972. Though disbanded in 1995 as part of the Contract with America, OTA provided analysis and reporting on complex policy problems usually involving science and technology. The OTA was also one of the central forces making possible the electronic availability of government documents. Thus, it served not only members of Congress but also helped drive improvements in the transparency of government activity.

In 1974, the Budget Control and Impoundment Act expanded congressional influence in federal administration through two powerful legislative bureaucracies. First, it created the Congressional Budget Office (CBO), which was a powerful counterbalance to the president's Office of Management and Budget (OMB). The CBO's initial role was to generate information about the federal budget, especially by providing an independent analysis of the president's budget and an unbiased economic forecast for members of Congress. From this initial mission, CBO's analytic purview has expanded to preparing issue-specific budgetary analyses of various foreign and domestic policies – everything from disaster management to immigration policy.

The Budget Act also greatly expanded the reach of the Government Accountability Office (GAO), formerly the Government Accounting Office. Congress had transferred the function of accounting and audits from the Treasury to the newly created GAO with the Budget and Accounting Act of 1921. In 1974, Congress expanded GAO's authority. Where the GAO once only conducted audits of agencies and programs, it was then charged with analyzing the degree to which government programs and agencies were meeting their policy objectives. This change has been most easily seen in the staff of the GAO, which until 1974 had been mostly accountants and thereafter included policy and issue area experts and analysts. The policy problem orientation of the GAO in recent years has become even more engrained. The GAO is now a key institution for identifying *potential* policy problems – meaning that its agenda for analysis and oversight is proactive.

Each of these institutions has evolved from performing very general overarching analysis of management and efficiency or bookkeeping functions to conducting substantive policy analysis, thereby greatly increasing their expertise and, by extension, that of Congress. These institutions have played an increasingly important part not only in the analysis of public policy but also in its development. Both the CBO and GAO routinely generate policy alternatives from their expertise and analysis. For the CBO, these alternatives come in the form of alternative budget projections for the overall budget and for those of particular program and regulatory areas. For instance, the CBO has played a particularly important role in debates about education and healthcare over the past decade. For the GAO, alternative policies are generated through its recommendations targeted directly at various agencies and programs. An important feature of GAO analyses is that they may focus on particular regulations or decisions or issue recommendations about entire programs, bodies of law, or regulatory regimes. This is in stark contrast to the president's Office of Information and Regulatory Affairs, which must generally approach issues one regulation at a time. For instance, in 2008, the GAO issued 1,261 separate recommendations to federal agencies concerning various regulations and programs. Where rulemaking is concerned, the GAO now has the authority to evaluate final regulations before they become law, providing members of Congress with information on the expected impact of each regulation on the economy, national security, the environment, and other important policy topics (Kerwin, 2003, p. 219).

It is often underappreciated that the process of bureaucratic policy making was created and designed by Congress (see McCubbins et al., 1987). Congress has gone from designing and honing a *process* for making policy, one that very much resembles legislating, to one in which bureaucracies are more conscious of congressional influence up front in setting policy agendas. The legislative development of the process has come about at the same time that Congress has undertaken the institutional development of its own set of bureaucracies. These powerful "analytical" bureaucracies do far more than address questions of program management and efficiency; they are now key resources for overseeing the regulatory process and steering how bureaucracies process information and set policy agendas (Workman, 2014). An examination of the process that Congress inaugurated in the Administrative Procedures Act of 1946 reveals the parallels to legislation, particularly how regulations are developed, how political and problem-oriented information is incorporated, and how success is an exercise in building consensus among pluralistic interests. In fact, West (2005a, p. 660) notes that rulemaking amounts to "the defining of policy goals through the accommodation of competing interests," something far more important than the implementation of laws and statutes.

3.3 THE PROCESS OF RULEMAKING

The Administrative Procedures Act (APA) is the basis of the modern process of developing and "passing" regulations, or rulemaking, and any scholar with an interest in the process should consult Kerwin's book on the subject (2003). Usually, the development of a rule begins with an agency's problem monitoring and policy priorities. The process begins with the agency's impetus for contemplating rulemaking, which is no small consideration given that rulemaking represents the largest single allocation of time and resources for an agency. If not initiated by the agency, rules begin with mandatory reviews, the administration of statutes, OMB prompt letters, GAO recommendations, or requests from interest groups, other federal agencies, or state and local governments.

If the agency determines that a rule is necessary given the nature of the problem or request, then the agency has three choices. First, it may issue a proposed rule and request comments. The proposed rule is published in the Federal Register, and Executive Order 12866 establishes sixty days as the length of the period for submitting comments (extensions are often granted). The OMB may review a rule if the agency has tagged it as "economically significant." During interviews I conducted with officials at the Regulatory Information Service they revealed that OMB review is not as onerous as it may seem. Agencies very often want OMB review out of risk aversion – to make sure that the rule is consistent in general with the administration's priorities. Alternatively, these officials also noted that agencies are able to craft rules in such a way as to garner considerable support in Congress as a counterbalance to the OMB. Finally, one official noted that skillful agencies are able to split more complex regulations into smaller ones in order to navigate the "economically significant" designation. In any event, agencies are not merely reacting to the OMB review, but are proactive in the development of the regulation in a way that builds or contrives consensus.

Second, the agency may begin negotiated rulemaking. Under the Negotiated Rule Making Act of 1990 (see Table 3.1), agencies may choose to bring together interest groups, citizens groups, and other parties affected by the regulation to negotiate the text of a proposed rule. This provides a direct mechanism for the aggregation of preferences and opinions about the rule. This process is especially useful when there is a high degree of conflict over the language of the proposed regulation or a high degree of uncertainty regarding the problem the regulation is meant to address. In the latter instance, policy problems often require more information about a technology, economic sector, industry, ecosystem, or the like than an agency possesses. Conflict and uncertainty are even more likely when the agency is asked to address a policy problem not traditionally within its realm of activities and occupied by interest groups and other federal agencies. As Chapter 5 shows, this is not an uncommon occurrence. Coglianese (1997) suggests that negotiated rulemaking has been important in furthering pluralism and consensus building in the process and outcomes of rulemaking.

The third option is for the agency to issue an Advanced Notice of Proposed Rulemaking (ANPR). Agencies use an ANPR when uncertainty about a policy problem is too high to formulate a proposed rule or when considerable information is needed from relevant interests and other agencies. This process is also useful when the issuing agency is not able to fully formulate the problem or is unsure of who the relevant stakeholders might be and how they might view the problem.

In all three rulemaking options, the process of developing a proposed rule hinges on information supplied by relevant stakeholders, other federal agencies, and political overseers. These options also suggest that a considerable amount of consensus building has already taken place by the time the rule appears in the Federal Register. With attentiveness to the politics of the issue, the nature of the policy problem, and building of consensus, the proposal process has all the hallmarks of the legislative process.

After publication in the Federal Register, organized interests, citizen groups, other federal agencies, and members of the general public are free to comment on the proposed rule. The agency issuing the proposed rule is then bound by statute to incorporate this feedback in its version of the final rule or be able to give justifiable reasons why it did not do so. Most often, the agency's formulation of the final rule is altered in response to comments received during the (usual) sixty-day notice and comment period.

The most prominent scholar of interest groups in the notice and comment period is probably Yackee (2005, 2012), who finds that organized groups exert considerable influence, including the ability to restrict the rulemaking agenda (Yackee, 2012). Although little research has focused on citizen participation and influence in the notice and comment period, Shulman (2009) links the quality and effectiveness of citizen participation to the provision of information. He finds that mass e-mail campaigns, like those for organizations such as MoveOn.org, are not effective because the mass e-mail (form-letter) submissions carry very little new information for the agency to consider (also see Schlosberg et al., 2008). In other research, Zavestoski et al. (2006) find that the adversarial nature of the regulatory process limited citizen influence in rulemaking on the National Organic Standard and the Roadless Area Conservation Program. This research suggests that consensus building and citizen influence are connected to the provision of new information.

In formulating the final rule, the agency again has three avenues. It may publish a "final" rule. In doing so, the agency moves the regulation toward law that has the force of an act of Congress and alters the Code of Federal Regulations (CFR). This version is then subject to OMB review, if deemed "economically significant." However, the agency need not directly move to issue the final rule. It may instead issue what is called an "interim" final rule. In doing so, the agency adjusts the rule in view of the comments it received, but again issues a request for public comments. The other option is that the agency may issue a "direct" final rule. In this option, the agency agrees to withdraw the rule if it receives adverse comments within the specified comment period. The rule would then proceed to become a final rule with the potential for OMB review. Final rules must be submitted to the GAO and to both houses of Congress. Afterward, rules are published in the Federal Register and the CFR and are the law of the land.

Information processing shaped by the politics and context of the problem undergirds the entire process. Furthermore, this information processing serves the goals of consensus building and the aggregation of preferences and opinion with regard to the problem. In these senses, the regulatory process closely resembles the development of legislation in Congress. However, rulemaking is unique in focusing the public's and interest groups' participation in crafting a specific piece of proposed law. Kerwin (2003, p. 35, 98) notes that the specificity of rulemaking makes crafting arguments about the regulation much easier and notes that it "changes information into law."

3.4 REGULATORY POLICY MAKING AND SYSTEM ADAPTABILITY

The adaptability of the policy-making system hinges on the proficiency with which it processes information, whether it involves the pluralistic, consensus-building activities discussed earlier or the recognition of a problem. That regulatory policy making serves as a source of adaptivity is a consistent theme in scholarship on the process. Rulemaking is important to system adaptivity for two reasons: its substitutive function in relation to the legislature and its place as an extension of legislation.

Kerwin (2003, pp. 2, 5) notes that a crucial function of rulemaking is to "allow action while democratic processes play out." Much of Chapter 2 discusses the ways in which bureaucratic policy making expands the agenda capacity of the governing system. The major branches of government are free to focus their attention elsewhere in part because bureaucracies have been delegated problem-solving authority. This substitution of bureaucratic attention for that of the major branches of government is adaptive for both the system and individual legislators' issue attention. For the system, issues of great salience receive attention at the highest levels of government, while bureaucracies go on building consensus and problem solving for issues less in need of "democratic processes." For individuals, the substitution that rulemaking allows frees up legislator attention for issues closely aligned with their priorities, especially their reelection priorities.

As an extension of legislation, bureaucratic rulemaking directly addresses the Elmore problem. Legislation generally delegates a great deal of authority to bureaucracies, which goes beyond the implementation of various regulatory regimes and program administration. This delegation very often results in bureaucracies defining problems relative to legislative intent. Legislation is limited by the range and depth of expertise found in the typical federal agency (Kerwin, 2003, p. 29). Because agency officials possess expertise and are generally the first to notice the emergence of problems, legislative delegation to the bureaucracy provides adaptivity and simultaneously steers policy making toward legislative intent. Although all regulations draw their authority from legislation, regulations are only loosely connected to statutes and laws passed in real time. This is because grants of authority to develop regulations can be drawn from any congressional act, whether the bill was just passed or became law seventy-five years earlier. Thus, regulations are as closely associated with the congressional oversight process as its legislative agenda.

Adaptivity is bolstered by the fact that there is no real-time connection between rulemaking and the passage of legislation in Congress. Bureaucracies perpetually administer not only newly passed laws, but also the existing body of law. This means that government is free to respond to pressing problems even as democratic processes bring the major branches toward a much more encompassing solution or, more likely, compromise. Given the prominence of campaigns and elections in modern American politics, the adaptivity provided by rulemaking becomes even more important. Elections cost time, resources, and, most importantly, attention: rulemaking especially provides adaptability in the election cycle so that democracy does not subvert governmental problem solving.

3.5 REGULATION AS INFORMATION

Legislating is but one of the major functions of Congress, oversight being the other. Rulemaking is closely related to congressional oversight of the executive branch, and it is through this connection that the informational value of rulemaking becomes apparent as a signal to political overseers. The few comprehensive empirical studies of oversight testify to the relationship between bureaucratic policy making and oversight. Probably the most comprehensive study of oversight is that of Aberbach (1990), who finds a strong correlation between the content of the Federal Register and congressional oversight activity. More broadly, Kerwin (2003, p. 219) notes that rulemaking "triggers" oversight.

As an attention mechanism, regulatory policy making is clearest with regard to this triggering of oversight. Rulemaking specifically acts as a signal to legislators about the nature of problems and, as importantly, the nature of politics in a given issue. In empirical research examining influences on rulemaking, legislators emerge consistently as the most influential force on rulemaking, once they are engaged. In fact, many of the other features of oversight built into the process, such as oversight panels, have their greatest impact as an additional signal to legislators. A case in point is Shapiro's (2007) study of OSHA's ergonomics rulemaking. Shapiro compares the impact of these oversight mechanisms: notice and comment, OMB review, a small business oversight panel, and congressional budgetary oversight. He finds that legislative attention was by far the most impactful oversight mechanism, but also importantly notes that the main effect of others, especially the oversight panel, was as a signal to legislators (see West, 2005a, p. 662). Eventually, legislators struck down the rule under the provisions of the Congressional Review Act.[1] The ergonomics rule illustrates all the features geared toward signaling legislators during the regulatory process, including the rule itself.

All of this raises the question of whether actors in the process are attentive to or aware of the proposed rules as they are developed. It is important to point out that the semi-annual Unified Agenda (UA), a publication of the Regulatory Information Service of the Office of Information and Regulatory Affairs (OIRA) is a catalog, or indicator of a regulatory process occurring day to day. Legislators are attentive to the regulations that bureaucracies are considering at any one moment in time and, furthermore, have immense and pervasive leverage on this substantive agenda. For instance, many of the regulations meant to implement important provisions of the consumer protection provisions of financial reform have been effectively "vetoed" by the House Banking Committee and financial lobby since 2010. In July 2014, Representative Ann Wagner of Missouri introduced a bill aimed directly at the EPA's "climate" rule. The bill

---

[1] Notably, this is the only time to date the act has been used to strike down a rule.

would force the EPA to alter its cost-benefit analysis to consider only benefits within the United States.

Studies like that of Shapiro described earlier highlight congressional attention as a blunting force on the development of rules, but congressional attention often aims to foster the development of rules. A case in point occurred in July 2014 when the Senate Committee on Homeland Security and Governmental Affairs urged the Department of Homeland Security (DHS) to develop federal standards for securing chemical plants from terrorist threats. In June of the same year, the GAO, Congress's chief oversight bureaucracy, issued a report urging the EPA to develop regulations to improve safety and oversight of hydraulic fracturing or "fracking" (GAO, 2014).

In another study, Golden (2003) interviews thirty-two officials across five federal agencies. She finds that legislators wield the most influence on the rule-making agenda compared to OMB and OIRA, interest groups, citizens' groups, and the media, but as importantly, finds that this influence is intermittent. Not only do agency officials cite members of Congress as extremely influential as their agencies go about setting regulatory agendas but this influence also works in the way a signaling model rooted in communications would be expected to work. Legislators attend to the issue and intervene when signaled, and because this signaling exists, they are free to divert their attention elsewhere before and after their intervention. Taken together, these studies of rulemaking suggest that legislators are attentive to rules issued by bureaucracies, that these rules provide information to legislators about problems or a signal about the politics of the issue, and that legislator attention is geared toward adjusting the bureaucracy's agenda rather than micro-managing policy implementation. Regulations serve many purposes, one of which is the implementation of laws and statutes, but these purposes do not preclude the provision of information, engagement in consensus building, and the involvement of pluralistic politics in the process of bureaucratic policy making.

My interviews with officials at the Regulatory Information Service (RIS; the governmental unit responsible for publishing the Unified Agenda [UA]) testify to the usefulness of the regulatory process as a signal. For example, the contact person for bureaucracies at the RIS told me that bureaucracies almost always include much more in their section of the UA than the law actually requires. When asked why this was so, this official responded that agencies viewed the process as a way to *communicate information*, issue positions, secure turf, and reduce the uncertainty of other actors, especially legislators, in the process.

The APA sets up a process for bureaucratic policy making that is geared toward generating and communicating information to members of Congress, interest groups, and the public. The notice and comment requirement for regulations ensures this communication. This information serves to communicate both problems in policy making and the need for revision and also to communicate information based in the politics of the issue – who cares and how preferences may be aligned among interested actors (more on this later). The administrative process itself may be viewed as a signaling mechanism in this regard – a type of early warning system.

3.6 PRESIDENTIAL PRIORITIES AND REGULATORY POLICY MAKING

The dual dynamics theory downplays the importance of the president in the process of issue prioritization and problem solving for two reasons. First, to highlight the processes associated with congressional interaction with the bureaucracy over the policy agenda, it is necessary to pay less attention to the president. All theories need to make similar sacrifices. Second, the types of dynamics described here occur, except in unusual situations, "below" the president.

The processes described here occur at the meso, or subsystem, level of government. Day-to-day problem solving between the bureaucracy and Congress occurs within and across subsystem arrangements, which usually involve a few committees, bureaucracies, and a small constellation of organized interests. For certain boundary-spanning policy problems, such as climate change, food security, renewable energy, and public risks, the dual dynamics occur across a set of subsystems (see May et al., 2009a,b; May, 2010; May et al., 2011; May and Koski, 2013). Within and among these types of arrangements, presidential attention and involvement are "transitory," according to Worsham (1997, 1998). Kerwin (2003, p. 30) also notes that presidential influence in relation to rulemaking is transitory and fragmented.

Subsystems are generally long-lived, and policy change through these governing arrangements comes about as issues evolve and information changes over a long period of time (Baumgartner and Jones, 1993; Sabatier and Jenkins-Smith, 1993). In other words, the political capital required for presidential involvement is high, as are the resulting political costs. In addition, presidential involvement in subsystem and, more broadly, regime politics has costs in terms of the president's own information-processing capacities. If attention is limited in nested, delegated organizations such as the Congress and the bureaucracy, it is even more so for the president. There are opportunity costs to presidential attention to subsystem politics although presidents can certainly reach down into subsystem politics, creating Worsham's (1997) transitory coalitions and influencing policy change.

Two recent cases in point are President Obama's recent forays into financial regulation through legislation (2010) and carbon emissions through regulation (2014). Both are instances of successful presidential efforts in influencing powerful subsystems. With regard to financial regulation, the president secured the cooperation of Congress in the passage of the Dodd-Frank Wall Street Reform and Consumer Protection Act,[2] illustrating that presidential influence on the

---

[2] P.L. 111–203.

agenda comes more often from the top down.[3] With regard to carbon emissions, the president has faced stiff opposition from legislators, particularly in coal states, and the broader energy lobby (Wallach and Abdun-Nabi, 2014). Nevertheless, he has used administrative tools to issue regulations on emissions. These protracted battles represent opportunities seized within one subsystem, but come at the cost of headway in others.

More often, presidents set broad regulatory agendas for the bureaucracy consistent with their overall issue priorities. These priorities are difficult to measure in a systematic fashion. I made attempts to connect regulatory agendas in federal agencies to presidential policy priorities using executive orders, State of the Union speeches, and OMB reviews. In the case of the first two, I could not statistically detect a relationship across issues. In the case of OMB reviews, I argue that the ease of data collection and availability and the visibility of important regulations have skewed scholarly views of the power of the OMB. In 2009, at the completion of my empirical work, OMB reviewed only about 12 percent of regulations. Of that 12 percent, 72 percent of regulations passed with no substantive change, and fully 89 percent passed muster with no change or with some small change. Less than 1 percent of regulations were "returned" across the entire federal bureaucracy. Similar figures for the George W. Bush administration were that 70 percent passed with no change, 93 percent passed with no, or small change, and less than 1 percent were returned to the agencies. These data indicated continuation of a long-term trend in presidential oversight (Workman, 2014). In an interview with an OMB analyst, I also learned that agencies are tremendously adept at manipulating OMB attention in two ways. First, agencies are often able to break apart and craft regulations such that they never reach the level required for review by the OMB. Second, agencies often flood the OMB with so many regulations that it simply cannot monitor them all.

Does this mean that the president does not influence the rulemaking agenda? Certainly not. It may be that so few regulations are returned by the OMB because they are crafted with the president's priorities firmly in mind at the start. If this is the case, then the influence of the president is already accounted for in the analyses to follow. Where presidential priorities matter, and I am certain that they do despite an inability to get a good measure of them, they feed into the process of information provision by the bureaucracy. As Congress reacts to the regulatory agenda, it is, in part, reacting to presidential regulatory priorities. I argue that the flow of information from the bureaucracy includes these priorities, even if indirectly. In fact, in Chapter 4 I claim that the administrative state arose, in part, in response to the administrative or imperial presidency.

---

[3] This is also apparent in presidential efforts to influence the bureaucracy through personnel policy. See Lewis (2008).

4

Problem Monitoring in the Administrative State

At the heart of the dual dynamics of the administrative state is the processing of policy problems by the bureaucracy and Congress. Bureaucracies communicate to Congress about aspects of emergent policy problems relevant for policy making at higher levels of government. They do so from the vantage point of functional differentiation and topical specialization, with expertise developed through the delegation of attention. From this foundation, the processes of problem monitoring, definition, and transmission of information influence agenda change, and efforts by Congress to prioritize among issues.

By contrast, elected officials in Congress communicate the systemwide priorities attached to the problems confronting government and blend problem definitions in an effort to steer policy making and orient bureaucratic problem solving. Elected officials must synthesize the disparate information generated by bureaucracy, fostering coordination or competition among agencies, and must do so with an eye toward making issue tradeoffs in setting the course for public policy. Elected officials decide which of the myriad problems identified and defined will be prioritized and, therefore, how bureaucratic problem solving will be adjusted in the future. Congressional issue shuffling, bundling, and promotion of competition in the provision of information are the functions embodied in congressional agenda setting.

More broadly, communications between the bureaucracy and Congress about the nature of the policy agenda form the linchpin linking bureaucratic problem solving and congressional prioritization to the system's overall adaptation and evolution over time. The ability of the bureaucracy to monitor problems and transmit information determines whether government addresses important problems or, bereft of information, finds itself unable to respond to changes in the issues on the agenda. For Congress's part, elected officials may expand or contract the supply of information from the bureaucracy by altering its prioritization of the problems, definitions, and information generated by bureaucracy. To this end, elected officials make the system more adaptive by ensuring a steady, broad-ranging supply of information on the policy environment: they foster constrained adaptation by constricting this supply. This error-correction function is vital to Congress. Policy makers can realign the entire system of information processing with their concerns or the exigencies of policy problems.

This chapter describes in detail several of the relevant trends in the administrative state over the past half-century. Chief among these is the rise of the bureaucracy–Congress nexus in the day-to-day policy making of government. This trend involves a transition away from activity centered on the passage of legislation as a catalyst for policy making toward a renewed vigor in subsystems as engines of policy making. This increased importance of meso-level policy making in the American system is best understood in the context of broader systemic and institutional developments in U.S. politics.

The rise of the Congress–bureaucracy nexus forms the context for the examination of the dual dynamics of the administrative state. This chapter offers an understanding of dual dynamics as signaling among institutions. The notion of signaling used here derives not from formal economic modeling, but from the field of communications.

The empirical foundation for understanding dual dynamics as signaling is an examination of the agendas of the bureaucracy and Congress over the past quarter-century. In all, the dataset on which this analysis is based contains 226,710 regulations: it represents a monumental effort in the collection, coding, and description of the policy agenda of the U.S. federal bureaucracy. The dataset is also the only one of its kind and is unique in its breadth. Scholars typically analyze budgets or enforcement activity when studying bureaucracy. In contrast, the approach taken in this chapter focuses on bureaucratic policy making. From this examination of the policy-making agenda of the bureaucracy, we can begin to understand bureaucratic problem monitoring as well as the way in which congressional prioritization has shaped the monitoring system. The information processing embodied in the dual dynamics of problem solving and prioritization rests on a particular notion of information provision, which occurs in the context of the regulatory process.

4.1 RISE OF THE CONGRESS–BUREAUCRACY NEXUS

Whether in response to the administrative presidency (Moe, 1985; Wood, 1988; Golden, 2000; Lewis, 2008; May and Workman, 2009) or the imperial presidency (Moe, 1987, 1989; Lewis, 2003; Rudavelige, 2005), or despite these developments, legislators have shown an increasing affinity for policy making that involves bureaucratic and subsystem processes, even when it does not involve bureaucracies directly (e.g., public contracting).[1] Legislators today pass fewer laws and spend more time in oversight than members of Congress in the past. In recent years, more than 90 percent of the hearings in Congress were held for the purposes of information gathering and oversight. Meanwhile, from an average of 300 to 400 laws passed annually in the early 1980s, the corresponding numbers have dropped to 200 to 300 in recent years. These two empirical trends suggest that policy making is increasingly carried out at the meso level and is governed by the dual dynamics of the administrative state.

Scholars have not paid much attention in recent years to the administrative state. This scholarly inattention does not reflect the real, empirically verifiable facts of the modern system of government. Policy process theorists hold diverging views on policy subsystems and their relationship to policy change. Punctuated equilibrium scholars view policy change as the result of subsystem information processing, in which disproportionate processing of information by subsystems leads to large-scale policy changes and, further, to subsystems weakened and left vulnerable to external competitors (Baumgartner and Jones, 1993). Advocacy coalition theorists view policy change as the result of learning or adaptation occurring within subsystems as coalitions battle it out by providing policy-relevant information (Sabatier and Jenkins-Smith, 1993). Despite these different conceptions of subsystems and policy change, most theorists seem to agree that policy subsystems, or any of the conceptual spins on the general notion, are the locus of the vast majority of policy making (Worsham, 1997); and that information is important.

Legislators and bureaucrats are in a much more powerful position within the political system than are far-flung actors such as presidents. Although presidents may certainly reach down into the bowels of the administrative state and influence policy change, doing so requires a tremendous commitment of political capital, not to mention of time and resources. Moreover, presidents will be faced with opportunity costs for diverting their attention. Presidents, no less than legislators or bureaucrats, are faced with the limits of attention. The dual dynamics of the administrative state result in the refinement of public policy, both its goals and the means to achieve them. The refining of public policy is an important aspect of policy making. Without the small changes that amount to "tinkering" with policies, the system is deprived of valuable feedback. An underappreciated aspect of the administrative state is that new legislation need not be passed in order to adjust policies. Much can be accomplished through

---

[1] It should be noted that the rise in contracting has placed tremendous strain on the ability of the government to govern or otherwise oversee contracts. One can easily envision the transformation of the administrative state from developing and administering policy to one whose institutions are leveraged in monitoring contracts. Many of the traditional sources of both bureaucratic and congressional problem expertise would be suited to monitoring contracts.

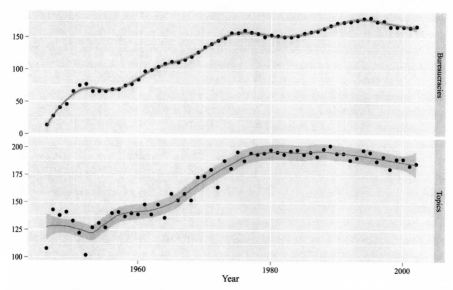

FIGURE 4.1 Bureaucracies and Topics on the Congressional Agenda.

the dual dynamics of the system, where institutions have evolved alongside the government agenda.

Figure 4.1 shows one aspect of this evolution: the growth in the number of bureaucracies (top) and the number of topics on the congressional hearing agenda (bottom) from 1946 through 2002. The line through the data is a loess smooth with bandwidth .25 and a shaded 95 percent confidence interval. The bureaucracy data were collected by Lewis (2002),[2] and congressional hearing topics data were obtained from the Policy Agendas Project.[3]

As these data show, bureaucracies, as measures of capacity and prioritization, are incredibly important. Unlike specific programs or budgets, which tend to mirror ideological and partisan dimensions of politics, bureaucracies directly affect the governing system's ability to process information about problems. The governing system must maintain some rough approximation of issues on the agenda and institutions available for processing them. Figure 4.1 is very

[2] David Lewis makes this data publicly available on his website at http://people.vanderbilt.edu/~david.lewis/. The website also contains details on the coding of newly created and terminated bureaucracies.

[3] Data and coding guidelines are available at http://www.policyagendas.org. The data used here were originally collected by Frank R. Baumgartner and Bryan D. Jones, with the support of National Science Foundation grant numbers SBR 9320922 and 0111611, and were distributed through the Department of Government at the University of Texas at Austin. Neither NSF nor the original collectors of the data bear any responsibility for the analysis reported here.

suggestive of this long-run equilibrium between issues or problems, broadly speaking, and bureaucracies.[4]

The growth of bureaucracy in terms of numbers of agencies very closely mirrors the growth in the number of issues confronting government. Figure 4.1 lends some credibility to the problem focus of the dual dynamics of the administrative state. Two points are worth noting about the expansion of administrative capacity. First, the expansion is a result of the pressures of agenda change. Attention is delegated to bureaucracies to expand agenda capacity and allow elected officials flexibility in issue politicking. Second, bureaucracies institutionalize the concerns held by interested publics. Bureaucracies represent the realization of demands placed on government. For example, the EPA was created not only because of the identification of very real problems of environmental degradation but also from the demands of the environmental movement itself.

Figure 4.1 is also suggestive of the limiting factor of the issue agenda. Normally, we think of bureaucracy – or the size and pervasiveness of government – as expanding steadily through time. However, the bureaucracy has not witnessed major expansions (in terms of institutions) since the 1970s, long before presidents Carter and Reagan set in motion the downsizing trend that continues through today.[5] Figure 4.1 also begs the question of whether the system has reached its carrying capacity for issues on the agenda. Even with the creation and maintenance of bureaucracies and the delegation of attention to these institutions, Congress eventually outstrips its capacity for providing oversight, including the meso-level policy making and policy refinements so vital to the operation of the system. Once capacity is outstripped, Congress must either create new bureaucracies and delegate attention, or allow the problem to fall from the agenda. The key point is that the administrative state expands and contracts to meet the demands of the problems on the agenda. Bureaucracy is geared toward problem solving, and bureaucrats influence policy making by conveying information about these problems. It is useful to think of their information as a signal emanating from a noisy policy environment.

4.2 DUAL DYNAMICS AS SIGNALING

The dual dynamics of the administrative state can be understood in terms of policy makers and bureaucrats signaling to one another through the din of everyday policy making and politicking. I borrow the model of signaling used in the field of communications rather than from economics. These two formulations of signaling differ over the nature and sources of uncertainty in information and its communication.

---

[4] This long-run equilibrium is confirmed statistically. A Phillips-Ouliaris cointegration test on the series has a test statistic of -22.52, which yields a p-value of .03.

[5] Note that the Department of Homeland Security, although certainly an expansion of the government's role in a number of areas, was created mostly from existing institutions.

Classical economic theorists view information as a scarce, privately held good and argue that securing information comes at a high price (Stigler, 1961). Preference-based theories of politics, especially principal-agent models drawn from the relationship between the bureaucracy and its political principals, tend to view information as a private good that must be induced via an incentive structure. This assumption undergirds most of the classical economic theorizing of overhead democracy. The central problem of signaling for the economists is then the underprovision of relevant information, or how to adjust for biased information, especially when agents have different goals and incentives from those who oversee them.

In contrast, the central problem of signaling in the communications field is the immense amount of noise in which signaling occurs. For this reason, mathematical models were developed to understand the effect of noise on the information conveyed in a signal (Shannon and Weaver, 1949). This noise is created by an oversupply of information. In the policy-making process, in turn, an oversupply of information demands prioritization (Jones and Baumgartner, 2005, p. 9). In pluralistic political systems with multiple, overlapping political coalitions and institutions, the classical economic characterization of information breaks down, as information is freely generated in the competition to control different policy issues.

Bureaucratic problem solving is in part a signal to policy makers about what is important or relevant for decision making at higher levels of government. Similarly, congressional prioritization is a signal to bureaucracy about broader shifts in the importance or definition of issues, which ones will be bundled, and which problems and definitions will be privileged at higher levels of government. What effect does bureaucratic signaling about policy problems have on the policy agenda of Congress? When will politicians move to expand or constrict the supply of information emanating from the bureaucracy more generally or within specific policy areas?

Social and economic indicators change, unemployment rises, corporations go bankrupt, interest groups rally behind particular problems, nascent social movements converge on a set of underlying social ills, and all of these changes demand a response from government. Any of these changes may also represent a departure from current understandings of policy problems, new policy problems, or underperforming policy solutions; in general, these changes lead to discrepancies and disturbances that may be identified as problems. These bridgeable gaps between status quo policies and changed problems form the inputs to the dual dynamics of bureaucratic problem solving and congressional prioritization. As political institutions respond to these gaps, our understanding of problems change, and policies change.

I define discrepancies and disturbances as the set of exogenous factors to which all governing institutions, whether the bureaucracy, committees in Congress, members of Congress, or even the president, respond. These are the factors in society and the economy – real-world phenomena – to which governments of all types must respond. The theory of dual dynamics emphasizes the substantive dimensions or attributes of issues. The focus is on the problems confronting government, rather than on solutions generated to address these problems.

Bureaucrats and other policy makers notice the fissures between policies and problems; these fissures have two characteristics. First, they are problem oriented. For instance, the financial crisis of 2008 in the United States might be defined as a consumer credit problem, especially a low propensity to save, or it could be defined as the result of corporate greed and irresponsibility. The crisis could also be framed in terms of increasing economic globalism and resultant interdependence.

From the space race to the green revolution, from Social Security to homeland security, wherever policy is made, bureaucracy plays the central role in defining problems. The modern bureaucracy was born and cut its teeth during the Great Depression when the government confronted unique problems as social ills were linked together in the modern, urban, and industrialized economy in a way never seen before. Bureaucracies then and now are the institutional embodiment of government's attempts to deal with such problems.

However, disturbances are not always picked up by the system – and even when they are picked up, policy makers do not always respond appropriately (or at all). The second characteristic is that disturbances may or may not be bridgeable or represent opportunities for policy making. Moreover, some disturbances not initially relevant for policy making become so over time. Steroid use in professional sports, for example, was originally seen as a problem better left to professional sports leagues to monitor. However, over time it became clear that steroid use by sports stars was having a deleterious effect on young adults, who looked up to their idols and began to mimic them. Then Congress got involved in a classic issue-expansion move, and steroids became a "public policy" problem (Downs, 1972).

Disturbances in the policy environment are sometimes too large to be ignored. The terrorist attacks of 2001 called into question standard notions of civil defense and disaster management (May and Workman, 2009). In contrast, the Security and Exchange Commission's decision in 2004 to eliminate the "net capital rule" went largely unnoticed, despite its contribution to the greatly unstable, overleveraged position many large financial institutions found themselves in by fall 2008 (Labaton, 2008b). In this instance, a disturbance thought to be very small led to an avalanche of problems in the financial sector.

Even seemingly small disturbances sometimes accumulate to the point of becoming an unwieldy problem. For example, some financial institutions, separated by a steel curtain since the Depression-era Glass-Steagall legislation, began to merge functions in dangerous and volatile ways (Worsham, 1997;

Eisner et al., 2000; Comiskey and Madhogarhia, 2009).[6] These cumulative and connected changes in the conduct of finance nearly brought about the collapse of any semblance of a regulatory framework for checking the excesses of the financial system (GAO, 2007; Labaton, 2008a).

It is important to think about bureaucracy as geared toward monitoring the policy environment (Feldman and March, 1981; Katzmann, 1989). If a given institution takes no note of a disturbance (when it should do so), another institution is likely to alert its peers to the emergence and importance of the disturbance. For this to happen, institutions must communicate. Communication cannot merely be top-down dictation by elected officials to bureaucracy, as depicted in classic models of overhead democracy. There must be room for bottom-up influence as well (Krause, 1999). Communication about disturbances in the policy environment is important not only laterally, when different institutions communicate with another (for example, the EPA works with the USDA to address a new source of pollution) but also vertically, so bureaucracies ill equipped to handle emergent policy problems can signal this deficiency in capacity to policy makers.

Because disturbances are problem oriented, they underscore the role of agenda setting in policy making. By communicating problems to Congress, the federal bureaucracy helps set the government's agenda. Bureaucracies also serve an agenda-maintenance function, allowing the system to economize on scarce attention.[7]

Figure 4.2 illustrates bureaucratic monitoring of the policy environment for disturbances (d). Information about these disturbances is then transmitted to congressional committees via the emission of signals (s), which sharpen the general outlines of issues deemed most relevant for decision making at a given moment. The backbone of the administrative state is the bureaucracy and the congressional committee system.

The figure illustrates several facets of bureaucratic problem monitoring and generation of information. First, note that not all disturbances in the policy environment are picked up and communicated to higher levels of government. In the figure, disturbances α, γ, and ϕ are not transmitted, either because they went unnoticed or because the set of bureaucracies did not deem them important for choice. Second, some disturbances are amplified (e.g., δ) in the generation of information, whereas others (e.g., ε) are downplayed in the process.

---

[6] Some have even suggested that this is symptomatic of a larger failure of government (Jacobs and King, 2009). Still, others have noted that there is a general tendency not to monitor sectors of the economy that seem successful, even as this success contributes to enormous crises over time (Marjit, 2003).

[7] The literature on the various aspects of agenda setting and its connection to policy change is immense in its theoretical, empirical, and methodological scope (a sample might include Schattschneider 1960; Cobb and Elder 1972; Downs 1972; Kingdon 1984; Hilgartner and Bosk 1988; Stone 1989; Baumgartner and Jones 1993; Riker 1993; Sabatier and Jenkins-Smith 1993; Jones and Baumgartner 2005).

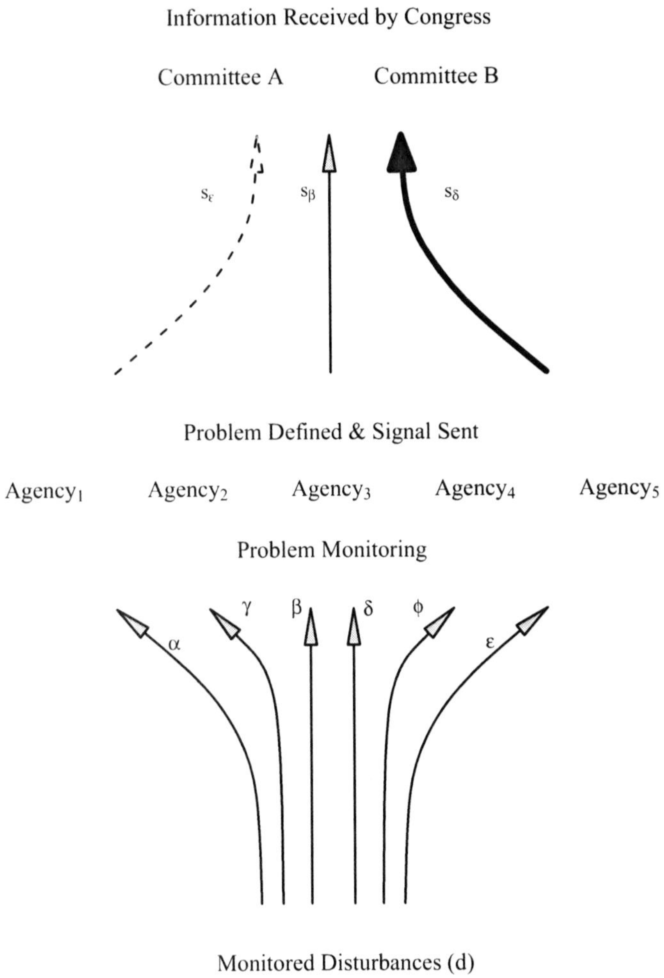

Information Received by Congress

Committee A   Committee B

s_ε s_β s_δ

Problem Defined & Signal Sent

Agency$_1$ Agency$_2$ Agency$_3$ Agency$_4$ Agency$_5$

Problem Monitoring

γ β δ ϕ

α ε

Monitored Disturbances (d)

FIGURE 4.2 Problem Monitoring and Signaling. Bureaucracy monitors the policy environment for disturbances (d) and generates information about the problem. This information is transmitted to Congress by way of signals (s).

Bureaucratic signaling is a process of winnowing and weighting disturbances from the policy environment in the course of generating information in the system and constructing a problem definition.

Note also that Figure 4.2 illustrates that disturbances in the policy environment are rarely monitored by only one federal agency. Rather, multiple agencies monitor any given issue. Likewise, the information generated by bureaucracy and passed on as signals may be attended to by multiple congressional committees. The competition and overlap that are often a feature of the administrative state foster the provision of information by providing multiple outlets, or venues, for the information as well as multiple sources of its generation. It is this characteristic that ensures information will be oversupplied because actors must oversupply it to have any hope of steering the course of policy making.

The information generated about potential disturbances to the system bears the markings of the particular bureaucracies that attended to the disturbances. Dery (1984, p. 35) notes that the "institutionalization of solutions requires the institutionalization of problem definitions." This means that discrepancies and disturbances picked up by the bureaucracy will be conveyed upward with a particular problem definition. As mentioned earlier, bureaucracies are the institutionalization of a problem definition. They leave an *institutional trace* on the signals sent to higher levels of government. Bureaucratic signaling is associated with the allocation of attention and the emphasizing or deemphasizing of, the attributes of policy problems communicated to political overseers. Monitoring these discrepancies and disturbances, and constructing problem definitions around them, means tying them to specific attributes or dimensions of issues.

Signals are also ways of garnering attention. Although I conceptualize bureaucratic signaling in terms of attention-attracting and attention-directing behaviors, signaling is a continual process over time and space, rather than a series of discrete actions by individual bureaucrats. Scholarship on the bureaucracy that addresses signaling in the principal-agent setting suggests that top-down signals must be repeated in order to trigger action by the bureaucracy. For instance, Carpenter (1996) considers budgetary decisions in Congress as a measure of congressional signaling about policy preferences and finds that these decisions (as the signal) must be repeated several times before the bureaucracy acts, because of its risk-averse stance.

It is unlikely, given the scale of the federal bureaucracy, that any discrete action by an agency could be counted on to garner attention from elected officials. Government must process information on a plethora of policy problems simultaneously, each and every day. This means that bureaucratic signals occur in the context of competition for issue areas as well as for issue prioritization. Agencies signal to higher levels of government, but their voice is only one among many. The largest, loudest, and most persistent "signalers" often receive the most attention. This means bureaucratic signals are weighted by the competitive environment in which they occur. Thus, bureaucratic signaling is best understood in terms of the larger pattern of consistent attempts to attract or direct attention in the course of problem solving. This suggests the bureaucracy actively anticipates problems in setting the agenda.

There is good reason to believe that bureaucrats actively intend to signal policymakers. While bureaucracies toil on the frontline of the government's ever-changing policy agenda, they draw their authority to act from the elected branches of government. Even if a bureaucracy views a particular problem as important, it does not always have the authority to act. This is especially true as bureaucracies attempt to alter problem spaces and reweight issue attributes. Aiding in this effort, relationships between bureaucracies and political principals at higher levels of government, especially between federal bureaucrats and congressional committee staff, are both institutionalized and regularized. Subsystem arrangements and the organization of the federal bureaucracy ensure bureaucrats' routine contact with policy makers and members of their staff in the legislative branch of government. Bureaucracies are influential players in the crafting and maintenance of problem definitions.

Three elements of bureaucratic signals make them particularly useful to politicians in need of information to shape their policy and political calculations. First, bureaucratic signaling alerts elected politicians to changes in *content*. Perhaps new disturbances have arisen in the policy environment that imply that the salient attributes of a given issue have changed. If the bureaucracy changes its substantive focus with regard to a particular policy issue, then this alerts elected politicians that the problem definition, which comprises the parameters of choice – the dimensions of the issue most relevant for decision making at a given point in time – may have changed.

Look again at Figure 4.2. The bureaucracy monitors disturbances in the policy environment and signals a sample of these disturbances chosen based on professional expertise, organizational exigencies, and past alterations of its problem-monitoring system by congressional prioritization. Whether these disturbances are viewed as potential policy problems partly depends on whether the changes are bridgeable or represent opportunities for bureaucrats and policy makers. Some of these disturbances, say, the ϕ and α disturbances, represent emergent problems that were not detected or had yet to develop. The bureaucracy chooses to transmit the δ disturbance and ignores the ϕ disturbance.

Second, bureaucratic signaling can influence policy agendas at higher levels of government by affecting the salience of a given issue attribute in the problem definition. The substantive content of bureaucratic signaling need not change for the bureaucracy to exert influence on agenda setting at higher levels of government: amplitude matters. If the substantive content of bureaucratic signals in a given policy area remains the same, but a given attribute of an issue becomes more prominent in the signal, this discrepancy alerts politicians to pay attention. In effect, changes in the amplitude of bureaucratic signaling are associated with the relative weighting of different issue attributes. Changes in amplitude influence importance by downplaying or amplifying given issue attributes.

In Figure 4.2, the bureaucracy ratchets up the amplification of the δ signal. The δ signal may have been a persistent feature of the information generated and transmitted by the bureaucracy, but now the bureaucracy transmits it with greater amplitude. This is not a change in content, but rather a change in the perceived importance of this information to decision makers. The bureaucracy signals the bridgeability and opportunity presented by the new information. The ε signal is only weakly transmitted. Though it may have been more prominent than the δ signal at one point, the bureaucracy now downplays its importance for decision making. Although this information does not disappear from the choice context, it no longer holds the salience of the δ or β signals.

Third and finally, politicians rely on a steady supply of information from the federal bureaucracy to make informed policy decisions and reduce uncertainty. Bureaucracy's provision of information is even more important and timely now, given trends in Congress over the last thirty years related to the reauthorization process and what amounts to the routinized nature of oversight and policy making generally (Cox, 2004; Adler and Wilkerson, 2012). The dynamics of information supply may potentially introduce uncertainty and instability to these highly routinized modes of policy making. A stream of information that is a trickle at one point in time and a raging torrent the next severely taxes the attention limits of legislative institutions. Faced with information overload from the bureaucracy or within a given policy area, legislative institutions might produce disproportionate agenda and policy outcomes, where the legislature both over-responds and under-responds to information, as processing the information becomes increasingly problematic and too many issues demand attention. Likewise, when bureaucracies reduce the information supply, legislators face uncertainty as the information allowing for policy and political calculations dries up. Especially with regard to new or redefined issues, political institutions will then confront problems that are not well defined or have changed without detection by the system. A stable, consistent supply of information allows politicians to adapt to the changing policy agenda more smoothly and make proportionate, efficient, and incremental adjustments to the policy, which in turn will reduce volatility in agenda setting and policy outputs.

The theory of bureaucratic signaling gives greater agency to the federal bureaucracy in setting the policy agenda for the administrative state. Nevertheless, federal bureaucracies do not strong-arm the elected branches of government. Politicians, constrained by limited time and attention, have many reasons to let the federal bureaucracy economize on their attention limits. I argue that politicians economize by delegating, which necessarily entails bureaucratic influence. The delegation of attention is often a net gain to the system in terms of policy, political calculation, and certainly agenda capacity.

4.3 BUREAUCRATIC POLICY MAKING

The federal bureaucracy is unique among American political institutions in that it combines all three major functions of government. Bureaucracies perform an array of functions that very closely mirror legislating, executing, and adjudicating responsibilities. However, in the theory of the dual dynamics of the administrative state, bureaucratic policy making, or "legislating," is of prime importance for two reasons. First, the substantive policies issued by bureaucracies as regulations are problem oriented. Second, regulatory policy has primacy over the other two functions: the other aspects of bureaucratic activity that amount to executing or implementing law and adjudicating usually occur as a result of regulations.

Most studies of bureaucracy focus on enforcement activity or agency (Wood, 1988; Huber, 2007). This is not surprising, because the study of the federal bureaucracy relies on statistical approaches to theory testing and enforcement activities and budgets are particularly amenable to the formulation of formal models that examine incentive structures. This work is commendable in its rigor and clarity. These measures are easily quantified, and their reliability rarely comes into question. However, these measures are ill suited to examining the dual dynamics of problem solving and prioritization. The bureaucracy's substantive agenda is much harder to reduce to more enforcement or less, to increases or decreases in budgets. In general, agendas are difficult to quantify without reference to the substance of policies.

Few studies of the bureaucracy in the overhead democracy or classic public administration tradition give serious consideration to substantive bureaucratic policy making, and those that do tend to give more attention to interest group influence on regulatory policy (Yackee, 2005, 2006). The model of dual dynamics as signaling provides the basis for an empirical examination of the policy agenda of the federal bureaucracy. The rest of the chapter describes and summarizes the policy agenda of the entire U.S. federal bureaucracy over the last quarter-century. This is an approach unique in the study of bureaucracy in American politics, not least because it represents a major empirical challenge.

In this chapter, I introduce regulatory policy making as one indicator of the agenda of the bureaucracy. My approach is the first systematic effort to quantify the regulatory agenda in terms of its issue or problem focus. In this section, I describe the methods used to classify or categorize this agenda topically. This collection and classification of data set the stage for describing the regulatory agenda over the last quarter-century and for relating it to the agenda-setting process in Congress. Yet in itself, this description of the agenda of the federal bureaucracy represents a unique contribution to the study of bureaucracy in the United States.

4.3.1 An Indicator of Bureaucratic Policy Making

My model of dual dynamics as signaling requires an indicator of the substantive agenda across the entire bureaucracy for a substantial period of time. The indicator underlying my empirical analyses of bureaucratic policy making is the Unified Agenda, which is published biannually (usually April and October) in the Federal Register and includes the regulatory and deregulatory actions that executive branch agencies are developing or have recently completed. The Unified Agenda is published by the Regulatory Information Service Center (part of the General Services Administration) in consultation with the Office of Information and Regulatory Affairs (part of the Office of Management and Budget).

The Unified Agenda has been published since 1983 by Executive Orders 12291 and 12498 signed by President Reagan in 1983 and 1985, respectively, and modified by Executive Order 12866 signed by President Clinton in September 1993. Clinton's order provided additional processes for the development of regulations, while keeping Reagan's provisions for OIRA review. These executive orders built on the Regulatory Flexibility Act in 1980[8] and represented a response to the growth industry of social and environmental regulation in the 1960s and 1970s; these orders attempted to balance regulatory aims with other values, particularly economic growth and small business concerns. Since its inception, the Unified Agenda has continued to be leveraged to balance regulation with other societal and governmental imperatives (e.g., regulation's impacts on federalism or on energy policy priorities).

Agencies of the executive branch are required to publish all regulations they expect will be issued within twelve months in three categories: Advanced Notice of Proposed Rule Making (ANPRM), Notice of Proposed Rule Making (NPRM), and Final Rules.[9] Although these entries are statutorily required, bureaucracies often list actions outside these categories, for reasons easily deduced from the discussion of bureaucratic signaling. My interview with a senior official at the Regulatory Information Service indicated that bureaucracies take a liberal approach to publicizing regulation in the Unified Agenda – meaning the Unified Agenda is an inclusive indicator of the regulatory agenda.

Bureaucracies establish their turf and define issues in order to steer policy debates. In addition, they want to maintain the legitimacy of regulations promulgated – a concern stemming from their position in the constitutional order and by the Administrative Procedures Act.[10] The consequence is that bureaucracies often list various "Prerules" and "Long-Term Actions" that may or may not fall under the three categories listed earlier. For instance, bureaucracies have listed 7,737 pre-rules since 1986 and 24,901 long-term actions since 1995. The result is that the Unified Agenda is a very comprehensive archive of the agenda items contemplated by the federal bureaucracy. With such a comprehensive archive, the central task was to categorize its entries to get a sense of how the agenda has changed over time across substantive issues and bureaucracies.

---

[8] 5 U.S.C. 602.

[9] Note that legislative bureaucracies such as the Government Accountability Office (GAO) or the Congressional Budget Office are exempt from these requirements and are not of concern for the analyses presented here.

[10] 5 U.S.C. 500 et seq.

Given that this dataset includes 226,710 entries, this was a monumental under-taking.

4.3.2 Categorization of Entries in the Unified Agenda

The unit of analysis for the categorization of regulations was each entry in the Unified Agenda, not each regulation. The Unified Agenda contains several bits of information about each regulation, or rule, including the regulatory iden-tification number (RIN), the bureaucracy or subagency issuing the rule, the rule's title, and an abstract describing the problem the regulation is meant to address. Each regulation appears more than once over time and I count each appearance. If specific regulations were the unit of analysis, the size and scope of the bureaucracy's agenda through time would have been obscured. Because regulations may be withdrawn for any reason, their continued appearance in the Unified Agenda represents continued commitment to the development of the policy. Kerwin (2003) suggests that developing regulations is one of the most time-consuming and intensive activities performed by bureaucracies. As such, regulations are important indicators of the policy priorities of bureau-cracies. Further, the earlier discussion of signaling suggests that signals must often be repeated to be effective. If a regulation appears in the Unified Agenda more than once, it remains on the agenda and is in some sense an ongoing problem.

To gauge the extent to which the bureaucracy paid attention to various issues over time, a coding scheme adaptable to the set of Unified Agenda entries was necessary. Since 1993, the Policy Agendas Project has used a topical coding scheme to categorize policy activity by issue. I used that same scheme to cat-egorize regulations by issue. The Policy Agendas Project topic coding scheme has the advantage of reliability across time and across institutions of the U.S. government, enabling issue attention to be compared across these institutions, most importantly, the Congress.[11] The Policy Agendas Project houses signifi-cant time series of congressional hearings and public laws categorized by topic using the same scheme. In this analysis, I compared regulations developed by the bureaucracy to congressional hearings.

Using the abstract and title for each entry in the Unified Agenda as the unit of analysis, I assigned each entry a topic code. The size of the Unified Agenda for the time frame under study (226,710 entries from 1983 through 2008) made hand-coding infeasible. Therefore, three automated text classifiers were used to code the Unified Agenda entries by topic. Machine coding of regulations required the construction of a base "training" dataset. After constructing a sizable training dataset and establishing acceptable levels of reliability across topic categories, I used the text classifiers to code the entries in the Unified

---

[11] A more detailed description of the coding scheme is available at the Project's website at www.policyagendas.org.

Agenda. With each pass through the data, the text classifiers agreed on a code for a large proportion of the data (on average around 80 percent). I hand-coded a sample of the remaining data with no agreed-on code and added it to the dataset used to train the automated coder for each successive round of coding. A second pass with the text classifiers was conducted on the entries lacking a topic code. This process was iterated until the coding of the entire Unified Agenda was complete. In all, the process required the hand-coding of approximately 40,000 entries. With the coding complete, the UA data afford a reliable and consistent indicator of the issues on the agenda of the federal bureaucracy for the last quarter-century.[12]

Table 4.1 shows two proposed regulations that appeared in the 2012 edition of the Unified Agenda as examples of typical units of analysis. The first entry, issued by the Fish & Wildlife Service of the Department of Interior, demonstrates the updating and adjustment functions inherent in bureaucratic policy making. A related regulation on the Fish & Wildlife Service's agenda, in the same edition of the Unified Agenda, pertained to prohibiting falconry in national parks where hunting and fishing were permitted but regulated. The second entry in Table 4.1 addresses the interdependence of agriculture and national defense. Table 4.1 shows how even large-scale problems are addressed with regulation. These entries illustrate the range of policy problems contained in the development and promulgation of bureaucratic regulations. The substantive breadth and importance of bureaucratic policy making justify increased scholarly attention to this process and its role in the broader administrative state.

4.3.3 On the Importance of Regulations

Whether merely changing the placement of a name on a form or outlining a new approach to management of national forests, bureaucratic policy makers require the regulatory process to handle emergent policy problems. This process is governed by three prominent features of the American political system, which draw power and legitimacy from both law and politics.

The first feature is the Administrative Procedures Act (APA) passed in 1946.[13] The APA is the cornerstone of administrative law in the United States and of the rule of law. It establishes judicial review of agency policy making and procedures for involving the public in the process of developing and finalizing regulations.

The second feature is subsystem politics. Regulations are a product of the development of problem definitions and coalitions in the confines of policy subsystems, and they change through the process of subsystem politics. Both

---

[12] A detailed discussion of the challenges of and coding procedures for, the entries on the UA is included in Appendix A. This discussion also includes strategies and reliability measures for the process.

[13] P.L. 79–404, 60 Statute 237.

TABLE 4.1 *Two Proposed Regulations, Unified Agenda, Spring 2011*

Title	Abstract
Revising Regulations Implementing the Wild Bird Conservation Act of 1992[a]	We propose to revise our regulations implementing the Wild Bird Conservation Act of 1992, which have not been substantively updated since 1993. We plan to revise these regulations in light of our experiences in implementing the legislation and regulations over the past 15 years, and also to streamline and clarify certain aspects of the current regulations.
Agriculture Priorities and Allocations System[b]	The Secretary of Agriculture is authorized to establish a system of priority performance contracts and allocations of certain agriculture-related resources, as necessary, to meet national defense priorities. Current Department of Agriculture "stand-by" procedures to implement this authority are out of date and generally inadequate to meet Government or National needs should a situation arise that calls for exercise of the authority. As a result, the Farm Service Agency is proposing permanent regulations to allow USDA to efficiently place priority ratings on contracts or orders with respect to resources within its authority should the need arise. The new Agriculture Priorities and Allocation System (APAS) regulations will be similar to the Department of Commerce's Defense Priorities and Allocation System (DPAS) for establishing priority ratings for contract performance.

[a] RIN 1018-AW83; Department of Interior, Fish & Wildlife Service.
[b] RIN 0560-AH68; Department of Agriculture, Farm Service Agency.

legislators and organized interests are powerful influences on the development of regulations through the institutionalized and routinized process of congressional oversight. Subsystems are tools of meso-level policy making as much as tools of democratic accountability through oversight.

The third feature is the pluralistic arrangement of the American political system. Bureaucracies are the institutional realization of demands placed on government by interested publics. These organized groups then become a prominent influence on bureaucratic policy making and subsystem dynamics in general. By examining regulatory policy making over a long period of time, influences from the subsystem, the president, and interest groups can be incorporated into the analysis of bureaucratic influence on congressional issue prioritization.

Bureaucratic policy making begins when a federal agency either decides to develop a regulation authorized by Congress in legislation or when Congress or the president asks the agency to develop regulations. During this initial phase, comments are taken from interested publics, and the general public and the agency can respond where necessary.[14] Once the regulation has been refined in response to public comment, the agency publishes a "final" rule in the Federal Register along with the date the rule will become law. Agency rules then become regulations in the Code of Federal Regulations and have the same force of law as a normal congressional statute.

Laws – whether important, salient, mundane, dire, or esoteric – come to life in the course of bureaucratic policy making: the importance of this process cannot be overstated. By helping refine congressional intent, bureaucracies go beyond the mere implementation of statutes promulgated by Congress and signed into law by the president. Although bureaucracies do engage in a tremendous amount of mundane policy implementation, taking Dodd and Schott (1986) seriously means recognizing that bureaucracies adjust not only vague and sprawling legislation to observable realities on the ground but also the goals of the policies themselves, along with the expectations and demands we place on government.

The role of bureaucracy goes to the heart of the system's ability to adapt to the problems it confronts. Kerwin (2003, p. 7), probably the most prominent scholar in the study of bureaucratic rulemaking, notes that "statutes and rules depend on one another . . . statutes provide legal *authority*, while rules provide for detail and *adaptation*" [emphases added].[15] Rules codify nearly everything public bureaucracies undertake, from reordering entries on a form to mobilizing for war. In an institution where legal process is front and center, we often fail to recognize the overarching importance of the substance of bureaucratic policy making.

4.3.4 Studying Regulations

Although analyzing regulations is ideal from the standpoint of examining the dual dynamics of the administrative state, this study has a few limitations. First, bureaucracies also influence policy through enforcement activity or adjudicatory proceedings. Bureaucracies use different mixes of these approaches to policy making, though scholarship has ignored the question of the mix and choice of strategy. Just as bureaucracies differ in the degree to which they employ regulatory policy making to influence policy, some issues are more or less amenable to this avenue of questioning. Regulations are better indicators of agenda setting and policy making for some bureaucracies or some issues than for others.[16]

---

[14] For research on interest group influence in the notice and comment process, see Yackee (2005).

[15] See Yackee (2005, 2006).

[16] Other indicators might include intra-agency budgets, enforcement activities, suits filed, and so on.

Concerning regulatory policy making, it is also important to note that there is a difference between analyzing regulations for their substantive issue content and analyzing them for the solutions they recommend. The fact that we have bureaucratic regulations on environmental issues does not mean these regulations take a pro-government stance toward the environment. Regulations both further the role of government in the economy and society and retrench its role. As I have attempted to do throughout, it is useful to distinguish the problem from the solution space. In the solution space, basic preferences will play a much larger role in determining the form of the regulation. From the perspective of dual dynamics, the environment may either present an emergent problem that is dealt with by expanding government involvement or discrepancies may move government to a private sector solution. Where the bureaucracy is concerned, both scenarios will be implemented by way of issuing regulations.

Related to the problem-solution space discussion in the preceding paragraph, scholars and citizens alike often mistakenly assume that more activity by bureaucracy is associated with a liberal approach to government, whereas decreased activity is associated with a conservative approach. It cannot be stressed too much that whether the goal is expansion of government through regulatory policy or retrenchment through deregulation, each goal is achieved through the standard regulatory process. To deregulate, conservatives must initiate regulations that hand off change to private sector mechanisms. It is therefore dangerous to infer liberal or conservative approaches to government by looking at regulatory activity.

4.4 BUREAUCRATIC PROBLEM MONITORING

Bureaucratic problem solving begins with monitoring the issues on the agenda and identifying problems to address. As an indicator of bureaucratic problem monitoring, regulations provide information, best conceived in terms of signals, about the problems or issues confronting government.

Table 4.2 displays the frequencies, percentages, and descriptive statistics for each of the major issues comprising the agenda of the bureaucracy from spring 1983 through fall 2008. In all, 226,710 entries in the Unified Agenda – the entire population for the indicator – were coded according to the Policy Agendas Project topic coding scheme. The issues are ordered from top to bottom in terms of decreasing issuance and development of regulations. As Table 4.2 shows, attention varies across issues. Some receive substantial amounts of attention, whereas others receive only scant attention in terms of the development of regulations.

The first point to note is that the bureaucracy was very active in issuing and developing regulations during a decidedly conservative era of American politics when members of both political parties adopted the language of smaller, leaner government. Control of Congress was roughly split between the two political parties, though Republicans took control of the House after decades as a

TABLE 4.2 *Issue Composition of the Bureaucracy's Agenda*

Issue	Frequency[a]	Percent[b]	Mean[c]	St.D.[c]
Environment	37,128	16.38	1,428.00	364.51
Business & Finance	29,523	13.02	1,135.50	131.16
Government Operations	28,055	12.37	1,079.04	225.32
Transportation	24,842	10.96	955.46	178.36
Labor & Immigration	15,596	6.88	599.85	65.06
Health Care	14,027	6.19	539.50	78.41
Public Lands & Water	11,976	5.28	460.62	77.15
Macroeconomics	10,531	4.65	405.04	133.02
Energy	9,628	4.25	370.31	66.55
Agriculture	8,206	3.62	315.62	69.16
Housing	7,788	3.44	299.54	98.17
Civil Rights & Liberties	7,039	3.10	270.73	42.92
Social Welfare	4,909	2.17	188.81	39.66
Science & Technology	4,582	2.02	176.23	51.59
Trade	3,928	1.73	151.08	53.59
Education	3,194	1.41	122.85	64.12
Defense	3,186	1.41	122.54	18.18
Law, Crime, & Family	1,957	0.86	75.27	22.80
Foreign Affairs	615	0.27	23.65	6.32
Total[d]	226,710	100	8,719.62	725.56

[a] Frequencies (counts) of activity across the time period 1983–2008 falling into each of the nineteen major issue categories of the Policy Agendas Project.
[b] Percentage of all activity over the entire period contributed by the given issue.
[c] Annual mean and standard deviation for each issue.
[d] Totals for all issues over the time period. χ^2 167,515, df = 18, $p < .001$.

minority party in that chamber. The prominence of bureaucracy in this era shows that members of both political parties in Congress relied on regulatory policy making to achieve objectives.

Table 4.2 gives a very rough impression of the issue priorities in regulatory policy making. These priorities derive from three sources. First, bureaucracies pay attention to issues and identify some disturbances as problems within issue areas. Second, congressional prioritization both bundles and shuffles issues. Third, some issues are far less amenable to the development of regulations than others, so policy making around these issues occurs using different tools, such as enforcement or adjudication.[17]

[17] Table 4.2 also cannot give a sense of the importance attached to each rule or entry in the Unified Agenda. Some issues contain very few rules, yet these rules are incredibly important. A good example of this is trade policy. In the issue of trade policy, there are fewer rules, but they tend to be very important, pertaining to issues of national security, national defense stockpiles, technology transfers, and so on.

The issues near the top of Table 4.2 anchor partisan tussles in Congress and relate to the infrastructure of the economy and role of natural resources in economic growth. Bureaucrats grappled with the collision of business and environmental problems during this period; government operations became more important than ever as policy makers debated not only what government would do but also how government would go about doing it. Other subjects under debate included public administration versus privatization, negotiated regulation, and performance management. Issues such as agriculture, public lands & water, energy, and transportation pertain to various aspects of economic infrastructure and natural resources and are not as easily understood in terms of partisan conflict.

Issues near the bottom of Table 4.2 display three characteristics. First, they tend to be on the wane, peripheral to partisan conflict, and less important to the infrastructure of the economy. Second, some of these issues, such as science & technology, are dominated by experts and have no real organized publics (May, 1991) or historically have had low levels of federal involvement compared with state government involvement (e.g., education or law, crime, & family). Third, in some of these issues the policy-making function of bureaucratic policy making takes a back seat to other activities (e.g., defense, foreign affairs, and trade). These issues are also more amenable to presidential management and stay closer to the White House. For these issues, presidential management strategies are more persistent modes of policy making than are the issuance and development of regulations.

Apart from these exceptions, bureaucratic monitoring and identification of problems fueled attention to the set of issues on the agenda. During the time period under study, free trade became prominent in the increasingly global economy, bringing the promise of free, competitive, global markets, along with a host of labor and environmental regulatory issues. The stock market in the United States saw unparalleled growth. Scandals spurred change in the system of corporate accounting. The terrorism of the mid-1990s and the first decade of the new century brought immigration and federal law enforcement problems. Natural disasters challenged the role of the federal government in assisting and rebuilding shattered communities. A bridge collapse in Minnesota highlighted the need for infrastructure improvement, and in the spring of 2008, major financial institutions began to fail. Thus, although partisan and ideological trends broadly structure the issues to which bureaucracy attends, much of the agenda is dictated by circumstances. This feature becomes more apparent when examining the issues over time.

Figure 4.3 displays the frequency of entries in the Unified Agenda biannually by issue.[18] Whereas Table 4.2 focuses on the relative prominence of the

---

[18] Each panel of the figure includes a smoother with bandwidth .25 and confidence intervals around the smooth. In this case, the smooth is a lowess estimate. Note that the scales for each issue differ.

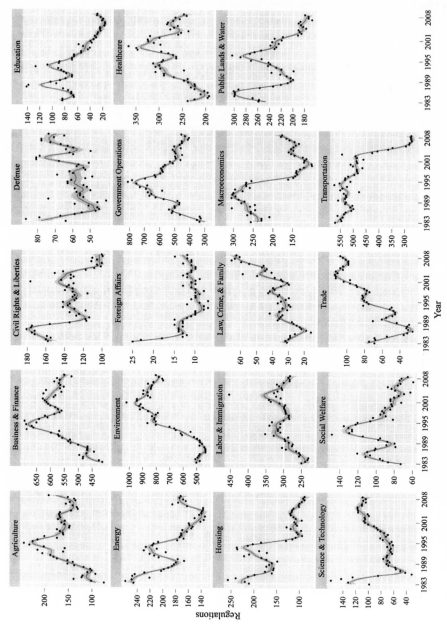

FIGURE 4.3 Issue Trends in Regulation. *Source:* Compiled by the Author.

issues on the bureaucracy's agenda, Figure 4.3 draws attention to their time dynamics. There is a strong and persistent characterization of bureaucratic policy making as inertial or static. At the time of this writing, for instance, typing the term "inertia" into Google brings up "bureaucratic inertia" as an example of the usage. Despite the inertia usually associated with popular notions of bureaucracy, Figure 4.3 suggests that almost no issue under the watchful eye of the bureaucracy displays anything approaching this characterization. The regulatory agenda changes dramatically over time.

Congressional prioritization is linked to overall movements in the bureaucracy's agenda by two mechanisms. Congress is able to alter the broad parameters of bureaucratic problem monitoring and identification by shuffling the priority the bureaucracy assigns to issues or by bundling groups of issues. Reprioritizing may occur by direct act of law or by the dynamics of congressional agenda setting (see Chapter 2). Issue shuffling is never more evident than when parties switch control of Congress.

The most important feature of Figure 4.3 is that many, if not most of the issues, changed dramatically after 1994, when Newt Gingrich helped bring Republicans to power in Congress. On issues such as agriculture, energy, macroeconomics, housing, government operations, and public lands & water, this change was stark (although this shift seemed to occur in every issue).[19] The connection between congressional change and regulatory change supports the theory of dual dynamics in policy making because it posits a closer connection between Congress and bureaucracy than claimed by recent presidential scholarship. Figure 4.3 suggests that issue shuffling is more consistent with changing congressional priorities than with changing presidential administrations.

Presidency scholars have noted that presidents in this era commit considerable time and resources to various strategies for *managing* the bureaucracy (Golden, 2000; Lewis, 2008). Further, data suggest they spend increasingly less time attempting to shape regulation, at least overtly, because the process requires spending so much time, effort, and political capital, not to mention the opportunity cost of focusing attention elsewhere. OIRA reviews of regulations peaked at just over 2,500 in 1991, but fell precipitously after 1994, falling below 700 annually after 2003. Among these reviews, less than 20 percent make requests for changes to the regulation. Presidents set broad regulatory priorities for the bureaucracy. If a president prioritizes energy policy or environmental policy, there will be on average more activity on these issues as presidents compromise the subsystem and create a transitory coalition (Worsham, 1997). However, this prioritization will come at a cost in other issue

---

[19] These seeming changes, or issue shuffling also occur at the time the Clinton presidency shifted ideologically to the center. Yet, this shift was primarily in response to, or even in anticipation of, the turn to the right in Congress and its expected consequences, both electorally and in terms of policy-making opportunities. Republicans began to shift policy debates even before coming to power.

areas, because attention is more limited for presidents than for Congress. An analysis of presidential regulatory priorities would gauge this ability to shift attention broadly, but still take into account the costs associated with focused presidential efforts to set the agenda.

All that said, the primary power of the president to set regulatory agendas seems to be through the power of appointment of high-level bureaucrats (Lewis, 2008). To the degree that the preferences of appointees approximate those of the president, the OMB figures above reflect a responsive bureaucracy. Yet estimations of the ideological positions of bureaucracies (Clinton et al., 2012) demonstrate that even partisan appointees are often far away from the president in ideological space. Moreover, scholars have yet to systematically connect these predispositions to regulatory behavior.

The fact that there are clear and dramatic increases and decreases in most issues during the period under study demonstrates two additional features of the administrative state. First, due to the rule of law and regulatory policy making as a mode of governance, conservatives in many cases adopt the regulatory mode of policy making to achieve policy objectives. In the administrative state regulatory policy making is a prominent tool for achieving policy objectives of either government expansion or retrenchment. The development of regulations on the environment is a good example. Bureaucratic attention to the environment generally increased over the period of study, and reached its zenith under the Republican-controlled Congress of the late 1990s. This does not mean that conservatives looked fondly on environmental regulation, but it does suggest that "getting the EPA off the backs of business" meant working through the regulatory process.

The second feature of the administrative state that begins to appear in Figure 4.3 is the powerful influence of congressional issue prioritization. The broad contours of bureaucratic problem monitoring are in no small portion a reflection of issue shuffling by the two political parties. Although some issues uniformly receive attention because they animate partisan conflict in Congress, some issues just drop off the agenda because they are not priorities for the legislators (e.g., housing).

Much can be learned about the trajectories of issues from Figure 4.3. Education, for instance, witnessed a drastic decline in activity over the period. This decline occurred at a time when the federal government was paring down its role in higher education and moving into secondary education, mostly by implementing a testing or performance regimen through incentives and fiscal federalism rather than regulation. The policy changes in energy in the earlier part of this decade and the emerging energy crisis surely influenced the uptick in bureaucratic attention to this issue. In contrast, the drastically decreased attention to transportation came at a time when many viewed the country's infrastructure as outdated and crumbling. In the same period, the expansion of free trade and the increased global interdependence that resulted, certainly fueled bureaucratic attention to trade. Though few in number trade regulations tend to be very important and increasingly relate to national security, as well as to economic security.

These patterns in regulatory policy making are the product of an interwoven response to real-world problems and the issue shuffling and bundling that result from congressional prioritization. As bureaucratic problem solving flows into congressional prioritization, bureaucratic efforts at policy making are signals to elected officials about the nature and severity of problems.

Issue signals convey the most information when they change. A supply of information that departs from what is the norm and does so for an extended period of time yields a clear signal that the nature of the problem has changed. Figure 4.4 presents a waterfall plot of the deviations from the mean frequency of regulations on the bureaucracy's agenda through time. The waterfall plot is meant to illuminate two features of the data on changes in bureaucratic signaling. First, the peaks and troughs show how extreme the signaling is, compared to the historical average. Second, the filled portions of each issue draw attention to the length of time that signaling goes above or below this average. Figure 4.4 thus gives a sense of whether bureaucratic signaling has departed from the norm and for how long. The longer that signaling is abnormal, especially drastically so, the more likely it is to draw the attention of policymakers.

Figure 4.4 also shows that signaling for some issues spends extended periods of time considerably below or above their averages. Some of these departures are easily explainable by particular events or acute policy problems. Labor and immigration issues, for instance, display a sharp uptick around the time of the terrorist attacks of fall 2001, when concern for border security intensified. Business and financial regulation is above the norm during the period building up to the passage of the National Securities Markets Improvement Act of 1996.[20]

It is worth considering whether the issues exhibiting longer term departures from the norm closely anchor partisan politics and are subject to substantial and extended efforts by parties to reverse the progress of their predecessors. If so, it follows that these issues would be less responsive to the emergence of policy problems as communicated by bureaucracy (e.g., environment, macroeconomics, and government operations). Congressional prioritization may facilitate the adjustment of problem monitoring, such that much-needed information is supplied to the system. Where partisan and ideological conflict structure congressional prioritization, bureaucratic problem solving often leaves the system with an over- or under-abundance of information on particular issues. Where competition is based on issues, information is increased; where competition is ideological, issue attention may not reflect problem priorities.

As a point of comparison, Figure 4.5 presents a waterfall plot of the period-to-period changes in regulations appearing in the Unified Agenda from spring 1983 through fall 2008. Rather than assuming there is some mean level of

[20] P.L. 104–290.

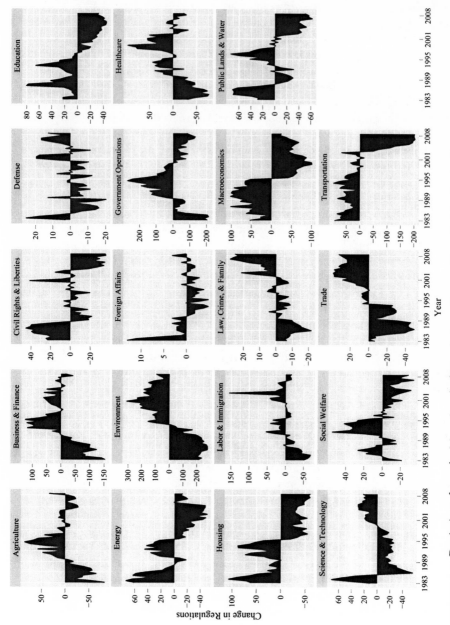

FIGURE 4.4 Deviations from the Mean Level of Regulations. *Source:* Compiled by the Author.

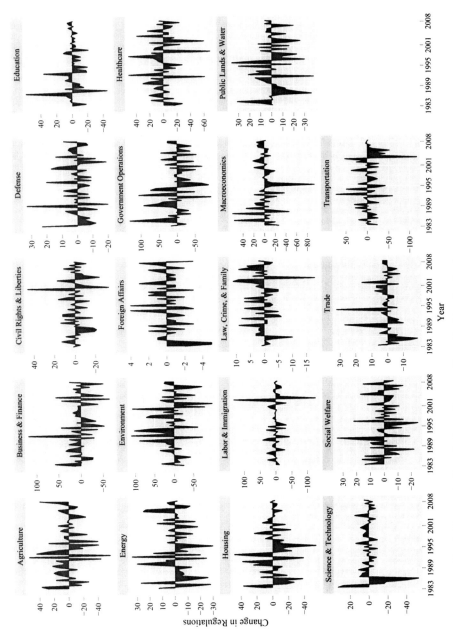

FIGURE 4-5 Real Change in Regulations. *Source:* Compiled by the Author.

regulations associated with each issue, Figure 4.5 takes as its baseline the previous period's level of regulations. One of the properties associated with bureaucratic signals is the degree to which they represent a varying information supply. Figure 4.5 illustrates clearly the variability in the supply of information from the bureaucracy. The supply of information across issues varies widely, but just as important, however, is that variability is nonconstant through time within issues.

As discussed earlier, even a highly variable supply of information, if constant and "expected," is useful to policy makers. Within several of the issues in Figure 4.5, however, long stretches of low constant variance are followed by increased variability. The labor and immigration issue area is an example, as are education and trade. These issues exemplify the switch from a trickle of information to a torrent, which taxes the attention limits of decision makers at higher levels of government. Nonconstant variance, or volatility, introduces tremendous uncertainty into policy-making efforts in both Congress and the bureaucracy.

The information provided by bureaucracy via these signals presents two problems for elected officials. First, the actual amount of information contained in signaling varies over time. Second, this natural, or true, variation occurs amid a tremendous amount of noise, making the amount of information hard to discern. Figure 4.5 also gives an impression of the amount of noise associated with bureaucratic signaling.

Noise is a persistent and troublesome feature of the administrative state as political and administrative institutions attempt to communicate, influence policy, and mitigate uncertainty. Noise is introduced by over- and under-reactions by the bureaucracy, Congress, or both to real-world problems (May et al., 2008). Overreactions on one issue are dangerous for institutions charged with monitoring several aspects of a problem at once. These overreactions occur because of the scarce nature of attention, which has opportunity costs in other areas when attention is focused on a given issue. They circumvent the system's built-in protection: delegation. As all units begin to focus on one issue, problems arise in other areas as policy does not adjust to new realities through time. For instance, the Department of Homeland Security's overreaction to the threat of terrorism destabilized policy-making arrangements reaching all the way to the state and local levels in disaster management (May and Workman, 2009).

Noise is also introduced by congressional prioritization. The process of congressional prioritization is influenced by both intra-institutional conflict in its many guises and interbranch conflict with the president. For example, although most of the blame for the Deepwater Horizon Oil Rig explosion on April 20, 2010, and its aftermath fell on a bureaucracy (Minerals Management Service of the Department of Interior) that was seemingly unwilling to regulate, this disaster was in part the culmination of at least a decade of prioritizing oil exploration and production over environmental and safety concerns.

Noting that the blame did not lie entirely with lax regulation at the Minerals Management Service (MMS), the GAO (2010) found that MMS lacked the substantive guidance its analysts needed to prepare National Environmental Policy Act (NEPA) documents. The MMS had formally requested such guidance from Congress multiple times, receiving no clear response. What was clear was the signal from Congress: oil development and production, especially in light of rising fuel prices, were to be prioritized over environmental and safety concerns. Congressional prioritization introduces noise to bureaucratic problem monitoring, and this effect is even more pronounced where partisan issue alignment is prominent.

Of course, noise does not excuse wayward bureaucracies, but reforming the regulatory process involves recognizing that policy making in the administrative state is an interdependent process. Bureaucrats rarely venture beyond latitudes drawn by Congress or the president. Two of the more pressing problems early on in the Obama administration involved the nation's crumbling infrastructure and financial regulatory reform, especially of financial instruments called derivatives. Yet these issues were sidelined by a year-long battle to pass health care reform legislation. Likewise, the Bush administration's neglect of these two issues, especially of transportation, is shown prominently in Figures 4.3 and 4.4. The president has considerable power to introduce noise into the system by influencing congressional priorities.

Noise also enters the system when bureaucracies get it wrong. Bureaucracies may misinterpret disturbances in the policy environment, identify the wrong problems, or mischaracterize an issue. For instance, bureaucracies charged with regulating financial institutions failed to perceive the threat posed by an enormous bubble in the housing market in early 2007. Further, the bureaucratic action taken over this period served to amplify the negative consequences when the bubble burst. Banks became overleveraged partly because regulations governing reserve requirements and risk had been dismantled. The result was noise about the true nature of the problem and its consequences. Thus, the influence of noise in the system goes beyond defining the problem, but cascades through the solution space as government subsequently overreacts.

The fields of communication and engineering offer a way to think about signaling and noise in the dual dynamics of bureaucratic problem solving and congressional prioritization. Bureaucratic signaling carried in regulatory policy making may be characterized both by a signal-to-noise ratio (SNR) and by amplitude. The SNR refers to the level of a signal compared to the background noise. For the present discussion, the SNR is simply the ratio of the mean of the signal for an issue to its standard deviation.[21] In other words, it gauges the strength of a signal compared to its variability or noise.

---

[21] This is one among many possible ways to measure the SNR. Formally, the SNR is simply $SNR_k = \frac{\mu_k}{\sigma_k}$, where k indexes for each issue. This measure of SNR is also the inverse of the coefficient of variation.

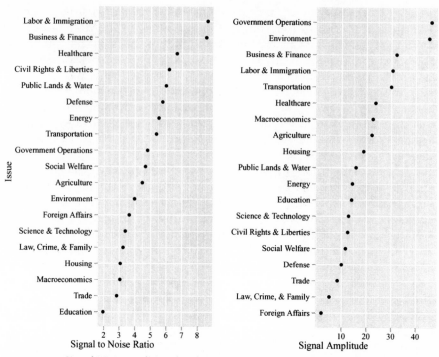

FIGURE 4.6 Signal Noise and Amplitude. *Source:* Compiled by the Author.

Amplitude measures the magnitude of change in an oscillating variable. Although there is no fixed level of regulation in any issue area, Figures 4.4 and 4.5 show that bureaucratic policy making does oscillate as bureaucracies attempt to adjust to changes in the policy and political spheres. Regulation is a process of continual approximation to the realities of problems. Bureaucracies, and policy-making institutions in general, tend to over- and underreact to problems. The result is a disproportionate response to the information available. For purposes here, amplitude is measured as the root mean square of the issue series.[22]

Figure 4.6 displays the SNR and amplitude of signaling of each issue across the set of bureaucracies; as such, they are averages for each issue. The greater the SNR, the more distinguishable the signal emitted by the set of bureaucracies monitoring the issue is from background noise.[23] Labor & immigration

---

[22] Formally, the root mean square amplitude of each issue is $AMP_k = \sqrt{\frac{x_{ik}\cdots x_{jm}}{n}}$, where i indexes the observations over time for each issue k.

[23] Note that all SNRs in the bureaucracy's agenda are greater than one. This occurs because the variables are counts over time and the mean and variance of count processes are not necessarily independent. Smaller SNRs mean smaller variance.

issues, along with Business & finance, display the strongest signals compared to attendant noise. Education has the least discernible signal from its background noise. Government operations and the environment have the largest signal amplitudes, closely followed by a group that includes business & finance, labor & immigration, and transportation policy.

Three features of the issues in Figure 4.6 provide a measure of order to the SNRs and amplitudes. The SNRs and amplitudes are ordered by issue in terms of the strength of the signal or size of the amplitude. Issues such as transportation, energy, public lands & water, and business & finance are addressed by powerful bureaucracies and independent regulatory agencies. Further, these bureaucracies regulate and cultivate organized interests that have considerable resources and political savvy. Issues with the highest amplitude tend to be those over which there is intense political conflict. Because amplitude measures the magnitude of oscillations in policy direction, partisan conflict fuels intense, wide-ranging oscillations, or corrections, in bureaucratic policy making.

4.5 SIGNALING AND INFORMATION

Bureaucratic inertia does not convey information. Elected officials, however, do not face a bureaucracy with its feet hopelessly stuck in the mud. There are always fluctuations in bureaucratic policy making, which convey certain types and amounts of information to elected officials. Bureaucratic policy making exhibits tremendous variability both across issues and within issues over time. This chapter's systematic cataloging of regulations demonstrates great variability in bureaucratic policy making and, hence, the types and quantities of information elected officials might glean from it.

This variability derives from the dual dynamics of the administrative state. Bureaucracies monitor problems and issue regulations. These regulations are valuable both as the implements of policy making at higher levels of government and also for the information they carry to elected officials about relevant dimensions of problems and relevant publics or organized interests. The dynamics of bureaucratic problem solving also tell elected officials something about which issues the system will detect and how it might deal with them. The likely content of the agenda tells elected officials how the dynamics of bureaucratic problem solving align with their efforts at prioritization and how bureaucratic problem solving might be adjusted. Congress adjusts the broad parameters of the system based on the information that flows from below.

Congressional prioritization in turn depends on bureaucratic efforts to monitor, identify, and define emergent policy problems. Problem definition depends on which bureaucracies are paying attention. This delegation of attention plays a role in which issues are noticed, how they are defined, and ultimately how Congress responds. The Elmore problem is very much alive and well in the modern administrative state.

The following chapters examine the juncture in the administrative state at which bureaucratic problem solving flows into congressional prioritization. Congressional prioritization structures bureaucratic problem solving in at least two ways. First, through the dynamics of agenda setting and shifting congressional attention, Congress fosters issue shuffling and bundling, erecting walls between some issues and tearing them down between others. In this regard, Congress helps define the broad issue space facing bureaucracies. Second, elected officials are able to foster either separability or competition among bureaucratic institutions in supplying information to Congress. By issue shuffling, bundling, and making bureaucracies compete to supply information, Congress steers the course of government responsiveness to problems.

5

Problem Prioritization and Demand for Information

Agenda setting in Congress profoundly influences signaling about policy problems by the federal bureaucracy. The prioritization of problems by Congress makes congressional influence on the federal bureaucracy so pervasive that it is intrinsic to the system of dual dynamics and operates even in the absence of structured incentive systems. The U.S. Constitution mandates that Congress takes up the authority position in Elmore's problem, while bureaucracy supplies the bottom-up expertise for government decision making. The process of prioritizing problems for attention in Congress creates a demand for information that tunes signals about problems from the bureaucracy and structures the supply of information.

These top-down influences are different from the more formal methods of controlling bureaucracy. The key baseline assumption of most characterizations of the system is that bureaucracies hold private information that must be induced through incentives and disincentives. Therefore, absent a fully adequate contract and system of monitoring, bureaucracies undersupply information relevant to the policy and political calculations of legislators.

The dual dynamics of prioritization and problem solving depart from this key assumption of the nature of the information supply in the policy process. The ability to steer policy change is predicated on influencing how problems are defined and understood at upper levels of government. Bureaucracies supply information in an effort to craft problem definitions beneficial to their organizations, constituencies, and their own interests in policy making. In this model, undersupply is not a concern. Instead, the problem for policy makers lies in influencing the types, quantity, and nature of the massive amount of information generated by the federal bureaucracy.

Congress shapes the supply of information from the bureaucracy through three mechanisms. All three mechanisms relate to agenda setting in Congress and the way members of Congress choose to allocate scarce attention to the array of problems on the agenda. The mechanisms of prioritization so influential for the supply of information do not bear the heavy cost of contracts embodied in legislation or the burden of intensive monitoring. Instead Congress shapes the information supply through issue shuffling, issue bundling, and fostering competition in the provision of information on policy issues. Using the measures of signal-to-noise ratio and signal amplitude developed in Chapter 4, this chapter examines how congressional agenda setting shapes the information supply generated by the bureaucracy and sets the dual dynamics of the administrative state in motion.

5.1 ISSUE SHUFFLING

Through issue shuffling, Congress alters the set of issues on the agenda or, more likely, reprioritizes the set of issues in terms of importance. The classic conception of Congress as controlling the bureaucracy holds that Congress stacks the deck against administrative agencies, ensuring administrative responsiveness. Yet Congress is also able to "shuffle the deck," altering bureaucracy's information supply by shifting attention to new or redefined issues. In many ways, issue shuffling thus reformulates classical notions of agenda setting in Congress to explain congressional influence on the federal bureaucracy.

When Congress alters its agenda or reprioritizes the issues already on the agenda, the supply of information coming from the bureaucracy is changed in two ways. First, bureaucracies previously in a prominent position because of particular issues on the agenda, along with other interests and actors, change the supply of information they give to Congress because they want to influence policy change. If congressional attention has shifted to a different set of issues, it behooves bureaucracies to incorporate these issues into their own way of defining problems. Second, issue shuffling switches some bureaucracies on and switches others off. For example, if Congress shifts attention broadly toward issues such as homeland security and immigration and away from other broad issues such as infrastructure development, then different federal bureaucracies become relevant as suppliers of information to Congress. In this example, the Department of Homeland Security and the Department of Justice would become more relevant than the Transportation or Energy departments. Simply altering the agenda alters the nature of the information supply. Yet this alteration changes more than the set of agencies doing the signaling. Changing the prominence of given bureaucracies as suppliers of information also changes the nature of how problems become defined and what particular strategies emerge for addressing the problems.

Chapter 4 introduced regulations as an indicator of signaling by the bureaucracy about policy problems. The signal-to-noise ratio and signal amplitude are measures of the information carried in the regulatory agenda of the federal bureaucracy. Two aspects of information are relevant when considering bureaucratic signals about policy problems, as assessed by these measures.

First, stable, robust signals convey information about the continued importance of given issues or relevant bureaucracies. Second, the degree to which information is changing, thereby causing uncertainty, matters greatly. Stability and volatility have different implications for policy issues and the bureaucracies monitoring these issues.

Signal-to-noise ratios (SNRs) tap into the stability or robustness of a signal. The SNR is the ratio of the mean quantity of regulations on a given issue over time to the standard deviation or variance. The higher the SNR, the more distinct the signal is from the noise around it. The lower the SNR, the less information conveyed by the signal.

Signal amplitudes indicate the magnitude of the variance in a changing signal, and thus the portion of information that changes over time. The simplest measure of signal amplitude is the root-mean square of the signal, in this case, over time. The measure is constructed by taking the period-to-period changes in a signal and squaring these. Then, the mean is obtained and its square root taken. The amplitude assesses the magnitude of the variation over time in regulations on a given issue or from a given bureaucracy.

A simple way to assess the effects of congressional prioritization is to compare periods with different party control in Congress. Issue politics is clearly important to members of Congress in terms of campaigning and governing (Petrocik, 1996; Petrocik et al., 2003; Sulkin, 2005, 2011). Increasingly, research demonstrates that issue ownership is a direct result of the priorities of the major parties (Egan, 2013). Given this, it is worth considering the partisan differences associated with the bureaucracy's supply of information about problems. Theoretically, Democrats and Republicans prioritize different issues and face unique sets of problems through time (although legislators of either party could not ignore the attacks of September 11, 2001, or the ravaging of the Gulf Coast by Hurricane Katrina). Figure 5.1 provides one way of assessing changes in signal clarity and volatility from the bureaucracy that are associated with party control. It shows the change in SNR (left panel) and signal amplitude (right panel) associated with the move from Democratic control of Congress in 1983–1994 to Republican control from 1995–2006. In each panel, issues on the left of the dotted line at zero are those in which the SNR or amplitude decreased under Republican control. Issues on the right of the dotted line at zero in each panel are those in which the SNR or signal amplitude increased under Republican control of Congress.

Figure 5.1 shows three things about bureaucratic signaling. Signal clarity (left panel), measured using the issue SNRs, varies with party control in Congress. Signals for some issues (e.g., business & finance or the environment) become much clearer and distinguishable from background noise, whereas others become less audible (e.g., transportation or public lands & water). When there are stronger or more audible signals, the set of bureaucracies making policy in these areas have either ramped up their regulatory attention to the issue or decreased the background noise characterizing attention to the issue. In the

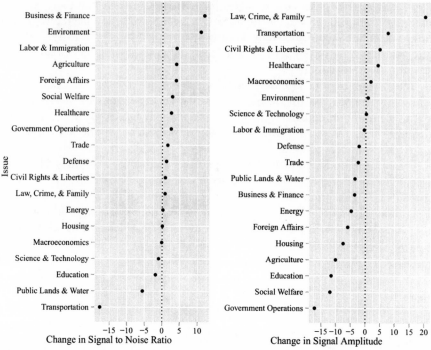

FIGURE 5.1 Party Control in Congress and Change in Issue Signaling by the Bureaucracy. The left panel in the figure displays the change in signal-to-noise ratio associated with moving from Democratic control of Congress from 1983–1994 to Republican control from 1995–2006. The panel on the right in the figure displays the same information for signal amplitude.

case of issues with decreasing SNRs, the set of bureaucracies making policy have either reduced overall attention to the issue or increased the background noise. Thus, signals become more or less clear in part due to changing party control of Congress, including changing issue priorities on the agenda. The distinction between signal clarity and strength is subtle, but also very important. Some issues remain stable on the agenda even when attention flags. A small, but clear signal is still important to the overall agenda.

For example, agriculture contributed 3.62 percent of the federal bureaucracy's attention across issues. Yet, its SNR increased dramatically across party control of Congress. This was due in part to the increased importance of agriculture in an era of global food crises related to climate change, and the use of ethanol as an alternative fuel in an effort to increase energy independence. These problems reframed agriculture as a national security issue, especially given terrorism-related concerns for safety of the food supply. Agriculture garnered a moderate amount of attention from the bureaucracy when compared across issues, yet the signal from the federal bureaucracy was clear and increasingly relevant to these other issues. In this context, levels of attention to an issue can be deceptive.

Figure 5.1 also shows that, like SNRs, signal amplitude varies by party control in Congress. As in the case of issue SNRs, some issues become much more volatile as party control of Congress changed, whereas others settle down. Some issues display increased signal amplitudes because of party interest in these areas. As Congress moves into issue areas, it often has a destabilizing effect on the issue (Redford, 1969; Baumgartner and Jones, 1993; Worsham, 1997). A good example here is the modern Republican party's interest in social regulation. This type of party-induced fluctuation is key to understanding the law, crime, & family issue. Arguably, the destabilization in this issue area resulted from increased importance of the issue on the agenda (at least in terms of partisan conflict). The issue area of Civil Rights & Liberties also experienced this same type of destabilization. Many of the themes of civil rights and liberties are closely related to those concerning social regulation (e.g., the debate over same-sex marriage). These issues experienced fluctuations that may make them more central to an understanding of overall congressional agenda dynamics.

However, issue destabilization may also mean the decreased visibility of an issue on the agenda. Transportation is a good case in point. Professional associations, including the American Society of Civil Engineers, have noted the dismal state of infrastructure in the United States (Cooper, 2009). This general neglect is borne out in part by dramatically reduced attention to transportation, which reflected the difficulty that set of bureaucracies had in transmitting signals about its importance, as well as broader trends in Congress. For example, much transportation policy is made through the use of earmarks and logrolling. In the current political context, Congress has found it difficult to engage in these activities because of election rhetoric and polarization. The result is a fading signal from the bureaucracies charged with making policy in this area. The signal often falls on deaf ears, becoming lost not only in the noise of the agenda more broadly but also in the background noise of changing politics and institutional processes.

This discussion highlights the fact that variable SNRs and signal amplitudes reflect congressional agenda setting, including changing modes of policy making that favor some issues and downgrade others. Some of this change is endogenous to the system of dual dynamics and processes of agenda setting in Congress and the bureaucracy. However, signal variability also arises from changing circumstances on the ground and the way bureaucrats and members of Congress exploit these circumstances. Congress's interest in the issue area of labor & immigration used to be mostly about ensuring a cheap, stable labor supply for American businesses. Now the perceived threat of terrorism by immigrants has strengthened the signal in this broad area, as legislators, bureaucrats, and organized interests all attempt to redefine the issue.

Figure 5.1 shows that the SNRs increase for the majority of issues addressed by the bureaucracy as one moves from Democratic to Republican control of Congress. This makes sense when considering historical patterns of party control in Congress. Republicans gained control of Congress in 1995 after almost a half-century of Democratic control of the House of Representatives and only a few instances of party changes in the Senate. Given unbroken Democratic control for so long, it makes sense that Republicans made changes in many issue areas after taking over. It is important to note that we would expect differences in the signaling on issues regardless of the temporal grouping if there were enduring upward or downward trends in the data. Appendix B contains an analysis of trends in the signaling data and finds only six of the nineteen issues contain trends. Of these, partisan differences are undetectable for only two after controlling for the trend. In other words, party differences in bureaucratic signaling remain even after controlling for the time dynamics of the signal for any given issue.

Signaling by the bureaucracy on business & finance and the environment provides evidence of this party shift and the clarifying of signals in these areas. First, regulation in these two areas anchors the modern party conflict evident not only in Congress but also more broadly in American politics. In terms of SNRs, business & finance and the environment ranked seventh and thirteenth respectively, under Democratic control of Congress. Under Republican control, these issues rose to the first and second positions, respectively, in terms of SNRs. Looking at the panel of Figure 5.1 measuring signal amplitudes, it is clear that this increased signal clarity, as evidenced in higher SNRs, is only partly due to decreasing signal amplitude. This means that some of the change must come from greater regulatory attention. Consistent with this view, the correlation between the SNR ratios of congressional hearings under Republicans and the bureaucracies' regulatory attention over that era is a moderately strong .6. Republicans in Congress set out to clarify or refine signals from the bureaucracy on these issues, which necessarily meant engaging the regulatory process. Even deregulation required the development of regulations. Data on congressional hearings during this time period suggests that Republicans held fewer hearings and passed fewer laws than the earlier period under Democratic control. Republicans perhaps had an affinity for inducing policy change through administrative means, especially by altering the set of signals about various issues from bureaucracies.

Within the dual dynamics of the administrative state, bureaucracies monitor policy problems, generate information about them, and engage in a struggle to define these problems for policy makers. Issue shuffling, partly the result of the processes of congressional agenda setting, profoundly influences which problems are monitored and the strength of signaling by bureaucracies about these problems. Congressional issue shuffling alters the problem-monitoring agenda of the bureaucracy and the supply of information about this set of problems.

One effect of congressional issue shuffling is to change the relative importance of an issue on the agenda. Behind the scenes, however, it also changes the relevance of various bureaucracies sending the signals in the first place. Each communication in a system has a sender, message, and a receiver. In a governing system with jurisdictions, authority, and expertise such as the dual dynamics of the administrative state, shuffling issues means shuffling senders. For example, the decreased clarity of transportation as an issue likely means the bureaucracies engaging in problem monitoring also have a decreased ability to generate and transmit clear signals about the problems within Transportation. In this case, the Department of Transportation and the Surface Transportation Board, among a few, might lose their ability to transmit clear signals about transportation policy problems.

Issue shuffling presents two possibilities for bureaucratic signaling. First, issue shuffling alters the relevance of particular bureaucracies when compared to bureaucracies in other broad issues (e.g., the Department of Transportation loses ground as a signaler to the EPA), because one issue is now more or less prominent than the other. Second, bureaucracies may recede in relevance as signalers within their own issue. For example, the redefinition of immigration in terms of terrorism rather than its labor economics means a greater role for the Department of Homeland Security and a reduced role for the Department of Labor.

Figure 5.2 addresses both possibilities of how congressional prioritization influences the senders of issue signals. It displays the change in SNR (left panel) and signal amplitude (right panel) associated with the move from Democratic control of Congress from 1983–1994 to Republican control from 1995–2006. Because of the limitations of displaying data for each of the institutions in the federal bureaucracy, Figure 5.2 collapses departments and makes use of only the bureaucracies most active in regulatory policy making. As in Figure 5.1, in each panel, bureaucracies on the left of the dotted line at zero are those whose SNR or amplitude decreased under Republican control. Bureaucracies on the right of the dotted line at zero in each panel are those whose SNR or amplitude increased under Republican control of Congress. However, in contrast to Figure 5.1, Figure 5.2 measures these changes in terms of the bureaucracies doing the signaling within these issues.

Figure 5.2 shows that congressional issue shuffling not only affects signaling by the bureaucracy but also influences which bureaucracies predominate in the supply of information transmitted to Congress (note the left panel documenting change in SNRs). It does so in two ways. First, some issues become more prominent on the agenda, and consequently, the bureaucracies tasked with these issues become more prominent in the supply of information to Congress. Second, the reverse process occurs when issues recede in prominence. The USDA and the Department of Transportation (DOT) are instructive on this point. With the increased clarity of signaling on the agriculture issue, the USDA benefits from increased prominence as a provider of information in that issue

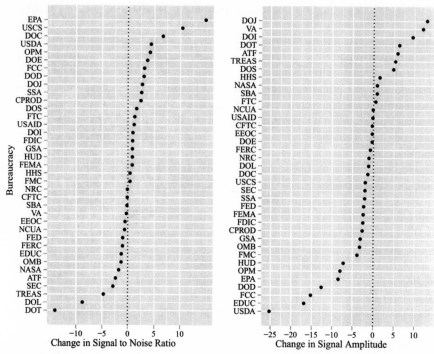

FIGURE 5.2 Party Control in Congress and Change in Signaling by Bureaucracies. The left panel in the figure displays the change in signal-to-noise ratio associated with moving from Democratic control of Congress from 1983–1994 to Republican control from 1995–2006. The panel on the right in the figure displays the same information for signal amplitude.

area. The opposite occurred with transportation. This issue area decreased greatly in prominence in the overall supply of information, and consequently, the Department of Transportation decreased in importance as a supplier of information.

Issue shuffling's effect on the prominence of particular bureaucracies in the supply of information extends beyond the overall prioritization of the agenda across issues to the relative prominence of particular bureaucracies within issues. All issues in American politics are addressed by several bureaucracies that monitor problems and generate information, sometimes in competition with one another.[1] The diverse array of bureaucracies within an issue area means there are many potential definitions of the problems they collectively monitor. The bureaucracies associated with energy and business & finance are good examples.

---

[1] This fact directly underpins the different economics associated with information supply under a communications, rather than an economic, framework.

Again, looking at the left panel of Figure 5.2, as we move from Democratic to Republican control of Congress, the Department of Commerce (DOC) and the Department of Energy (DOE) become more prominent as signalers on these issues as evidenced by increased SNRs. Meanwhile, other agencies in these issue areas, such as the Federal Energy Regulatory Commission (FERC) or Nuclear Regulatory Commission (NRC) for energy, or the Department of Treasury (TREAS), Federal Reserve (FED), or Securities and Exchange Commission (SEC) for business & finance, recede in importance as suppliers of information. Note that the DOC and DOE are cabinet bureaucracies responsible not only for regulating these sectors of the economy but more importantly for administering many programs including subsidies, research, and development in these issue areas. The bureaucracies (e.g., FERC or TREAS) receding in importance as suppliers of information are those with primary responsibility for regulating behavior or fallout associated with these sectors. From Figure 5.1, it is also notable that this change in prominence of the bureaucracies within energy comes about even though the prominence of the issue in the overall information supply does not increase.

This alteration to the information supply within the energy and within the Business & Finance issue areas makes sense in light of the transition from liberal to conservative control of Congress. From the dual dynamics perspective, this transition was important because the very definitions of problems in these issue areas changed with the prominence of particular bureaucracies as suppliers of information. Problem definitions likely changed at an abstract level from those focusing on the need to regulate the behavior and practices of businesses and energy suppliers and the externalities these industries generate to definitions encouraging expansion of the sectors, lessening of regulatory burdens, investment, and increasing supply. The difference between a problem definition favoring government intervention or unwillingness to aid these sectors is crucial for understanding the issues and resultant policy change.

Finally, it should be noted that popular discussions of regulations generally miss the point. The conventional wisdom is that regulations mean government intervention in business or personal behavior or practices. Social scientists and journalists alike would benefit from the recognition that regulations do many things, including implement programs that benefit sectors of the economy, particular business interests, interest groups, and the public at large. If the bureaucracy, with the blessing or acquiescence of Congress, wishes to adjust a program that distributes benefits, it must do so via the regulatory process. It is also the case that regulations are very often about inducements, incentives to innovate, or the distribution of subsidies or other benefits. Such regulations do modify behavior, but are far from the heavy-handed popular, and rhetorical, notion of government regulation.

Looking at the right panel in Figure 5.2, issue shuffling also influences the variation in the information supply generated by bureaucracies. Congressional prioritization of the issues on the agenda destabilizes the information supply from some bureaucracies and stabilizes others. Destabilization in the information supply from the set of bureaucracies results from both congressional intrusion into an issue area and from congressional deemphasis of other issues. Congressional attention or inattention may destabilize the supply of information from bureaucracies, even in the absence of structured incentive systems. The information supplied by the Department of Justice (DOJ) is destabilized by congressional prioritization of the law, crime, & family policies. In contrast, the information supplied by the Department of Transportation is destabilized as a result of congressional de-prioritization of transportation and infrastructure policies.

Congress influences the information supplied by the federal bureaucracy through issue shuffling. This mechanism is similar to what classic social science theory called agenda setting, but it is only one of the ways in which Congress influences the information supplied by the bureaucracy. Congress also has the ability to bundle issues, precisely tuning the information generated by bureaucracy.

5.2 ISSUE BUNDLING AND THE "TUNING" OF THE INFORMATION SUPPLY

Issue bundling is the second mechanism of congressional influence. Whereas shuffling involves shifting emphasis or reprioritizing issues to create separation and division among and between issues on the agenda, bundling brings clusters of issues together. Rather than altering only the relative priority of issues, issue bundling alters the very relationships between issues or sets of issues. It changes the nature of the agenda space on which issues and bureaucracies may be mapped.

Issue bundling occurs in the course of normal agenda setting in Congress, including interdependencies and tradeoffs among issues or clusters of them. Like issue shuffling, bundling does not necessarily involve the high costs involved when Congress writes a contract or monitors intensively. Legislators bundle issues simply by altering the way issues relate to one another and changing their demand for information accordingly. May et al. (2009a, 2009b) show that Congress bundled the issues around what would become homeland security policy, significantly altering both the agenda and the actors involved in the process. The attacks of September 11, 2001, led to a fundamental restructuring of what had earlier been the issues of civil defense and disaster management. With a focus on terrorism, the homeland security policy that arose out of those attacks bundled together such diverse issues as food safety,[2] domestic preparedness, border protection, and public health.

The example of homeland security displays three typical and instructive characteristics of congressional issue bundling. First, it brings together diverse

---

[2] "Food safety" has itself come to be associated with "food security."

issues to form a new understanding of a problem. Second, by doing so, bundling alters each of the subsystems within the established issues in both substance and participation. In the case of homeland security, a focus on terrorism became increasingly evident in the substantive policies of the organizations. For example, the public health subsystem had to incorporate terrorism-relevant aspects of the problem such as anthrax preparedness, where before it had focused mainly on epidemics such as flu. Bureaucracies and private organizations focused on food safety now had to consider the prospect of willful chemical and biological contamination of the nation's food supply. Third, May et al. (2009b) also show that this bundling affected not only the substance of the policy agenda but resulting participation profiles as well. The participation of bureaucrats, private interests, and other actors was fundamentally altered as a result of the bundling of these issues on the congressional agenda. The bundling mobilized new and old interests, altered the diversity of participants, and created spillover of interests as actors in other areas flooded into homeland security. The debate surrounding the issue increasingly meant that a focus on terrorism became increasingly prominent for both public and private actors involved in the policy.

Issue bundling alters the information supply from bureaucracy by "moving" some issues together and others apart. For example, if legislators historically considered agriculture and public lands & water as collective concerns, but then choose to add the environment alongside these issues, they alter the overall supply and mix of information. This amounts to "tuning" or "seasoning" the information supply on agriculture and public lands & water with information on the environment. Issue bundling generates a mix or basket of information from the bureaucracies monitoring bundles of issues. It amounts to disconnecting an issue from one bundle and plugging it into another, altering the information supply in both. It is also important to note that issue bundling not only alters the proximity of issues to one another but by extension, it also alters the proximity of the bureaucracies monitoring these issues in the space. This helps generate competition in the supply of information.

It is instructive to consider how bureaucracies might respond to issue bundling in Congress. Faced with bundling, bureaucracies have two basic choices. They could patiently wait for the issues they monitor to become important once again or otherwise gain prominence in the bundle, or they might recast their agenda in terms of more prominent issues on the congressional agenda.

For example, if transportation issues recede in Congress or get bundled with other issues, bureaucrats at the Department of Transportation can either sit back and wait for transportation and infrastructure development to become important again, or they can recast transportation in terms of its importance to prominent issues on the congressional agenda. Like legislators, bureaucrats want to be influential in the policy process. To gain that prominence most often means recasting issues in terms of others. Returning to the discussion of homeland security, the percentage of hearings involving public health and food safety (two subsystems unrelated to terrorism prior to 9/11) that focused on terrorism increased after 2001. Terrorism comprised 15 percent of the food safety hearings in Congress and 75 percent of the public health hearings.

If one set of bureaucracies recasts the issue it collectively monitors in terms of the others in the bundle, it comes into direct conflict with other agencies for defining the bundle of issues. Bureaucracies handle this conflict by altering the information they generate in three ways. First, they might compete with others to define the bundle of issues. Second, bureaucracies might differentiate themselves from others in the bundle, effectively creating a niche supply of information. Third, bureaucracies might mold their supply of information on the issues in the bundle with that of other agencies, creating a mixture of information unique to them.

For example, let us assume that congressional prioritization has bundled agriculture, energy, and the environment. The EPA then will compete directly with the DOE and USDA to define the environmental bundle for members of Congress. However if the EPA were to differentiate its information supply from those of DOE or USDA, the agency would create a niche supply distinct from that provided by USDA or DOE. By engaging in issue bundling, Congress has in effect created a market for the supply of information on these issues. In the business world, companies try to compete and gain market share by marginalizing their competition or differentiating their products to create a niche market. Similarly, the EPA competes and tries to gain market share in the supply of information to Congress or it differentiates and creates a niche supply.

The third possibility is that the EPA molds or integrates its information with that of the USDA and DOE, presenting a cooperative supply. This was the case in recent debates about climate change and the effectiveness of cap-and-trade legislation. The EPA, USDA, and DOE worked together to provide information within their respective issue expertise to give Congress an overall picture of climate change and suggest potential solutions in a cooperative fashion. It is clear that any of these three responses by the bureaucracy greatly influences the bundle of information supplied to Congress.

In sum, issue bundling during the course of congressional prioritization alters the interrelationship of issues on the agenda and the proximity of various bureaucracies monitoring these issues and generating the information. Again, one simple way to assess the influence of Congress on the bureaucracies' agenda space is to examine party control of Congress. Biplots can show how the relationships between issues change in the agenda space and how the proximity of bureaucracies changes within the space.

Using data on the amount of regulations each bureaucracy develops within the broad issue categories, biplots generate a simple two-dimensional model of that matrix. This is much like projecting the shadow of a multidimensional object onto a wall to achieve a simple two-dimensional representation that retains the important features of the object.[3] Biplots are generated from a multivariate measurement model. In the analysis that follows, the biplots are generated from a simple principal-components analysis of the number of regulations issued by each bureaucracy within each of the issue categories separately for the period of Democratic control of Congress (1983–1994) and for Republican control of Congress (1995–2006).

Biplots allow us to see several features of the data simultaneously. First, the axes represent the underlying dimensionality of the data matrix. Second, the vectors in a biplot display the information contained in the columns of a matrix, in this case, the issue categories. Third, the points in a biplot display the information contained in the rows of the matrix, in this case, for the bureaucracies.

The length of the vectors approximates the variance associated with an issue. The longer the vector the greater the variance. Longer vectors are therefore more important in defining the dimensional space mapped by the biplot. The vectors also display information about the relationships between the variables and the dimensions. The cosine of the angles between the issue category vectors approximate the correlations between issues. Acute angles signify positive association, whereas obtuse angles signify negative associations. For instance, an angle of zero degrees represents a correlation approaching one, whereas an 180-degree angle represents an almost perfect negative association among the issue variables. Issue variables that are perpendicular to one another signify a correlation approaching zero.

The points in the biplot map the position of the bureaucracies in the dimensional space and approximate their values on the issue vectors based on their agenda compositions. The points also display the proximity of the bureaucracies to one another in space using Euclidean distances. Points close to one another signify bureaucracies whose agenda compositions are similar, and vice versa.

To sum up, a biplot displays the defining characteristics of the agenda space within which bureaucracies are making policy. The issue vectors display the strength or power of given issues in defining the space, as well as the relationships between issues. The points display the composition of bureaucracies' agendas through their proximity to the issue vectors, as well as the proximity of bureaucracies to one another in the space. The biplots are useful in getting a sense for which bureaucracies occupy similar positions in the overall supply of information and how alterations to the space may affect this supply. The following two biplots map only the domestic policy space of the bureaucracy

---

[3] Credit for this very apt analogy belongs to Bill Jacoby and was gleaned during a long summer studying measurement at Inter-Consortium for Political and Social Research (ICPSR) in Ann Arbor, MI.

pursuant to party control in Congress.[4] The discussion mostly ignores speculation about the nature of the two underlying components, or dimensions, in order to illuminate congressional issue bundling within the space and changes in proximity of the bureaucracies.

Figure 5.3 displays the biplot for the domestic policy agenda of the U.S. federal bureaucracy from 1983 through 1994 under Democratic control of Congress. It shows that issues are indeed bundled and that there are three large bundles. The first issue bundle is defined by the prominence of business & finance, but also includes transportation, macroeconomics, and law, crime, & family policy. The second issue bundle contains public lands & water, the environment, agriculture, energy, and housing policies, though the public lands & water issue area is most influential in defining the bundle. The third major issue bundle contains government operations, labor & immigration, civil rights & liberties, and, to a lesser extent, education and science & technology policies.

The issue bundles apparent in Figure 5.3 indicate that the agenda compositions (across issue categories) of the bureaucracies monitoring these issues are similar. Bureaucracies within the bundles must monitor and generate information on similar problems. However, each issue bundle contains one or a few issues with more leverage in defining that bundle. This is important in terms of congressional prioritization, because it influences how bureaucracies go about developing their agendas. For instance, given the prominence of business & finance within its issue bundle, bureaucracies monitoring transportation, macroeconomics, and law, crime, & family issues must either wait until their issues are prominent again – that is, rebundled – or recast their issues in terms of business & finance. Because bureaucrats want to be influential in policy change, they must recast the problems they monitor in terms of the prominent issues within the bundle. Note, for example, the proximity of the DOT to the vector defining business & finance, as well as the location of the U.S. Customs Service (USCS) relative to law, crime, & family policy and to business & finance. Similar points could be made for the other two broad bundles of issues.

In addition to recasting or refining the issues they monitor in terms of their bundle's most prominent issues, bureaucracies may engage in other strategies.

---

[4] This is primarily because foreign policy bureaucracies rely less on regulation as a tool of policy making than do domestic policy bureaucracies. Much of the work of foreign policy bureaucracies occurs beyond the very public process of engaging in the development of regulations, and necessarily so. As a result, there is less information on which to construct an accurate representation of foreign policy issues and their bureaucracies within the space. Another consideration is that foreign policy introduces another dimension not well related to the rest of the space. Congress is arguably less important than the president in determining the overall direction of foreign policy and how issues within this area are bundled. Although foreign policy is relevant to the overall policy agenda, the biplots forego considering it in an effort to illuminate more clearly the dynamics of congressional prioritization highlighted in this chapter.

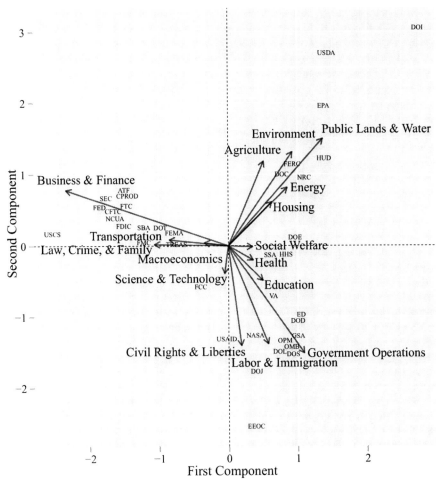

FIGURE 5.3 Issue Bundling under Democratic Control of Congress. This figure presents a depiction of a principal-components analysis of the regulations data under Democratic control of Congress.

They may differentiate their information to create a niche supply within the bundle, compete directly with other bureaucracies monitoring issues within the bundle, or adapt a more cohesive, coordinated supply of information for the legislature in concert with the other bureaucracies. Because of their interest in shaping policy, bureaucracies should have incentives to adjust their supply of information depending on how Congress has bundled the issues in the overall agenda space. By prioritizing issues and altering the agenda space, Congress alters the problem definitions and information generated by the bureaucracy.

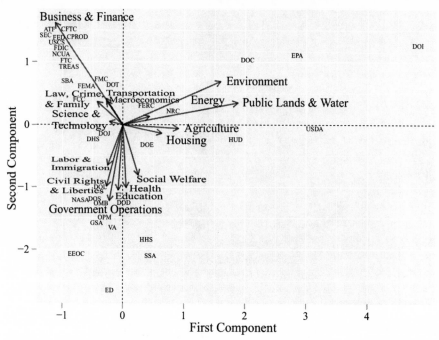

FIGURE 5.4 Issue Bundling under Republican Control of Congress. The figure presents a depiction of a principal-components analysis of the regulations data under Republican control of Congress.

Figure 5.4 displays the same principal-components analysis for Republican control of Congress from 1995 through 2006. In general, the three major issue bundles evident under Democratic control of Congress are evident under Republican control, though some significant differences emerge. The issue bundle previously defined by the business & finance vector is even more prominent under Republican control. Transportation, macroeconomics, and law, crime, & family policy recede in relation to the business & finance issue vector. Furthermore, transportation and macroeconomics become increasingly correlated with business & finance. Again, bureaucracies within the bundle have similar agenda compositions. When a bundle becomes overwhelmingly defined by one or a few issues, bureaucracies hoping to influence policy feel pressure to recast their issues in those terms. Retaining influence as a supplier of information means crafting problem definitions in light of the issues dominant in Congress.

The issue bundle including agriculture, the environment, public lands & water, energy, and housing becomes defined more by the environment and public lands & water. Agriculture recedes, and energy's prominence within the bundle is greatly reduced.

Looking past the issue bundles, note also that congressional prioritization leads to issue differentiation. For example, agriculture in the Congress under Democratic control occupied a position within the overall agenda space between business & finance and the environment. The business & finance vector and the agriculture vector were nearly perpendicular, indicating little association between them. Under Republican control of Congress, agriculture became negatively correlated with business & finance.

The issue bundle defined under Democratic control by civil rights & liberties, labor & immigration, and government operations was joined by social welfare and health care under Republican control of Congress. The issues in this bundle were also of more equal prominence.

The prominence and association of these issues in the overall space mean something very real for bureaucracies' monitoring of problems and generation of information within the system. Issue prominence within a bundle and positive associations with other issues reinforce the tendency to recast other issues and redefine problems in terms of the more prominent issues. When issue bundles contain several issues of equal prominence, and when issue associations are nonexistent or even negative, the agenda space reinforces bureaucracies' tendency to differentiate their information supply from that of other issues and from other bureaucracies. This altering of the market for information via congressional prioritization in turn alters the nature of the information supply emanating from the bureaucracy.

5.3 COMPETITION AND THE MARKET FOR PROVISION OF INFORMATION

Issue shuffling and bundling bring bureaucracies in direct competition with one another as they monitor issues on the agenda and generate information. Congressional influence hinges in part on the potential for issue shuffling and bundling to introduce new or altered problem definitions by altering the array of and relationship between bureaucracies monitoring the issues.

An easy way to see how competition among agencies might change is to count the number of agencies issuing regulations within each of issue areas. Figure 5.5 displays this measure for 1983 through 2008. The figure speaks to the broad variability in the numbers of agencies that make policy within given issues, from around one hundred agencies in government operations to three in macroeconomics. Because the government operations issue area deals with much of the internal functioning of agencies and their relationships with other governing institutions, it is not surprising that so many agencies issue regulations here. However, even within more neatly defined issues such as the environment, energy, and public lands & water, many more agencies are involved than a simple interpretation of agency missions would predict. In addition, there is striking within-issue variation over time in the numbers of agencies issuing regulations in the same area. Energy, for instance, goes from twenty-nine agencies making regulations in 1984 to around ten by the end of the twentieth century, and rises above twenty again by the end of the series. In general,

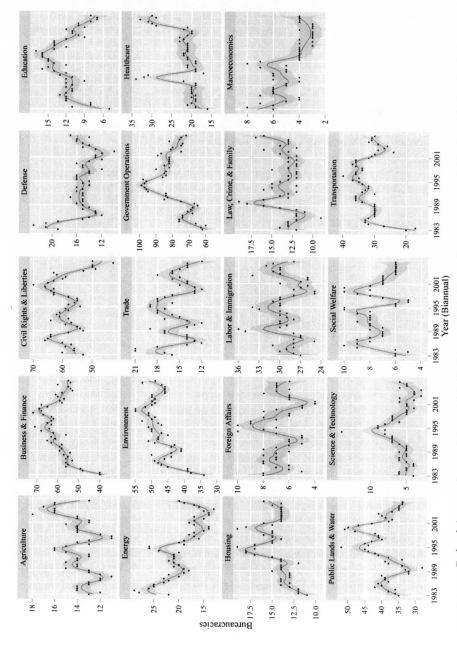

FIGURE 5.5 Federal Agency Competition within Each Issue. This figure shows a count of the number of federal agencies issuing regulations within each issue from 1983 through 2008.

the figure shows the danger in conflating the institutional labels and structure of bureaucracies with the substantive policies the agencies pursue.

A comparison across issues in Figure 5.5 reveals three classes of dynamics. First, there are issues that display low competition early on, but become more competitive over time. Business and financial regulation, the environment, and agriculture fit this general pattern. The second group consists of issues that were competitive early on, but have become less so over time. Energy and macroeconomics fit this pattern. The third grouping contains issues that transition between periods of low and high competition. Housing, public lands & water, and labor & immigration display these characteristics. Education and science & technology are interesting in that the number of agencies making policy in those areas reached a crescendo in the mid-1990s and then began a long and slow consolidation in that number.

Education illustrates well the ebb and flow of competition among bureaucracies. In addition to the Office of Elementary and Secondary Education and the Office of Post-Secondary Education, which have traditionally been active, the Office of Education Sciences and Office of Management were especially active in issuing policies. Beyond the walls of the Department of Education, other prominent players included the Veteran's Administration, the Public Health Service within the Department of Health and Human Services, and the Secretary of the Department of Defense. By 2006, only the Veteran's Administration had continued its prominence within the issue.

To assess the influence of congressional prioritization on competition among bureaucracies in the supply of information, two measures are necessary. The first is a measure of the competition for market share among bureaucracies within issues. Are issues dominated by one or a few bureaucracies supplying information, or are there relative competition and dispersion among bureaucracies? The second measure is the dispersion of bureaucracies' attention across the issues on the agenda. This measure is important because congressional issue shuffling and bundling sometimes disperse agencies' attention across issues, amplifying or dampening competition to supply information within issues. Through issue shuffling and bundling, congressional prioritization may induce a more uniform information supply, with few bureaucracies generating most of the information, or it may diversify the information supply, inducing many bureaucracies to monitor an issue and generate information.

Herfindahl-Hirschman indices have been used extensively in economics to parse out market share held by various companies or sectors of the economy and to measure competition. The HHI is measured by summing the squared proportions of a variable across its categories.[5]

---

[5] Formally, the Herfindahl-Hirschman Index is measured as $HHI = \sum_{i=0}^{n} s_i^2$, where s_i is either the share of an agency's agenda falling into issue category n, or the share of total attention to an issue held by bureaucracy i. HHI is equivalent to the Simpson Diversity Index used in ecology and other measures of diversity, such as entropy.

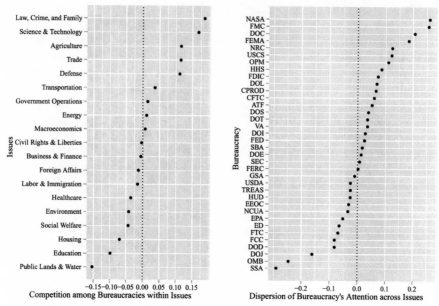

FIGURE 5.6 Congressional Prioritization and the Information Market for Bureaucracy. Left panel displays the change in Herfindahl-Hirschman Index moving from Democratic control of Congress from 1983–1994 to Republican control from 1995–2006 for issues across bureaucracies. Right panel displays the same information for bureaucracies across issue categories.

The data for examining competition among bureaucracies in the provision of information are compiled in a matrix of bureaucracies and issues containing the quantity of regulations issued by each agency in each issue during Democratic and Republican control of Congress. For the analysis to follow, HHI is calculated for each issue across bureaucracies to yield a measure of competition among bureaucracies within each issue and also for each bureaucracy across the set of issues to yield a measure of increasing or decreasing diversity of each bureaucracy's problem monitoring across issues.

Figure 5.6 displays the HHI measure for competition among bureaucracies within issues in the left panel and for the dispersion of attention for bureaucracies across the set of issue categories in the right panel. Once again, one of the simpler ways to gauge change in congressional issue priorities is party control in Congress. Figure 5.6 displays the changes in competition among bureaucracies on the left and changes in the dispersion of bureaucracy's attention across issues on the right, both with reference to changes in party control.

In the left panel of Figure 5.6, issues on the left of the dotted line became more competitive under Republican control of Congress, whereas issues on the right of the dotted line became less competitive. In the right panel of Figure 5.6, bureaucracies on the left side of the dotted line diversified their regulatory attention or spread it across issue categories. The regulatory agendas of bureaucracies on the right of the dotted line compressed into one or a few issues under Republican control of Congress.

Figure 5.6 suggests that congressional prioritization alters the market for information supply within issues. Some issues become less competitive (e.g., science & technology), meaning one or a few bureaucracies are doing the bulk of the problem monitoring and issuing regulations within the issue. Several issues go the other way under Republican control. These issues (e.g., housing) become more competitive as issuance of regulations is more evenly divided among the set of bureaucracies monitoring the issue area. Within the issue categories, some bureaucracies gain "market share" for providing Congress with problem monitoring and generating information, whereas other bureaucracies lose market share and prominence in the information supply. Bureaucracies have different missions and predilections for defining policy problems in particular ways. Altering the prominence of bureaucracies within the stream of the information supply directly affects the type, quantity, and diversity of information that legislators glean from the bureaucracy.

Turning to the right panel in Figure 5.6, the adjustment of competition among bureaucracies for supplying information within issues has an impact on the agenda compositions of bureaucracies. Bureaucracies on the left of the dotted line in the right panel of Figure 5.6 have more diversified regulatory agendas under Republican control of Congress. The regulatory agendas of bureaucracies to the right of the dotted line (and at the top) have become concentrated on one or a few issues.

Through issue shuffling and bundling, congressional prioritization alters the issue markets in which bureaucracies compete for the provision of information on policy problems. The alteration of the composition of bureaucracies' agendas is a byproduct of congressional influence on competition for information supply within issue areas. Congress's ability to alter the agendas of bureaucracies might be viewed in a positive light, as a way of adjusting the information supply fueling policy decisions – the tuning of signals described at the outset of this chapter. A second possibility is that, by altering the number of issues bureaucracies must monitor, Congress strengthens or amplifies signals from some bureaucracies, while weakening signals from others. Either of these interpretations is likely in Figure 5.6, depending on the bureaucracy.

5.4 CONGRESSIONAL PRIORITIZATION

This chapter sheds light on one-half of the theory of dual dynamics. The ability of Congress to shape problem monitoring and the information supplied by the federal bureaucracy sets in motion the dual dynamics of congressional prioritization and bureaucratic problem solving. Based on the assumption that the two political parties in the United States hold different issue priorities, this chapter takes a simple approach to hypotheses about congressional control of, or influence on, the bureaucracy; this approach is unrelated to contract theory or the development of incentive systems. Agenda-setting processes in Congress shape not only what problems bureaucracies monitor, but also the nature of the information they generate and transmit to Congress.

This chapter identified three mechanisms linking congressional prioritization to influence on the bureaucracy. The first of these, issue shuffling, is most consistent with classic understandings of agenda setting. It must be noted, though, that issue shuffling occurs amid signaling about problems by government institutions. Given the communications framework that is the basis for the dual dynamics of congressional prioritization and bureaucratic problem solving, attention must be given to the noise surrounding signals from the bureaucracy. Noting levels of attention to issues is not enough when multiple issues compete for attention from government. These issues are potentially being monitored by multiple bureaucracies seeking prominence in the supply of information.

The second mechanism, issue bundling, relates to the emphasis that policy process scholars place on the interdependency among issues, known as trade-offs. By bundling issues, Congress can customize the information supply from bureaucracy – blending some issues and adding shades of meaning to others – to create the desired mix of information and problem definitions. In the process, issue bundling requires bureaucracies to decide whether they will compete with, differentiate from, or coordinate with other bureaucracies monitoring problems within the bundle.

The third mechanism is competition among bureaucracies in the supply of information to members of Congress. Given that congressional prioritization often leads to issue bundling, congressional influence alters the "market" for the provision of information. Bureaucracies compete to influence policy by monitoring problems and providing information that help steer policy debates, altering the parameters of choice for members of Congress. Yet, congressional prioritization may increase the competition faced by bureaucracies within particular issue areas or broadly within issue bundles. This brackets their influence on the process. Likewise, congressional prioritization may decrease competition for the provision of information, giving bureaucracies more leeway in defining problems for congressional action. Finally, competition among bureaucracies alters the composition of the agendas of these same bureaucracies. By increasing or decreasing competition for problem monitoring and generating information, congressional prioritization amplifies or muffles the signals from particular bureaucracies.

Congressional prioritization influences bureaucracy even in the absence of more formal levers of control. It is the ultimate "deck-stacking" control, in that it structures the bureaucracy's information on policy problems. It requires nothing of members of Congress save altering the way they talk about and understand policy problems. Issue shuffling and bundling do not require Congress to write or pass legislation. Normal modes of agenda setting, particularly congressional hearings, are enough to alter the supply of information flowing from the bureaucracy.

The dual dynamics of congressional prioritization and bureaucratic problem solving assume that both legislators and bureaucrats want to influence policy change. Bureaucracies willingly supply information in an effort to steer policy debates, but congressional prioritization is a powerful force in shaping that supply. I now turn my attention to how bureaucratic problem solving shapes the congressional agenda.

6

Problem Solving and the Supply of Information

Congressional efforts to shape the information supply via problem prioritization do not occur in a vacuum. First and foremost, congressional influence depends on the problems bureaucracies identify, how they define them, and what information about these problems they pass on to Congress. In classic systems models of politics, system control depends on feedback from the past performance of the system. The dual dynamics of the administrative state constitute just such a communications system oriented toward addressing problems. Congressional problem prioritization in this system depends on being attentive to and, in part, reacting to information generated by the bureaucracy about various policy problems. In such a system, bottom-up influence by the bureaucracy is inevitable.

This chapter sets out to assess the bottom-up influence of the federal bureaucracy, the second half of the dual dynamics of agenda setting in the administrative state. I argue that the influence wielded by bureaucracies comes at the front end of the policy process – during and before agenda setting. This perspective is a major departure from the way in which both scholars and the public at large understand bureaucracy. Typically, the influence of bureaucracy, if it exists at all, is envisioned as playing a role in the implementation and evaluation stages of the policy process – after Congress, the president, and often even interest groups have had their say. In contrast, the dual dynamics of problem prioritization and problem solving highlights the influence of bureaucracy at the very early stages of policy making. The federal bureaucracy influences not only which problems are identified for government action but, importantly, also how these problems are defined and understood.

Problem solving by the bureaucracy entails three processes: the monitoring of the agenda for problems, the generation and maintenance of problem definitions, and the generation and provision of information about the problems to Congress. Examining the influence of these processes on the congressional issue agenda requires the introduction of another dataset. This chapter makes use of the congressional hearing dataset of the Policy Agendas Project,[1] which codes congressional hearings into the same set of topic categories that I used for the regulations issued by the bureaucracy. This makes the issue agendas of the two institutions directly comparable for the time period under study.

This chapter uses four types of statistical models to examine how bureaucracy influences problem solving. In all cases, the models relate regulatory agendas in the bureaucracy to congressional agendas measured using hearings. Where the dependent variable lies between zero and one, as is the case when using Herfindahl-Hirschman indices, beta regression is used to examine the influence of problem solving by bureaucracy. Where the dependent variable is a continuous positive integer, as with the Renyi entropies, regression based on the gamma distribution is used to assess the influence of problem solving. Where the dependent variable is a count, such as for the models of congressional hearing sessions, regression is based on the quasi-Poisson model, which figures in the likelihood that the counts are overdispersed. These models are particularly useful in examining the influence of problem definition on congressional issue attention. To analyze information and feedback in problem solving, fractional error-correction models (a time series technique) are used to gauge the influence of problem monitoring and system feedback through congressional issue agendas over time.

For all four models, I present figures showing the estimated response of congressional issue agendas to or, alternatively, the estimated influence of problem solving by the bureaucracy, with confidence intervals where possible. Many of the analyses also employ state-space models to show whether and how the influence of problem solving by bureaucracy on congressional issue agendas may vary over time. All model results are generated using simulation techniques, with ten thousand simulations for each estimate of an effect or a parameter value. The full model results are contained in Appendix B.

6.1 PROBLEM MONITORING

In the system of dual dynamics, congressional prioritization requires policy makers to be aware of a set of problems or potential problems. Problem monitoring by the bureaucracy provides this awareness. Though rarely highlighted in the study of bureaucracy in the United States, the legal and political framework for bureaucracy not only provides for but also charges bureaucracy with searching out and anticipating problems in policy making. The bureaucracy

---

[1] The congressional hearing data used here were originally collected by Frank R. Baumgartner and Bryan D. Jones, with the support of National Science Foundation grant numbers SBR 9320922 and 0111611, and were distributed through the Department of Government at the University of Texas at Austin. Neither NSF nor the original collectors of the data bear any responsibility for the analysis reported here.

monitors and locates problems at the juncture of the public agenda and the governmental agenda. It makes a first attempt to winnow the myriad problems confronting government into an agenda that our institutions can manage.

It is worth reiterating what it means for bureaucracies to monitor issues for problems. Problem monitoring has two components. Bureaucracies must pay attention to the issues on the agenda and also take some action to identify or address the problem. For our purposes, the bureaucracy's regulatory agenda is a good indicator of its ability to monitor problems. To the degree scholars or citizens think about bureaucracies monitoring issues for problems, they likely point to efforts of various bureaucracies to enforce existing laws and regulations.

However, within the system of dual dynamics, the bureaucracy is influential in helping alert policy makers to the changing nature of the agenda. Bureaucracies signal policy makers both when they detect new and important problems, and when old problems disappear. Bureaucracies monitor the changing nature of issues entrusted to their care and help determine which aspects of issues are most important for decision making at given points in time. Problem monitoring is not confined to gauging levels of compliance with regulations. Much more importantly, it looks to the substance of the policy agenda confronting government and sees how it may or may not be changing. The various federal bureaucracies work like antennae, sharpening the picture of the policy agenda for policy makers.

Problem monitoring by the bureaucracy has important implications for congressional prioritization and agenda setting. As members of Congress look out across the federal bureaucracy, they are inundated with information about problems detected or anticipated by federal bureaucracies. This information comes in the form of signals about the possible nature of the policy agenda. These signals have already been influenced by congressional prioritization, especially issue shuffling, bundling, and bureaucratic competition.

These signals convey two important characteristics of the agenda to members of Congress. First, at the broadest levels, problem monitoring by the bureaucracy indicates whether the policy agenda is broad and diverse – whether it contains many problems on which government must take action or it is narrow, in which only a few important issues must be tackled. Problem monitoring tells policy makers whether their attention should be dispersed or concentrated. It influences the relative density of the policy agenda at higher levels of government over time. Second, problem monitoring in the bureaucracy conveys the amount of information contained in the policy agenda. Agendas are generally characterized by two types of issues. Some persistently receive attention (e.g., the economy, foreign policy, and business regulation), whereas others occupy the agenda much less consistently (e.g., agriculture, science & technology public lands & water).

Taken together, bureaucracies naturally monitor all issues on the agenda with more consistency than does Congress. There are more bureaucracies than congressional institutions available to do the monitoring, and their consistency derives from missions given by Congress and maintained by congressional oversight. Thus, the bureaucracy monitors issues and detects problems across the range of issues on the agenda – those often on the congressional agenda and as those that rarely appear – on a consistent basis. The "information" contained in this problem monitoring is geared toward detecting problems.

The question then becomes whether members of Congress are collectively more sensitive to problems monitored and detected in persistent issues or to those that rarely appear on their own agenda. Members might be more sensitive to persistently salient issues because these issues are relatively more important or because members wish to control bureaucrats and direct agenda setting. Alternatively, members of Congress might be more sensitive to problem monitoring on the issues they encounter infrequently, simply because they monitor these issues sporadically themselves and rely on the bureaucracy for information gathering to a greater degree.

Likely, members of Congress are driven by both of these considerations when considering problem monitoring by the bureaucracy. The information contained in monitoring comprises problems and changes detected in both types of issues. This information should influence the relative concentration of congressional attention to the issues on the agenda as well as the amount of information (as characterized here) in the congressional issue agenda.

The connection between problem monitoring and congressional agenda setting requires measures of concentration in both. The measure for concentration of problem monitoring and the congressional agenda is familiar from Chapter 5. Herfindahl-Hirschman indices (HHIs), calculated on the regulations of the bureaucracy and on congressional hearings, yield a measure of the degree to which problem monitoring and the congressional issue agenda are concentrated on a few issues or dispersed more widely.

As problem monitoring in the bureaucracy becomes increasingly concentrated on a few issues, congressional attention should follow suit. Conversely, if problem monitoring in the bureaucracy is dispersed more evenly across issues, congressional attention should also be distributed evenly. The agenda-concentration hypothesis should hold if problem monitoring in the bureaucracy is useful to members of Congress in setting their agenda. Problem monitoring distributed more evenly across multiple issues on the agenda signals Congress about the need for higher level decision making in greater numbers of issue areas.

The measure of the amount of information contained in problem monitoring by the bureaucracy is less familiar in the study of politics and public policy. Using the regulations issued by the bureaucracy across the various issue categories already identified, I calculated Renyi (1970) entropy for problem monitoring and for the congressional issue agenda. Notions of entropy are well known and defined in the analysis of communications systems, biology, physical systems, and the study of imaging, x-rays, and radio frequencies. Entropy is a summary measure of the changes across the issues on the agenda, taking into account their relative probabilities. Renyi's entropy allows for the weighting of information for sensitivity to issues appearing more or less frequently or with higher probability.[2]

An increase in the amount of information contained in problem monitoring by the bureaucracy should influence the congressional agenda in two ways. First, increasing it should lead to less concentration in the congressional agenda, as evidenced by the Herfindahl-Hirschman indices of concentration. Higher levels of information mean increased sensitivity, for the reasons outlined, to problems detected across the range of issues. In essence, these higher levels alter the probabilities of given changes in problem monitoring, yielding unexpected issue attention in the bureaucracy and creating uncertainty for policy makers. Increased information in problem monitoring should also lead to increased information in the congressional agenda because of congressional sensitivity to problem monitoring by the bureaucracy.

Figure 6.1 displays two regression models based on the beta distribution of concentration in the congressional agenda. Panel (a) displays the estimated effect of a beta regression of congressional agenda concentration on problem solving, each measured using HHIs. Panel (b) displays the estimated effect of information contained in problem monitoring by the bureaucracy (measured using Renyi's entropy) on concentration of the congressional issue agenda.

Figure 6.1 shows two things. First, when problem monitoring becomes concentrated, the congressional issue agenda also becomes concentrated. Second, increasing information contained in problem monitoring by the bureaucracy leads to less concentration or dispersion across issues in the congressional agenda. The data suggest that the information in the agenda of bureaucracy occurs temporally before the response in the congressional agenda.[3] Although the changes to the HHI of congressional agenda concentration are numerically small, it is important to remember that they summarize all the changes in allocation of congressional attention occurring across all issues on the agenda. In other words, small movements in the index are meaningful in terms of the overall makeup of the issue agenda.

At this broad level of the agenda, the evidence suggests that the characteristics of problem monitoring by the bureaucracy influence the nature of the

[2] Renyi's entropy is formally defined as $H_\alpha(x) = \frac{1}{1-\alpha} \log(\sum_{i=1}^{n} p_i^\alpha)$, where x is a category and p is the proportion of activity falling in the category x. Positive values of α bias the measure increasingly toward events with higher probability (i.e., occurrences in the center of the distribution). Negative values of α bias the measure increasingly toward lower probability events (i.e., occurrences in the tails of the distribution).

[3] A test of Granger causality yields evidence that the series for bureaucracy granger-causes those of Congress. For concentration (panel a), $F = 3.71$, $p < .06$. For information (panel b), $F = 4.05$, $p < .04$. Neither test for congressional agenda concentration granger-causing concentration in problem monitoring or information was statistically significant at levels less than $p < .1$.

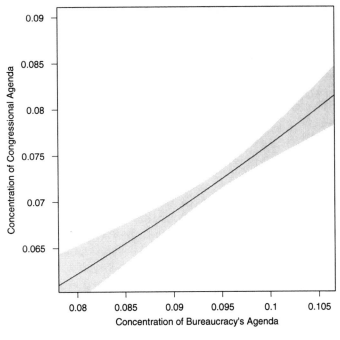

(a) Problem Monitoring

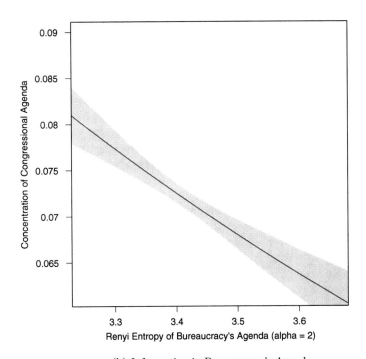

(b) Information in Bureaucracy's Agenda

FIGURE 6.1 The Influence of Problem Monitoring on Congressional Agenda Concentration.

congressional issue agenda. Congress delegates to bureaucracies responsibility not only for implementing its various policies and directives but also for paying attention to issues and providing information about the problems confronting government more broadly. Paying attention to the general nature of problem monitoring by the bureaucracy yields important clues for how members of Congress at a broad level might allocate their attention to the range of issues. Congressional allocation of attention is reflected in the changing concentration of the congressional agenda.

Problem monitoring by the bureaucracy gives members of Congress enough information to prioritize issues on the agenda. When facing an agenda with low information and few issues, Congress might find prioritization easier, given its members' limited attention, than when information is high and dispersed across many issues. Problem monitoring by the bureaucracy offers a general picture of a concentrated or diverse issue agenda. This general response occurs within the broader institutional context of American politics.

However, it is likely that congressional response to problem monitoring by the bureaucracy is not constant across time. Organizational concerns, presidential politics, and party agendas may dampen or amplify congressional response to problem monitoring, depending on the "fit" of the current problems to these broader institutional concerns.

Figure 6.2 displays two models of the influence of problem monitoring on the information contained in congressional issue agendas by applying the Renyi entropy measure to both the congressional issue agenda and the regulatory agenda in the bureaucracy. Panel (a) displays a regression model based on the gamma distribution of the estimated effect of increasing information in problem monitoring on the information contained in the congressional issue agenda. This model suggests that Congress is sensitive to the changing probabilities associated with problem monitoring by the bureaucracy across the issue agenda. Panel (b) contains a state-space model of variation in the value of the parameter estimate for the influence of problem monitoring by the bureaucracy over the time period under study. Figure 6.2 suggests that information contained in congressional issue agendas is indeed responsive to the information contained in problem monitoring by the bureaucracy.

Figure 6.2 also suggests that congressional responsiveness to the information contained in problem monitoring has decreased slightly over time. The period under study, 1983–2008, is a time in modern American politics when conservative approaches to government administration dominated political debate. However, although there is evidence for a decline in the responsiveness of Congress to problem monitoring in the bureaucracy, it is worth noting that the decrease is fairly small.

Yet the nature or outline of the congressional issue agenda is responsive to problem monitoring by the bureaucracy. Problem monitoring and detection offer some information to members of Congress about the general nature of the problems facing policy makers. These processes provide a signal about the

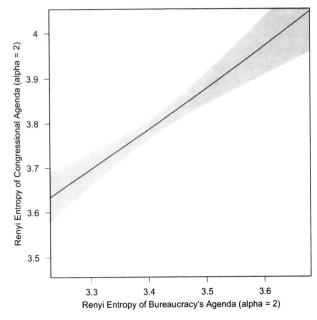

(a) Influence of Information from Bureaucracy

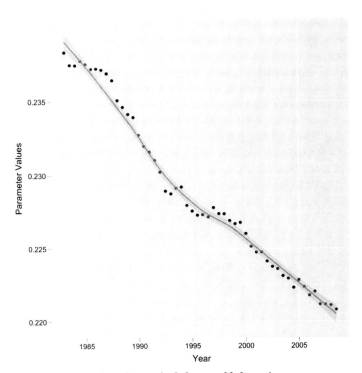

(b) Decline in the Influence of Information

FIGURE 6.2 The Influence of Information and Its Decline over Time.

nature of the agenda facing government, telling members of Congress how they might allocate their attention to various issues. They also offer the first bits of information Congress may use to engage in the processes of prioritization. This signaling is useful both in the sense of addressing the problems faced by policy makers, bureaucrats, and citizens alike and in showing whether prioritization will place severe limits on congressional attention or not.

6.2 PROBLEM DEFINITION

Bureaucracies do more than monitor problems and send signals about the overall character of the agenda. They help define problems for congressional action. By describing the most important aspects of a problem, problem definition enables policy makers to generate solutions. It is an important and underappreciated part of the policy process (but see Dery, 1984). Any examination of solutions presupposes that a working problem definition has been developed.[4]

Yet problem definitions are more than conceptual frames for making sense of an issue: they are institutional realities. Bureaucracies are the institutional realization of a problem definition; they are the embodiment of the definitions of the problems they monitor and help define in policy making.

Moreover, problem definitions cannot be broken down neatly into categories such as societal or economic regulation or program administration. Bureaucracies are created and imbued with missions from Congress. These missions orient bureaucracies toward achieving a certain set of goals. Thus that bureaucracies, even absent subsystem arrangements, are organizationally biased toward certain understandings of a problem or issue. Given these biases, bureaucracies will view some information or indicators as fundamental to addressing the issue. Alternatively, bureaucracies will view other bits of information or indicators of the problem or issue as tangential or unimportant, and will likely ignore these in formulating a working definition of the problems they monitor. Of course, these definitions then also narrow the types of solutions that might be developed later in the process.

By way of example, consider the activities of the USDA and the EPA in monitoring soil and groundwater problems. The USDA's mission and organization are geared to helping produce and maintain a stable, cheap supply of food, so it will perform soil analyses directed at the soil's quality as a medium for producing food. The EPA's mission and organization reflect a concern for soil quality in maintaining ecosystems and protecting the integrity of groundwater. Note that even the choice of what type of water to monitor is different. The USDA

---

[4] The generation of a problem space must necessarily precede the generation of a solution space. This point has long been appreciated by scholars of decision making (Newell and Simon, 1972; Jones, 2001).

is likely interested in soil moisture in a particular location, whereas the EPA's examination may take place miles from the point at which pollution actually occurs. Given these divergent initial concerns, the types of information and indicators relevant to the two agencies might be vastly different. Yet, agreement between them on soil quality sends a powerful signal to Congress that two agencies, though worlds apart in terms of missions, agree on a particular problem definition. This was the case in the recent debate over cap-and-trade legislation, in which the USDA and EPA ended up on the same side of the problem and even solution for climate change.

The problem definitions embodied in bureaucracies affect not only which types of information or indicators bureaucracies attend to but also how they understand this information in the context of the issues they monitor. For example, the same soil organism that may be viewed by the USDA as a pest and a hinderance to the productive capacity of the land might be seen by the EPA as an indicator of the health of the ecosystem.

Note that different problem definitions may operate even in the same bureaucracy but inside separate organizational units. Public lands & water policy in the United States is a great case for understanding the influence of problem definitions. Four major bureaucratic institutions oversee public lands and water in the United States: the departments of Interior, Agriculture, and Defense and the Environmental Protection Agency. Within these larger institutions, very different problem definitions emerge.

Take the Department of Interior (DOI) as an example. Within the DOI, a set of line bureaus is dedicated to the production, extraction, and exploitation of the nation's natural resources. DOI agencies such as the (now infamous) Minerals Management Service, Bureau of the Mines, and Bureau of Land Management are guided by a problem definition of natural resources conducive to the production of minerals and timber. This problem definition often biases these agencies toward extraction and away from conservation of the natural resource.

Yet the U.S. Fish and Wildlife Service (FWS) and the National Park Service (NPS), which are geared toward the preservation and continued maintenance of ecosystems and their plant and animal populations, work alongside these "extraction" agencies within DOI. This problem definition guides these bureaus' problem solving with regard to public lands. However, all line bureaus operating under the DOI, at the broadest level, share the problem definition of natural resources and land as properties that should be actively managed to benefit society and the economy. This broader definition is quite different from an environmental definition of public lands and water as resources to be preserved in their natural state.

A similar story could be told of the USDA. Many of its line bureaus are dedicated to promoting the productive use of the land as an engine of agriculture. However, the USDA also contains the Natural Resources Conservation

Service (NRCS) and the Cooperative State Education and Extension Service. The problem definitions of these two agencies differ greatly from those of the bureaus dedicated to agricultural productivity. Finally, it is worth noting that the Department of Defense (DOD) is an important institution in governing public lands and water. This function stems from one of its line bureaus, the Army Corps of Engineers, which oversees many of the nation's large public works projects (e.g., dams, reservoirs, seawalls, etc.). The Army Corps of Engineers organizationally embodies a problem definition with attendant policy goals distinct from those of the other agencies within the DOD.

Congressional prioritization guarantees that the influence of these various problem definitions will not be constant. Some problem definitions will be more influential for bureaucracy than others at different times. As bureaucracies monitor issues for problems and define them for governmental action, they leave their own "institutional trace" or signature on the information passed on to Congress. This institutional trace reveals the mission, organization, and problem monitoring of each bureaucracy. This trace informs the problem definitions crafted by bureaucrats and colors how members of Congress come to understand the information passed on by the bureaucracy.

Thus, if bureaucracies are the institutional realizations of problem definitions, then the bureaucracies most influential in a particular issue area will also generate the most influential problem definitions in policy making on the issue. It is also likely that the problem definitions or ways of understanding issues will change as the political context favors some arguments over others.

It is then worth asking which bureaucracies are influential in helping set the congressional issue agenda. To examine this question, it is necessary to measure the signals that bureaucracies send about issues. Yet it is not enough to examine the signals that bureaucracies send on particular issues, because these occur within the broader context of bureaucratic competition over the supply of information, as discussed in Chapter 5. Gauging any particular bureaucracy's efforts at signaling on an issue requires weighting this signal by the "noise" from other bureaucracies.

I calculated signal-to-noise ratios (SNR) for the analyses to follow as the number of regulations issued by a particular bureaucracy divided by the standard deviation of the signaling occurring across all bureaucracies active within a given issue. Therefore, the signal emitted by each bureaucracy is weighted by the noise generated by all the other bureaucracies within the issue area. I then used these SNRs to gauge the influence of the bureaucracy on the number of congressional hearing sessions held in a particular issue area. Given these estimates of the mean influence, I used state-space models to generate simulations of the relative influence of the bureaucracies over time.[5]

---

[5] Only bureaucracies reaching statistical significance at $p \leq .1$ are included in the state-space models of problem definition.

Figure 6.3 displays the results of such a model for congressional attention to the public lands & water issue area.[6] As noted earlier, this issue area is an interesting one by which to examine problem definition, because the DOI, the major bureaucracy within the issue area, houses bureaus dedicated to vastly different definitions of public lands & water. Within the DOI, both the extraction bureaus (e.g., Minerals Management Service, Bureau of the Mines, and Bureau of Land Management) and those dedicated to conservation (e.g., Fish and Wildlife Service and the National Park Service) experienced increased influence of or at least reception to their problem definitions over the time period under study. However, the influence of the extraction bureaus exceeded that of the conservation bureaus both in magnitude and rate of increase. Although positive and increasing over the period, the influence of the conservation bureaus leveled off considerably in the mid-1990s and again under unified Republican control of Congress during the George W. Bush administration.

Similarly to the conservation bureaus, the U.S. Forest Service (USFS) and Natural Resources Conservation Service (NRCS), within the USDA, generally enjoyed increased influence and prominence of their problem definitions through the mid-1990s. Thereafter, their influence began to wane.

The EPA provides another interesting case of congressional receptivity of problem definitions within the dynamics of larger scale political change. Its estimated influence fell completely on the negative side of the spectrum, generally meaning that increased signaling by the EPA fell on deaf ears in Congress. However, there was a clear linkage to larger presidential and congressional politics over time. The EPA was increasingly disassociated with congressional attention through the Republican administrations of the 1980s and early 1990s. Beginning with the Republican takeover of the House and Senate in 1995, Congress became relatively more apt to pay attention, likely because of the renewed prominence of the Clinton administration on environmental issues (especially Vice President Al Gore). This attention continued even through the early George W. Bush presidency, in part because Bush appointed Christine Todd Whitman to direct the EPA. Whitman was much more sympathetic to the EPA's mission than the president had expected. With the departure of Whitman and the increasing prominence of the failing economy, Congress was once again less likely to attend signals by the EPA.

The bottom two panels of Figure 6.3 display the estimated influence of the DOD and (together) the Bureau of Indian Affairs (BIA) and National Indian Gaming Commission (NIGC). Each of these bureaucracies greatly influences public lands & water policy. The importance of each increased over time, but the increase in the influence of the DOD exceeded that of the bureaus dealing with native Americans. The most important bureau within the DOD is the

---

[6] A test of Granger causality yields evidence that the series for bureaucracies granger-cause those of Congress ($F = 11.36$, $p < .001$).

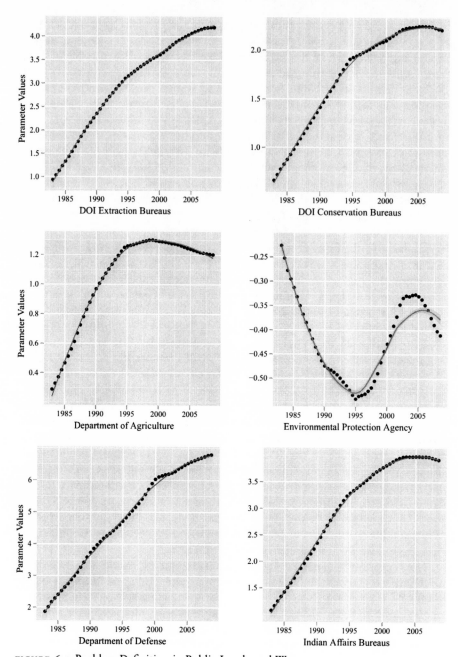

FIGURE 6.3 Problem Definition in Public Lands and Water.

Army Corps of Engineers, which monitors and maintains major infrastructure such as dams, canals, and flood barriers.

Perhaps the most interesting feature of Figure 6.3 is that the influence of most bureaucracies engaged in problem monitoring and definition in the public lands & water issue area increased over the period under study. This finding is important for two reasons. First, it suggests that the popular notion of bureaucracy as waning in importance may be issue dependent. Second, the quantity of legislation passed by Congress decreased over this period. Naturally, substantive policy must be made somewhere within the governing system for policies, laws, and governing institutions to adapt to the changing issues confronting government and society. If activity in Congress is not adequate, this policy is likely made by bureaucracy, if at all. This finding suggests the potential importance of bureaucracy under divided government and party polarization.

Figure 6.4 displays the same analysis for the issue of energy. The top two panels in Figure 6.4 display the influence of the departments of Energy (DOE) and Transportation (DOT) over time. The importance of the DOE to energy policy is obvious, but it is worth noting that the DOT is the major bureaucracy involved in the regulation of pipelines and also the transportation of fossil fuels over federal highways and railways. In each case, signaling by these two important bureaucracies was increasingly negatively associated with congressional attention to the issue of energy. The results for the DOE and DOT are important in the larger sense because they raise a question about how members of Congress collectively react to efforts by bureaucracies to monitor and define problems.

Two possibilities exist in the case where bureaucracies become significantly negatively associated with congressional attention. First, just because bureaucracies signal does not mean that Congress must pay attention. Members of Congress may collectively ignore the bureaucracy or the issue. This is likely the course of action when an issue is not salient to the larger political agenda or the larger political context is not conducive to the problem definition offered by the bureaucracy. Thus, there is a sort of substitution effect for bureaucracy in the system of government. Second, decreased congressional attention to the issue may be a direct result of acquiescence or, more likely, delegation to the bureaucracy. If problem definitions that bureaucracies offer are preferred by powerful members of Congress, especially when uncertainty reigns within the institution, members of Congress have an incentive to allow bureaucracy to make policy.

This strategy of delegation may be especially valuable to members of Congress when the distribution of benefits to constituents or "clientele" is important. The cases of willful ignorance or delegation on the part of Congress highlight the importance of the histories of policy and the institutions, as well as the larger political context, in understanding the influence of certain problem definitions over time.

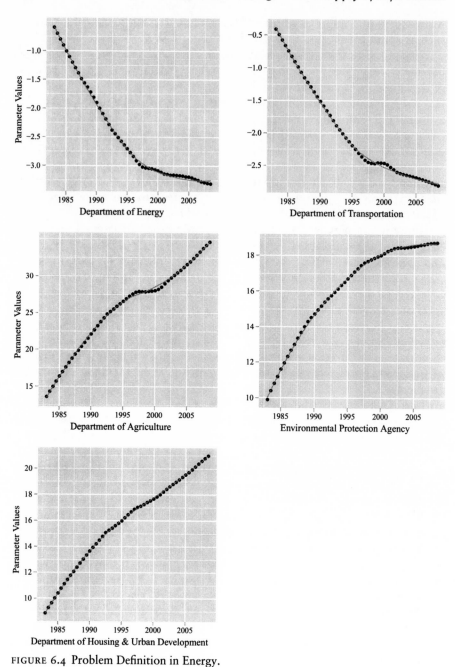

FIGURE 6.4 Problem Definition in Energy.

Figure 6.4 suggests the increasing importance of the USDA and Department of Housing and Urban Development (HUD) in energy policy. These findings demonstrate something important about the ability of bureaucracies to recast their missions in terms of important problems, thus altering the problem definitions they craft and send to Congress. During the mid-1990s, the USDA got caught in the cross-fire between Congress and the president over cutting the federal budget. Congress was eager to slash budgets, and in response the Clinton administration eventually went so far as to reorganize the USDA, making it organizationally much leaner. By the late 1990s, agriculture had a very tenuous prominence on the agenda. However, three broad trends worked in the favor of the USDA's ability to wield influence beginning in the 2000s. The first two, terrorism and worldwide food shortages, combined to offer the USDA the ability to define agricultural problems in terms of national security (as it had once been defined in the 1970s). The third trend was a growing concern over climate change, about which the USDA uniquely could offer novel problem definitions. The USDA began to integrate national security considerations and those of climate change into a very powerful problem definition for agriculture. The integrated problem definition generated solutions that seemed to work on both fronts (e.g., biofuels, reforestation, and the agricultural aspects of cap-and-trade legislation).

A similar story emerges for HUD. Observers everywhere, including scholars of urban politics, have bemoaned the demise of an integrated housing policy in the United States and this is borne out by HUD's decreasing influence. From the mid-1970s onward, HUD became much less important not only within the set of national bureaucracies but also on issues for which it had traditionally been the dominant federal player. Again, however, regulations in the time period under study bear out that HUD maneuvered well to integrate its standard problem definitions on housing issues with climate change. A mass of regulations now incentivize energy efficiency in public housing, home construction (including energy-efficient construction materials), and "greener" buildings.

Finally, Figure 6.4 suggests the openness of even traditional issue areas to novel problem definitions. This openness is borne out by the increased influence of the USDA, HUD, and EPA in a traditionally closed issue area such as energy policy. That problem definitions are malleable, even within the same bureaucracy, is a critical aspect of the government's ability to address the issue agenda and adapt to the ways in which issues change over time.

Problem definition allows bureaucracies to influence agenda setting at higher levels of government. The changing political context at the macro level determines which definitions succeed and fail. These constraints mean that some bureaucracies will succeed in defining problems for government action. Further, the constraints imposed by the broader political system rarely exceed the adaptability of bureaucracies where problem definition is concerned. To understand policy change in Congress, we must examine the way Congress responds to feedback about its policies provided by bureaucracies.

6.3 INFORMATION SUPPLY AND FEEDBACK

Systems of all types are guided, or steered, and adapt on the basis of information about their performance through time. For the administrative state, the major sources of information on the past performance of the system are the behaviors and information generated by bureaucracy. Note that a systems perspective on the dual dynamics of congressional prioritization and bureaucratic problem solving depends on the responsiveness of Congress to the information generated by bureaucracy.

This theorem holds true even if we assume that members of Congress have fixed ideas about how to address certain issues and want bureaucracies to fall in line with those ideas. In a systems perspective, control requires congressional attentiveness and responsiveness to the information generated by bureaucracy. This fact poses a problem for studies of bureaucracy and Congress aiming to examine democratic accountability of unelected bureaucrats. In the classic model, responsiveness to bureaucracy is assumed to be evidence of bureaucracy gone awry. In dual dynamics theory, in contrast, congressional responsiveness to bureaucracy is part and parcel of steering the administrative state: control of the bureaucracy hinges on it.

Figure 6.5 displays the results of a set of fractional error-correction models for congressional hearing sessions and the SNRs of bureaucratic regulations from 1983–2008. I used fractional error-correction models to gauge the responsiveness of the congressional agenda to information generated by bureaucracy because of the heterogeneity characterizing both hearings and regulations. Some hearings are held on a regular schedule and built into the larger process of reauthorization (Adler and Wilkerson, 2012), whereas others are more erratic as committees grapple with emergent problems on the agenda. The same holds true for regulations in the bureaucracy. Some regulations come about as a result of the lengthy process of lawmaking and implementation, whereas others address problems detected and defined by bureaucracy with little direction from above.

Figure 6.5 illustrates three important aspects of the influence of bureaucratic problem solving on congressional agenda setting. Estimates for the adjustment of the congressional agenda (the fractional error correction) are contained in Figure 6.5, along with their confidence intervals (both 67 and 95 percent). Significant (where confidence intervals do not cross the line for zero) and negative estimates indicate congressional adjustment.

First, informational feedback and resulting congressional adjustment is detected for half of the issues examined. Nine issues display considerable sensitivity of the congressional agenda to the information generated by bureaucracy. Nine issues do not display a statistically detectable influence, and one (government operations) is signed in the wrong direction given the parameters of the model. In short, there is ample evidence that the congressional agenda adjusts over time to the information contained in bureaucratic problem solving.

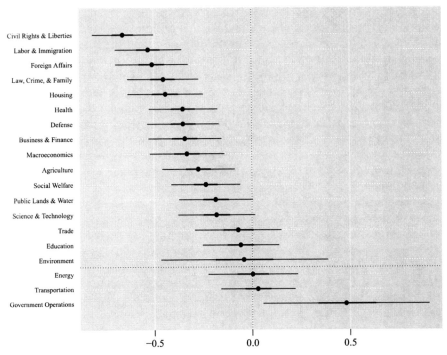

FIGURE 6.5 Feedback and Adjustment Within Issues.

Second, there is considerable variation in this adjustment depending on the issue. For example, the adjustment parameter for the environment is estimated at −.56. This indicates that when the SNR generated by bureaucracy diverges from its normal (compared in time) relationship with Congress, then the congressional agenda moves to restore this equilibrium at 56 percent per time period. Congress is thus adjusting its agenda based on the information provided by bureaucracy. This does not mean, however, that bureaucracy dictates Congress's response. Other issues, such as law, crime, & family policy, display much less pronounced sensitivity to bureaucratic problem solving.

The third aspect of the influence of bureaucratic problem solving displayed overall in Figure 6.5 is that congressional adjustment to bureaucracy is fractional – it is slow and partial. The slow and partial adjustment bears directly on the vitality of the system for government information processing. Although both Congress and the bureaucracy engage in communication aimed at addressing problems on the agenda, this communication comes in the form of signals, which also have noise. The result is that both Congress and the bureaucracy face uncertainty as to the meaning of the information carried in signals. A slow, partial adjustment means that the system tends to mitigate against overreaction to information, which is sometimes laden with uncertainty.

The slow, partial adjustment of the system is also evidence of the give-and-take of the dual dynamics of congressional prioritization and bureaucratic problem solving. Members of Congress attempt to steer the information processing system in real-world time. Only some of the information generated by bureaucracy influences decisions at higher levels of government. Other information is discarded or, more likely, gets "tuned" further during congressional prioritization. The partial adjustments indicated in Figure 6.5 show that members of Congress do not need to wait on *all* the information before attempting to adjust the system. Then, the process begins again, if not anew. The dual dynamics of congressional prioritization and bureaucratic problem solving are iterated through time as both institutions struggle to come to grips with the policy agenda.

This iteration highlights the dynamic nature of feedback. The estimations in Figure 6.5 should be understood as the sensitivity of the system to the supply of information about problems. Given congressional policy priorities, we should not expect that congressional sensitivity to feedback is static as represented in the models. Congress will be most sensitive to the feedback of bureaucratic problem solving when that information matches up with congressional priorities. To get a feel for the dynamics of feedback, Figure 6.6 displays a model for the issue of agriculture from 1983–2008. The figure is similar to the ones discussed in bureaucratic problem definition, showing simulations of the estimate through time. In reading the figure, increasingly negative (lower on the figure) values indicate greater sensitivity to information supplied by bureaucracy, whereas values nearer zero indicate the opposite.

Agriculture is an instructive case in the interplay between Congress and the bureaucracy over the agenda. Looking at Figure 6.6, two different types of situations emerge that speak to the give-and-take of congressional problem prioritization and bureaucratic problem solving. Broadly speaking, congressional sensitivity to the bureaucracy is variable over time. Interestingly, the narrative of agriculture policy over this period shows that Congress is most sensitive to bureaucratic policy making during periods where agriculture does not figure prominently on the congressional agenda. In other words, when agriculture is not on center stage in Congress, then Congress is more sensitive to policy making by the bureaucracy. Having delegated problem monitoring, members are more reliant on bureaucracy and other actors for information.

In the mid-1990s, both Congress and the president prioritized agriculture, in particular the USDA, introducing a spate of legislation that redefined the government's role in agriculture and reorganized the structure of key agencies within the USDA. Congress passed legislation amending many of the acts that define the government's involvement in agriculture, not to mention the USDA's mission. In 1994 alone it passed legislation related to rural development, nutrition labeling, food safety, insurance, and finance.[7] As Congress redefined what

---

[7] See Public Laws 103–248, 103–261, 103–276, and 103–376.

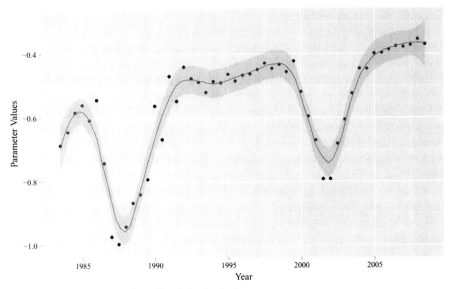

FIGURE 6.6 Dynamics of Feedback in Agriculture.

bureaucracies in agriculture monitor, the chief organization in the issue area was reorganized to buttress the redefinition.

For example, the Department of Agriculture Reorganization Act of 1994[8] consolidated not only organizational units within the USDA but also consolidated substantive missions of the agency (GAO, 1998). In its briefing to the Senate's Committee on Agriculture, Nutrition, and Forestry, the Government Accountability Office (GAO) noted that the 1994 act consciously set out to streamline the USDA both administratively and, perhaps more importantly, substantively. Of USDA's seven general mission areas, six were altered significantly, and the seventh, "economics", was eliminated. The elimination of the economics mission area was significant because it brought the Economic Research Service and the Agricultural Statistics Service under one umbrella in the research wing of the USDA. The three agencies whose chief job was generating and analyzing information were now under one organizational roof. The act also added food safety to the core mission of the USDA. In other words, the act not only greatly streamlined the USDA administratively (e.g., from 43 agencies to 30 agencies, 20,000 staff reduction, 1,200 office closures) but also significantly tuned the information supplied in the future.

The figure shows that before and after this surge of legislation redefining both the issue area and the bureaucracies monitoring it, congressional attention to the agriculture issue was sensitive to bureaucratic information. Thinking about the delegation of attention, the hallmark of the dual dynamics of the

---

[8] P.L. 103-354.

process, this makes perfect sense. If Congress is not attending to the issue itself, it is heavily reliant on bureaucratic problem solving. The figure shows that once the system for supplying and processing information is out of kilter, Congress must step in to reconfigure the issue and the organizations making policy.

The new configuration of the substantive missions of the USDA figured prominently in the evolving governmental response to terrorism in the wake of the attacks of 2001. In the Bioterrorism Act of 2002,[9] the USDA was given both authority and resources to prevent potential problems in the food supply. In recrafting its brand, "food security" became a prominent feature of debates over the approach to homeland security. The reconfiguring of agriculture and the USDA allowed this by expanding the mission of the agency in terms of food safety and research. This is just one instance that testifies not only to the dynamic nature of prioritization and problem solving but also the potential for the system to be adaptive as its institutions process information about problems.

6.4 THE DYNAMICS OF PROBLEM SOLVING IN THE BUREAUCRACY

When considering the efforts of government institutions to address existing and emergent policy problems in agenda setting, the systems perspective of dual dynamics offers insight into the nature of bureaucratic influence on the policy process. The influence of bureaucracy rests, as Richard Elmore might say, on its proximity to the problem. At the system's most basic level, bureaucrats are paying attention.

Through problem monitoring, bureaucracies are often the first to detect and respond to emergent problems or issues. Given their location in the overall organization of government and the duty of paying attention delegated to them, bureaucracies are also often the first institutions to define a problem for action in the larger system. Their definitions have a profound impact on how issues come to be understood at higher levels of government. This information then feeds slowly back into the larger system of dual dynamics and aids in the system's adjustment to the agenda. Largely ignored in most discussions of bureaucracy, bureaucratic influence in the policy process is firmly rooted in agenda setting.

Chapters 5 and 6 collectively illustrated the dual dynamics that govern information processing between Congress and the bureaucracy as both confront the policy agenda. Both congressional steering of policy change and bureaucratic influence are innate to the policy process and to the organization of government generally.

[9] P.L. 107–188.

7

Information, Bureaucracy, and Government
Problem Solving

For democratic systems like the United States, the Elmore problem means that legitimacy and authority reside at the top of the governing system, whereas the expertise to monitor and define problems originates from below. Much has been written in scholarly disciplines and elsewhere about the problem posed by unelected officials who skirt the public will. But this is perhaps democracy's easier problem. After all, power resides with the people or their elected representatives by definition in a democracy. This power, sometimes ill informed and wielded awkwardly, brackets the ability of the larger governing system to address problems that are important to citizens and politicians alike. In fact, the argument laid out here takes congressional direction of the policy process as a given, as something so innate to the process of addressing problems and making policy that it occurs at the earliest stages of the process, even absent well-defined incentives or policy goals.

Although elections are often a handy redress for correcting wayward officials, they also sometimes act as an inefficiency on government information processing. Democratic systems are unparalleled in representing and aggregating preferences, but are far less adept at aggregating and synthesizing expertise. The system does respond to information, but slowly and/or sporadically. How does the system cope at the juncture of authority and expertise?

For the answer, we must examine the earliest stages of the policy process. At the point where the Elmore problem introduces tremendous stress on the system of government, the dual dynamics of congressional prioritization and bureaucratic problem solving create a two-way flow of information about the problems facing government. This two-way flow of information offers both members of Congress and bureaucrats an opportunity to influence the direction of public policy, even when they disagree on strategies for dealing with the problems.

7.1 FOUNDATIONS OF THE ARGUMENT

The conceptualization of information in the policy process lies at the core of the theory of dual dynamics. Information has three characteristics important for understanding the influence of bureaucracy in the policy process. First, it pertains most importantly to understanding problems (or the agenda) and not merely to the solutions generated and considered. This is important because bureaucracy is typically thought to matter after problems have been considered and solutions generated and applied. Contrary to this conventional wisdom, bureaucracies are perhaps most influential at the very early stages of the policy process, when government first notices or detects problems. Bureaucracies are delegated to pay attention when the elected branches of government are focused elsewhere. This means that bureaucracies are the first to monitor issues and detect problems. They are crucial to defining problems for action at higher levels of government.

Second, information is not a resource held privately by bureaucracies. This observation departs from current understandings of the relationship between bureaucracy and Congress. Bureaucracy's influence on the policy process and even the degree of bureaucratic autonomy depend on supplying information, which enables bureaucracies to influence the direction of public policy and help steer the debate on given issues. Bureaucracies that choose to hoard information will find it supplied by a competitor, who then will gain leverage in influencing policy debates. This competition occurs for two reasons: bureaucrats want to influence policy on some level, and members of Congress foster competition among bureaucracies as a standard, low-cost mechanism of congressional prioritization. In fact, this competition is often a byproduct of run-of-the-mill congressional agenda-setting activities.

Third, and pursuant to the notion that information is not privately held, information is oversupplied. Because information supply offers the prospect of influence, especially at the earliest stages of the process when problem definition occurs, bureaucracies will supply information in an effort to steer agenda setting. In addition, competition among bureaucracies for supply of information amplifies its overproduction.

The characterization of communication among bureaucrats and legislators as signaling is also central to the idea of dual dynamics. The information that governs the relationship between the bureaucracy and Congress in the policy process does not travel unabated through the machinery of government. Noise is part and parcel of the information transmitted at the juncture of the dual dynamics. The conceptualization of communication among institutions as signaling captures the noise caused by the dual dynamics of the system. The theory helps place the influence of bureaucracy and the attempts of Congress to "tune" bureaucracy within the larger context of politics.

The conceptualization of signaling also helps explain why well-intentioned bureaucrats and legislators often fail to characterize a problem or issue in a way useful to generating solutions or why some important problems fall off the radar, despite adequate government organization and information gathering. In other words, signaling strips any determinacy from the theory in cases where the goals of bureaucrats and politicians align. Yet it does more than infuse the process with variance. It means the system can adapt to the agenda as noise induces uncertain bureaucrats and politicians to consider problem definitions and solutions they may have ignored given clearer signals about a problem.

7.2 CONGRESSIONAL PRIORITIZATION

Congress and the federal bureaucracy constitute a communications system geared toward generating and using information about policy problems facing citizens and government institutions alike. Congressional influence on the policy process centers on synthesizing information from the bureaucracy and using this information to steer what bureaucracy attends to and the types of information it generates.

From above, Congress is able to tune the information supply emanating from the bureaucracy. This influence or even control is innate to Congress's interaction with the bureaucracy and does not require the development and maintenance of costly incentive structures: it stems directly from congressional agenda setting. To alter how bureaucrats define and generate information about a particular policy problem, members of Congress need only discuss issues in a different way or alter their own policy debate on the issue.

The first mechanism linking congressional prioritization and influence on bureaucracy is issue shuffling. Through normal agenda-setting activities, members of Congress prioritize issues for attention, and ultimately for public resources. When shuffling issues, members of Congress amplify the prominence of some issues and dampen the prominence of others – amounting to a reweighting of the priorities attached to the range of issues on the government agenda. Bureaucracies are susceptible to this issue shuffling. As issues rise in prominence on the agenda, the prominence of the bureaucracies monitoring these issues also rises. These bureaucracies become more influential and more prominent in the information supply.

The second mechanism is issue bundling. Members of Congress are able to greatly alter how bureaucracies monitor problems and generate information about them by bundling some issues with others. As issues on the agenda are bundled, bureaucracies working within them are apt to discover new dimensions to the issues they traditionally monitor. These discoveries in turn alter the types of information that bureaucracies gather about an issue. Issue bundling changes the character of the information supply generated by bureaucracies monitoring problems within the bundle as members of Congress infuse issues with new dimensions.

The third mechanism available to members of Congress is related, but not reducible to, issue bundling. The cultivation or mitigation of bureaucratic competition as a tool used for congressional prioritization is not well understood in studies of public policy or of the interaction between Congress and the bureaucracy. I have assumed that bureaucrats will not hold information private, because doing so would limit their ability to influence the direction of policy debates. But even if I grant that bureaucrats might hold information private, congressional adjustment of bureaucratic competition ensures that bureaucrats must provide that information or lose influence in steering policy. Information not provided by one bureaucracy will be provided by another. Members of Congress can alter the numbers of bureaucracies monitoring given issues, as well as the prominence of some bureaucracies relative to others.

7.3 BUREAUCRATIC PROBLEM SOLVING

Bureaucracy influences the policy process by generating information about policy problems. In the sense of the Elmore problem, authority and legitimacy flow from elected representatives in Congress downward to the bureaucracy and other actors in the process. However, the federal bureaucracy's ability to generate independent information is unparalleled in the U.S. system of government and perhaps the world over. This information-gathering function of bureaucracy is arguably more important than its ability to implement the directives of members of Congress or the president. On every issue confronting society and the economy, the bureaucracy forms the vanguard of government institutions that address policy problems.

The information-generating capabilities of bureaucracy depend not only on expertise but also, more fundamentally, on how government organizes for attention (May et al., 2008). Government delegates to bureaucracies the responsibility to pay attention to issues and problems within their spheres of expertise. Bureaucratic influence on the policy process is pervasive simply because bureaucrats pay attention, even when the issues they monitor are not salient enough to reach the Capitol or Oval Office.

Three mechanisms link attention to problems by the bureaucracy and its influence on agenda setting at higher levels of government. The first is problem monitoring. By virtue of their position in the broader organization of the federal government, bureaucrats monitor issues on a day-to-day basis. They pay attention to issues and how they change, when other policy makers may be distracted. As the antennae of government, bureaucracies alert legislators when new problems arise, old problems fade or are resolved, and existing problems change. The problems monitored by the bureaucracy offer the first signals to members of Congress about the nature of the issue agenda confronting government. As bureaucracies monitor problems, members of Congress glean information about the size and severity of problems – information that is relevant to their deliberations as they set the agenda.

Second, bureaucracies help define the problems they monitor for action at higher levels of government. This is a crucial step in the policy process, because problems must be defined in order to generate and consider solutions. By helping define policy problems, bureaucracies influence the parameters of choice at higher levels of government. These problem definitions are important because they elevate in prominence of some potential solutions and preclude others.

The problem definitions bureaucracies develop and maintain can be traced back to their mission and attendant policy goals. Broadly speaking, each bureaucracy is the institutionalization of a problem definition. When different bureaucracies offer conflicting problem definitions, the policy debate benefits from multiple perspectives, and these perspectives can inform integrated definitions. These integrated definitions are vital for important issues that span the boundary of traditional subsystems (e.g., climate change, critical infrastructure, homeland security, and food systems). Likewise, when competing bureaucracies define problems differently yet reach the same general conclusions, they send a powerful and reliable signal to Congress about the true nature of the problem.

Third, bureaucracies generate and transmit information about problems to policy makers in Congress. To engage in prioritization, policy makers in Congress must be responsive to the information supplied by bureaucracy. Feedback is an important part of any system, and the information generated by bureaucracy feeds into the system and ultimately helps steer congressional agenda setting. It is worth noting that this happens even when members of Congress want to tightly control or direct bureaucratic behavior. The main source of information for controlling a system comes from the system itself.

The end result is a signal from the bureaucracy to legislators about what has changed on the agenda, a definition or frame for understanding the problem, and a supply of information pursuant to this definition. Taken together, these signals feed back into the system and form the basis for congressional adjustment of the system from the top. Congressional prioritization then influences the information that members of Congress may glean from bureaucracy in the future. The dual dynamics of the system mean that authoritative decision making and legitimacy within Congress rest on a foundation of information about policy problems supplied by the bureaucracy.

7.4 THE EVIDENCE

Bureaucracies are unique among American political institutions because all three of the constitutional powers of government are vested in them. Policy making by the bureaucracy has been the empirical frame for this study of the dual dynamics of congressional prioritization and bureaucratic problem solving. The information feeding into congressional decision making shapes the policies that bureaucracies make as they struggle to adapt to the problems on the agenda.

Understanding the dual dynamics of congressional prioritization and bureaucratic problem solving was not possible until now because it required a dataset that not only captured the policy-making agenda of the entire U.S. federal bureaucracy but was also systematically comparable to the policy-making agenda of Congress. To create such a database, I collected 226,710 regulations comprising the entire policy-making agenda of the bureaucracy since 1983. I then coded these regulations into a set of issue categories comparable to hearings in Congress. I sacrificed some detail in the regulations and hearings and in the give-and-take between members of Congress and bureaucrats to illuminate the general properties of the dual dynamics of the system.

Data of all types are collected for a reason, and this collection is no different. The argument laid out here involves how members of Congress and bureaucrats work together to set the agenda through the provision and processing of information about problems. Understanding the dual dynamics of the system is not possible without examining the substantive policy making of the bureaucracy and how it compares to congressional agenda setting. It should be kept in mind that policy making is but one of the major ways bureaucrats influence public policy. Bureaucracies also undertake adjudicatory proceedings and, of course, implement and enforce the policy directives of Congress and the president. More importantly, it is an underappreciated fact that bureaucracies can often choose the activities to which they will devote time and resources. And if the dual dynamics of the system teach us anything, it is that these decisions influence policy makers at higher levels of government.

The information generated by bureaucracy spurs congressional responsiveness to the policy problems, as well as congressional efforts to steer the information supply through prioritization. Chapter 5 examines the influence of party control of Congress on bureaucratic problem solving; the evidence presented there suggests that congressional prioritization influences several aspects of bureaucratic problem solving.

When Congress engages in issue shuffling, it exerts tremendous influence on the prominence of given issues on the bureaucracy's agenda. This process alters problem monitoring by the bureaucracy by changing the allocation of bureaucratic attention and shaping bureaucracies' opportunities to influence policy change. Issue shuffling changes not only the signal for a given issue relative to others on the agenda but also the prominence of the bureaucracies doing the signaling.

Issue bundling changes the landscape of the issue agenda in which bureaucracies operate. A comparison of party control of government to the array of issues on the agenda shows that Congress does indeed bundle issues. The analysis of Herfindahl-Hirschman indices in Chapter 5 suggests that bundling increases or decreases competition among the bureaucracies signaling within and across issues on the agenda.

Using issue shuffling and bundling, Congress is able to amplify the signal from certain bureaucracies while dampening the signal from others. This amplifying and dampening are much like adjusting the bass or treble on a stereo.

By way of normal agenda-setting processes, issue shuffling and bundling affect whether bureaucracies are out in front or in the background in the overall information supply. As the prominence of given bureaucracies within the stream of information changes, so too does the understanding of the issue at all levels of government, as problem definitions linked to bureaucracies change.

Using issue bundling to generate differential competition among bureaucracies over time, Congress accomplishes two things. First, members of Congress skirt the problem of bureaucracies holding private information. If one bureaucracy fails to supply relevant policy information, a competitor will step forward. Second, members of Congress are able to fine-tune the signal for a given issue. The environmental and energy sector impact assessments now required for most policies demonstrate how this process works. Bureaucracies now must consider the energy and environmental dimensions of their traditional issues. Furthermore, this type of information is not only valuable for policy making but also helps members make political calculations about public support for issues.

The information stream generated by bureaucracy is the product of efforts by bureaucracies to deal with real-world problems on the agenda, as well as efforts by Congress to steer the information stream using prioritization. Congressional decision making rests on a foundation built by bureaucracy. Like antennae, bureaucracies serve as an early-warning or alert system to members of Congress. In this sense, the federal bureaucracy is also like a fire alarm within the policy process.

Bureaucratic problem monitoring gives the initial signal to Congress about the general nature of the issue agenda facing the governing system. Chapter 6 relates bureaucratic problem monitoring to the concentration of and information contained in the congressional agenda. As bureaucratic problem monitoring becomes concentrated on a few issues, congressional attention follows suit. It does likewise when the bureaucracy's problem monitoring is dispersed across many issues. The analysis in Chapter 6 also suggests that when bureaucracy's problem monitoring contains more information, members of Congress are less able to narrow their own agenda to one or a few major issues and must spread their efforts accordingly.

Problem monitoring yields bureaucratic influence on the policy process, but this influence does not end at this early stage. The bureaucracy's efforts at later stages to define problems and shape how issues are understood at higher levels of government are also a source of considerable influence. Chapter 6 demonstrates how the influence of particular bureaucracies changes over time within the issue areas of public lands and water and energy.

Bureaucracies institutionalize certain problem definitions. Therefore the prominence of a given bureaucracy as an information supplier indicates the importance of that problem definition to current policy making. The analysis in Chapter 6 shows that the prominence of the various bureaucracies within these issues varies a great deal over time. Problem definitions go in and out of vogue as bureaucracies gain or lose leverage in the battle to supply information on an issue.

Finally, Chapter 6 demonstrates that the information generated by the bureaucracy feeds back into congressional agenda setting in several key issue areas. Most notably, the congressional agenda shows considerable sensitivity to bureaucratic problem solving in issues such as the environment, health care, housing, and labor and immigration. To steer the system from the top, members of Congress must be responsive to or be influenced by the information generated by bureaucracies. This response is necessarily partial and happens over a period of time, rather than immediately, as each institution adapts to the others and to the problems on the agenda.

7.5 WHAT DO WE LEARN?

The dual dynamics of the administrative state highlight the importance of thinking about the organization of government in a more systemic way. Organization here refers to the configuration of both legislative and bureaucratic institutions in relation to the issue agenda confronting government. Political scientists have made major advances in understanding the interaction of our institutions, but have said much less about how the parts fit into the system and influence policy change.

The organization of bureaucracies is important because it tells us something about which institutions will detect a problem, what problem definitions emerge, and the quantity and character of the information that guides decision making in government. The dual dynamics of congressional prioritization and bureaucratic problem solving show how Congress is able to influence this organization through its normal process of debate and agenda setting.

The description of the policy agenda of the federal bureaucracy also draws attention to the importance of the issue structure of the agenda for policy change. Congressional prioritization greatly influences which issues become bundled or, alternatively, become delineated from others. However, the relationship among issues on the agenda is not wholly determined by congressional steering of agenda setting from the top.

The flow of factual information brings some issues together and moves others apart, even absent involvement by government. Put another way, problems exist absent any government framing. The bureaucracy also influences bundling or unbundling through problem solving, especially through problem definition. The existence or lack of an interrelationship among issues on the agenda goes a long way in explaining how and why policy changes. Understanding the structure of the issue agenda provides the background for examining politics in the context of the policy process.

The notion of bureaucratic competition is key to understanding theories of delegation in the context of policy making. If bureaucracies compete for influence in the policy process, then competition helps explain why the classical idea – that bureaucracies hold back information – is not a more pernicious problem in democracy. Bureaucratic competition is fostered not only by members of Congress looking to reduce their informational disadvantage (stemming from information asymmetry and bureaucratic proximity to the problems) but also by the evolving structure of the issue agenda. As they converge and diverge, issues bring the bureaucracies monitoring them into contact or, alternatively, isolate them.

Theoretically, the dual dynamics of the system push us to think about how information and attention could form the basis for delegation. More than forty years ago, Arrow (1974) discussed the limits of organization as it pertained to information. Knowing how organization and delegation affect who is paying attention and how they attend to issues is necessary for understanding the flow of information both within and across institutions. Social scientists should examine theories of delegation in systems characterized more by communication, information, and attention than by lines of authority and control.

Finally, the dual dynamics of the administrative state described here show that politics and policy change are an everyday affair. Members of Congress engage in a day-to-day process of attempting to steer the federal administrative apparatus in monitoring problems and generating information. Bureaucracies engage daily in adapting to the set of problems they monitor and attempting to influence policy change by providing information to policy makers at higher levels of government. All of this activity occurs even when it appears that the elected branches of government are unresponsive and macro politics seems stale. If anything, this strengthens the importance of meso-level politics to understanding politics and policy change.

7.6 IMPLICATIONS FOR GOVERNANCE AND REFORM

Given what has been learned from the dual dynamics of the system of government information generation and processing, it is worth concluding with two important observations about governance and reform. First, the importance of government information gathering and generation to the economy and society cannot be overstated. Second, social scientists need to come to grips with the dual dynamics of our political system in an era when government functions are increasingly carried out by the private sector through contracting. The bureaucracy's ability to monitor problems and generate information, even in an era of privatization and smaller, leaner government, must be preserved.

The information that fuels decisions in the economy and society is largely gathered, generated, and synthesized by the bureaucracy. Yet, bureaucracy's crucial role rarely receives attention by scholarship or the mass media (where the information is taken as a given). Unemployment, crime, the gross domestic product, the consumer price index, carbon emissions, and investment are just a few of the indicators formulated by government institutions. The bureaucracy gathers a plethora of indicators in specific issue areas, aimed at detecting problems as they arise. On an issue such as public lands and water for instance, the bureaucracies monitoring that area generate information on everything from available mineral deposits and the population of salmon in Pacific Northwest rivers to available stands of timber in the nation's forests.

The bureaucracy has a greater capacity to gather and generate information than other economic and societal institutions. Although nongovernmental, nonprofit, and other private organizations are adept at gathering information within specific issue areas, the information generated by these groups cannot match the comprehensiveness of that generated by bureaucracy. Economic interests and organizations face market pressures such that they generate information only where it directly bears on the survival or profitability of a business or a sector. Societal groups such as consumer and environmental organizations must be specific to be effective; otherwise, their message becomes muddled and loses much of its punch. In general, the bureaucracy generates not only the information currently related to an issue area but also information that may be relevant in the future.

It should be noted that bureaucratic information gathering, generation, and synthesis are most important when policy must be made or integrated across issues on the agenda. Government provides a synthesis of information on policy goals that may conflict or be difficult to reconcile. In general, it is beneficial to let the bureaucracy generate this massive amount of information, so that information gathering in many sectors of the economy and society is subsidized by government. At least in domestic politics, nearly everything the U.S. government finds or undertakes is made public, and this external provision of information allows special interests to compete from a base of common information.

This common base of information becomes obviously important in thinking about the basis for pluralistic governing systems or the role of government in promoting market competition. Pluralism tended to focus on the resources or members that groups could bring to bear on the policy process. Yet information yields considerable influence. Information is as important as resources or members in determining the general balance of influence in society.

Where market competition is concerned, bureaucratic information gathering accords with the classical economic view that government should primarily promote competition. An example is seen in an issue area such as financial regulation. In this issue, bureaucracies generate information, disseminate it, and ensure that investors have as much information as possible, thereby promoting competitive markets. Providing a base of common information is as important to promoting market-like competition as is the enforcement of regulations or the implementation of policies produced at higher levels of government.

Given the importance of information generation by the bureaucracy, how institutional and partisan politics influence information generation and synthesis is an important topic for future consideration. The information supplied by bureaucracy may be free of many social and economic biases, but it is surely affected by the institutional and partisan politics of the governing system. The discipline of political science has yet to turn its attention to how such important features as divided (or conversely unified) government or party polarization influence not only the information stream but also the bureaucracy's capacity to provide such information.

This leads to the question of the information-generating capacity of the bureaucracy in an era of smaller, leaner government, privatization of the provision of public goods, and government contracting. Since the mid-1970s, politics in the United States has taken a conservative turn, emphasizing the power of markets and smaller government. This conservative turn has been accomplished both by deregulation of various sectors of the economy and society and by government contracting for goods and services.

These broad trends raise concerns about the capacity and ability of bureaucracy to supply information. The key question regarding deregulation is how to make bureaucracy's footprint smaller, yet retain its problem-monitoring and information-generating capacity. Arguably, the bureaucracy's ability to generate information is more important in areas of policy that are deregulated than in those where the bureaucracy remains the major policymaker and implementer. Information in deregulated issue areas serves as a backstop for interests adversely affected by the absence of bureaucracy. Put another way, bureaucratic problem monitoring promotes and subsidizes competition at higher levels of government among competing interests.

Given its importance to the policy process, the information generated by bureaucracy may be useful even in the case where bureaucracy lacks the teeth to take any regulatory or enforcement action. Information aids in fostering competition and market-like behavior, which are often the stated goals of deregulation. Assuming an issue area should be deregulated, it is worth considering how to do so while retaining the capacity of bureaucracy to generate, synthesize, and disseminate information to all relevant policy actors.

The supply of information also bears directly on the ability to oversee or monitor contracts. Contracting transfers the principal–agent problem from the Congress–bureaucracy nexus to the Congress–private sector nexus. The government's ability to monitor these contracts has not kept pace with the expansion of contracting. Relatively few government bureaucracies have the power to monitor contracts. The notable exception is the Government Accountability Office (GAO), which is a congressional bureaucracy. There is much less issue-specific contract oversight expertise elsewhere in the executive branch. Senator Tom Coburn, a prominent member of the Republican Party in Congress, recently bemoaned the ability of Congress to keep up with contract oversight (McAuliff, 2011). Senator Coburn's concerns related directly to congressional efforts to trim budgets at the GAO, which is Congress's chief bureaucracy for gathering information about government programs and contracts.

Contracting for public goods and services does not eliminate the Elmore problem or guarantee that the system has sufficient information on contract performance. Nor can overseers manage problems arising on the agenda absent some information-generating mechanism. The dual dynamics of the system envision an information-generating mechanism at the earliest stages of the process. Contracting as a mode of governance often fails to generate a stream of information until the later stages of the policy process, most often after the contract fails.

The ability of the contracting process to generate information at the front end of the process is heavily dependent on the structure and design of auctions and bidding systems (Whitford, 2007). Supplying information about contract performance is made more difficult because a system for monitoring must be designed and implemented for a cadre of actors external to the system. By contrast, the generation, transmission, and use of information are innate to the system of dual dynamics.

The dual dynamics of congressional prioritization and bureaucratic problem solving remediate the Elmore problem. Though citizens and scholars alike bemoan bureaucracy's existence, and especially its pervasiveness, it is hard to imagine modern society absent a large, robust bureaucracy detecting and addressing our problems. This need is particularly evident in natural disasters, economic downturns, and crises of all types, when citizens persistently call on government to "fix it" or "do something." At such times nobody calls on the private sector or expects private interests to step up. Bureaucracies monitor and detect problems not only because the system of dual dynamics rests on a foundation of information but also because citizens expect government to detect and address problems. As citizens, we should therefore think about how our own preferences help shape the government's ability to address our problems.

APPENDIX A

Conceptualization and Measurement

The empirical foundation of my argument is a large database of all rules promulgated by the federal bureaucracy from 1983–2008. The database contains 226,710 rulemaking actions and represents the most comprehensive database of bureaucratic policy making that exists to date. This Appendix describes the nature of the data and the data collection, coding, and analysis of the rules.

This discussion proceeds from the conceptualization of the bureaucracy's agenda through indicators and measures used in the statistical analysis of the dual dynamics of agenda setting. I first offer several examples of rulemaking actions found in the Unified Agenda, the indicator of the bureaucracy's agenda used for this study. I then describe the topic coding of each entry in the Unified Agenda. This process involves expert-machine interaction in generating a dataset coded consistently and reliably over time. Finally, I discuss the measures associated with the communications model of agenda setting employed in the argument.

A.1 EXAMPLES OF RULES

To be clear, a rule is a regulation, in the same way that legislation can become a law. Rules are simply regulations that have not made it through the process of becoming a law. In Chapter 4, I offered two examples of rules, one issued by the Fish and Wildlife Service and one issued by the Farm Service Agency. Table A.1 contains two additional examples to illustrate the conceptualization and content coding of the bureaucracy's agenda. These rules happen to be extremely important in shaping public policy in two key areas in the United States. The first rule listed in Table A.1 concerns the establishment of the National Organics Program at the USDA. The rule represented a decade-long development of appropriate standards for organic certification, marketing, and substances that began with the passage of the Organic Food Production Act of 1990.[1] Given its statutory authority and the date when the proposed rule was issued, this rule testifies the USDA's ability to draw on authority delegated long ago to address problems in the present time.

The proposed version of the rule presented in Table A.1 also illustrates how rules, as an extension of legislation, lend adaptivity to the policy process and allow for consensus building. Building consensus on the standards, especially for prohibited substances, was an iterative process of rule development, feedback, and revision. The first proposed rule was issued in fall 1995 and reissued in all but two versions of the Unified Agenda (UA) until appearing as a final rule in late 2000.

The fact that it stayed on the agenda so long signifies its salience and its value as an information signal to legislators, organized interests, and other actors. Looking at the substantive content of the National Organics Program rule, it touches on everything from production, certification, and administration in the states to agricultural trade. This demonstrates not only the importance of the regulation to producers and the public at large but also the topical complexity of many federal regulations. As an indicator of the bureaucracy's policy agenda, the content of rules certainly has tremendous face validity.

The second rule listed in Table A.1 is the EPA's "climate" rule. This version was released in the spring 2014 edition of the Unified Agenda. Despite the acclaim and derision this rule received in summer 2014, it is, in fact, not the first time it has appeared on the EPA's agenda. The climate rule appeared first in fall 2011 as a "long-term action." This is an important point, because it shows how rules function to reduce uncertainty and to secure turf for policy making. It did not appear as a proposed rule until spring 2013, appearing twice that year. The rule represents a significant change in policy, establishing emissions standards for existing electric utility plants, and resorting to the authority of the Clean Air Act to do so. It has brought a firestorm of criticism from both sides – from those who think it does not go far enough and those who oppose the regulation altogether.

Together, these two examples show how rules serve as a conduit for salient and important programs and policies. Not all rules are created equal, however. Some rules simply carry more information than others.[2] The National Organics Program and the climate rule are particularly important rules in the broad scheme of things. Some rules do not approach this level of policy significance (e.g., those stipulating alterations to forms). It should be remembered that the analyses presented here represent efforts to illuminate general patterns and processes associated with the dual dynamics of agenda setting. The examples provided here and elsewhere in the book demonstrate both the value of rules as indicators of a substantive policy agenda and the ability to derive topical content that at times is quite complex from their text.

---

[1] 7 U.S.C. ch. 94, 7 U.S.C. §6501 et seq.

[2] I should note this is not different from any large-N empirical study. Equally, not all roll-call votes, laws, executive decisions, and the like are of equal importance.

TABLE A.1 *Examples of Rules*

Title	Abstract
National Organic Program[a]	The National Organic Program (NOP) would establish national standards for the organic production and handling of agricultural products. It establishes the 15-member National Organic Standards Board (NOSB) who advises the Secretary of Agriculture (Secretary) on all aspects regarding implementation of the NOP and particularly in developing the national list of approved and prohibited substances. It also would establish an accreditation program for State officials and private persons who want to be accredited to certify farms and handling operations that comply with the program's requirements. The program additionally would include labeling requirements for organic products and products containing organic ingredients and enforcement provisions. It further provides for the approval of State organic programs and the importation into the United States of organic agricultural products from foreign producers that meet or are the equivalent to the national standard.
Carbon Pollution Guidelines for Existing Power Plants: Emission Guidelines for Greenhouse Gas Emissions From Existing Stationary Sources: Electric Utility Generating Units[b]	On June 25, 2013, President Obama issued a Presidential Memorandum directing the Environmental Protection Agency (EPA) to work expeditiously to complete greenhouse standards for the power sector. The agency is using its authority under section 111(d) of the Clean Air Act to issue emission guidelines to address GHG emissions from existing power plants. The Presidential Memorandum directs EPA to issue proposed GHG guidelines for existing power plants by no later than June 1, 2014, and issue final guidelines by no later than June 1, 2015. In addition, the Presidential Memorandum directs EPA to, in the guidelines, require states to submit to EPA the implementation plans required under section 111(d) of the Clean Air Act by no later than June 30, 2016.

[a] USDAAMS; RIN 0581-AA40; Proposed Rule; 7 CFR 205; Legal Authority: PL 101-624, §2101-2123; 7 USC 6501-6522; Spring 2000.

[b] EPA; RIN 2060-AR33; Proposed Rule; 40 CFR 60; Legal Authority: P.L. 88-206, 77 Stat. 392; Clean Air Act §111; Spring 2014.

A.2 THE UNIFIED AGENDA AS AN INDICATOR

Officials at the Regulatory Information Service (RIS), which publishes the Unified Agenda, were very helpful in assisting me to understand not only the nuts and bolts behind the regulatory process but also the intuition behind what gets listed in the UA. After a series of discussions, the RIS released the 1983–2006 data to me in XML format. I then collected 2007 and 2008 data by hand and converted the XML data into a spreadsheet and later into a database for easier management and querying.

The UA is published biannually as part of the Federal Register. The particular months that the UA appears vary from year to year by a month, but are always in the spring and fall. The UA contains each regulatory action that each agency expects to pursue in the coming year (12 months). Rules listed in the UA run the gamut from those appearing for the first time to those that have become completed actions (law). Rules may appear in multiple editions of the UA over time as they progress through the stages of rulemaking. In addition, if the rule is not mandated by law, with deadlines, it may be withdrawn by the issuing agency for any reason.

All executive branch agencies are required to list rules that they expect to take action on within the coming 12 months in the UA. This includes powerful executive branch offices such as the Office of Management and Budget (OMB) or the Office of Information and Regulatory Affairs (OIRA), which are the president's chief agencies for steering regulatory policy. Congressional units, such as the Government Accountability Office (GAO) and Congressional Budget Office (CBO), are not required to publish in the UA.

The UA carries a wealth of information about each rule, including the regulatory identification number (RIN); edition of the UA; title; abstract; priority status; whether it requires various reviews; which department, agency, and office issues the rule; and the name of a contact person for the rule. For this study, the most important identifiers are the RIN, title, and abstract. The database is organized by RIN-UA Edition. That means that the unit of analysis for the content coding is an *entry* in the UA, and not a rule. The concept of interest through this book has been the bureaucracy's agenda. Because a rule may appear in multiple agendas as it is being revised by political overseers and organized interests, each entry of a regulation is counted as a separate agenda item for the purposes of coding. The logic here is that, because a rule may be removed at any time, its continuance on the agenda is meaningful.

In my discussions with officials at the RIS, they mentioned that agencies normally include most of their policies in the UA, even for issues not required by law or statute (e.g., the climate rule's listing as a long-term action in Table A.1). Officials told me that this occurs because agencies wish to convey policy directions well ahead of time, in an effort to share as much information as possible and especially to reduce uncertainty for political overseers.

A.3 ITERATIVE EXPERT-MACHINE TOPIC CODING OF REGULATIONS

For the topic coding of the UA entries, it was important to utilize a system that ensured both backward compatibility and comparability with other institutions (Baumgartner et al., 1998). The deductive scheme adopted for the topic coding was that of the Policy Agendas Project (PAP) at the University of Texas at Austin.[3] The PAP topic coding scheme is comprised of 19 major topics and about 225 subtopics. The scheme is geared toward the coding of substantive content, and not necessarily directionality, making it useful for gauging attention to a range of issues across a range of institutions in American politics.[4]

By "backward compatibility," I refer to a system such that substantive content is coded the same moving forward, so that one is left with a reliable dataset. Because my theorizing concerns the interaction of Congress and the bureaucracy in the dual dynamics of agenda setting, I also required a scheme that would allow me to compare issue attention in one institution with that in another. The PAP houses the key congressional hearings data that underpin the empirical portion for Congress in this argument. By using the same scheme for rules, the dataset of rulemaking in the bureaucracy was comparable to indicators of agenda setting in Congress. For the analysis presented here, I coded the rules by major topic only.[5]

Coding 226,710 UA entries by hand would have been infeasible, so I adopted an iterative expert-machine coding process. The first step was to generate a dataset of validly coded cases that served as a training set for the machine to "learn" the coding system and then to code a virgin set of observations. The machine's codes were then examined for validity, corrected where necessary by hand, and fed into a new, expanded training dataset that further coded virgin cases. This process was iterated until all the data were coded.

With the UA entries as the unit of analysis, I topic coded each entry by PAP major topic, using the text of the rules' abstract as listed in the UA. These abstracts are usually a paragraph or two long and contain brief summaries of the problem the rule is meant to address and of the proposed rule. In a limited number of cases, the entry contained no abstract. These rules were then coded using the title, where possible, or by hand.

Many researchers who utilize such an approach begin with a random sample from across the data. Instead, I began with the hand-coding of approximately 2,000 UA entries from 1983. In doing so, I hoped to take advantage of three

---

[3] Details of the Policy Agendas Project, its topic coding scheme, and available data can be found at www.policyagendas.org. The data used here were originally collected by Frank R. Baumgartner and Bryan D. Jones, with the support of National Science Foundation grant numbers SBR 9320922 and 0111611, and were distributed through the Department of Government at the University of Texas at Austin. Neither NSF nor the original collectors of the data bear any responsibility for the analysis reported here.

[4] Increasingly, this work is comparative as well. See www.comparativeagendas.info.

[5] Work is currently underway to code the rules further by subtopic.

features of the rules data that past experience showed to be uncommon in other elite political texts. First, the language of rules changes more slowly than in higher order texts such as congressional bills. For example, text saying there are 400 ppm carbon in the air in 2014 is very similar to text saying the level was 180 ppm during the last Ice Age. This example also highlights a second feature of rules that are advantageous in coding. They are, by nature and law, very specific, in contrast to congressional bills, which tend to be phrased vaguely. Third, rules normally appear on the UA more than once, so coding a few correctly rolling forward reaps benefits early on.

To code the data, I used a set of algorithms now bundled in the R computing language as the package RTextTools. This bundled package makes many of the more difficult aspects of coding and diagnostics very accessible. Fortunately, the author had the privilege of employing Paul Wolfgang's original set of algorithms when they were still written in DOS.[6]

The coding involved three separate algorithms, each of which independently applied a PAP major topic code to each entry in the UA. The three algorithms used at the time of coding were MAXENT, SVM, and LINGPIPE. MAXENT assumes maximum entropy and classifies based on the reduction of entropy. SVM seeks patterns and classifies cases in a way that maximizes the disparities of the categories. LINGPIPE is a naive Bayesian classifier. Thus, each of the algorithms went about classifying the data in a slightly different way. I examined a sample of the data for cases where there was disagreement among the algorithms over the appropriate topic code. These were corrected and then fed back into the training dataset. This process was iterated until all 226,710 entries in the UA were coded.

In such an analysis, the real danger is posed not by the cases where the algorithms disagree, but instead by where they agree, but are wrong. This means I needed a good sample of coded data and to be careful to examine some cases where the algorithms agreed as well, especially early on in the coding when the training dataset was small. The expert human coder is thus indispensable to the process. My target for agreement on the rules coding was 80 percent. Reaching this goal required the hand coding of some 40,000 entries from the UA.

A.4 COMMUNICATIONS MEASURES AND INFORMATION PROCESSING

The argument presented here relies on a communications framework for understanding the interplay of bureaucrats and legislators in setting the agenda. In

---

[6] Paul Wolfgang deserves tremendous credit in developing the initial implementation of the algorithms, without which this work would not have been possible. Paul's work can be found at www.cis.temple.edu/~wolfgang. See Collingwood et al. (2013). RTextTools: Automatic Text Classification via Supervised Learning. R package version 1.3.9. http://CRAN.R-project.org/package=RTextTools.

this framework, information is oversupplied, and the problem for information processing is the prioritization of signals amid noise. The signaling model that emerges from this depiction is rooted in communications theory, rather than economics. Actors in the process compete to provide information in an effort to steer the direction of the policy agenda.

I would not expect the legislators to be attentive to every rule that is issued by a federal agency. After all, studies of the process reveal the built-in warning system of reviews, oversight panels, and the like. Instead, I expect that legislators are attentive or aware of bodies of activity within issues, especially those they care about. For this reason, my analysis is attentive to streams of information from the regulatory process, rather than particular regulations.

Two notions are key in understanding dynamics in this signaling formulation. The first is the robustness of a signal compared to noise. The noise could be from the signal's own volatile past or from other actors in the process, who are also attempting to provide information. The measure relevant here is the signal-to-noise ratio (SNR). The volatility of an information supply comprises the second notion. Signal amplitude (AMP) measures the range of variation in a signal over time (or its period). Both of these measures are used in Chapters 4–6.

The measures of SNR used in Chapter 5 were geared toward examining issue and agency dynamics pursuant to party control. They concern a simple relationship between the mean of attention for an issue and its past variance. Where μ is the mean of the issue or agency series and σ is the standard deviation, this measure is defined as

$$SNR = \frac{\mu}{\sigma}. \qquad (A.1)$$

In the fractional error-correction models of Chapter 5, I made use of a moving SNR by calculating a moving standard deviation for each issue series. Using these, I constructed the SNRs for those models by dividing particular realizations of the rule counts by the standard deviation of the series as each matching point in time.

Where i indexes the observations over time for each issue k, signal amplitude is defined in terms of the root mean square such that

$$AMP_k = \sqrt{\frac{x_{ik} \cdots x_{jm}}{n}}. \qquad (A.2)$$

Chapter 6 begins with another important feature of information: its fragmentation or concentration among suppliers. For analysis of the overall agendas of the bureaucracy and Congress early in Chapter 6, I used the Herfindahl-Hirschman index (HHI) of concentration and Renyi's entropy (REN) to measure the amount of information contained in the agenda. The HHI is the summed squared proportion of a variable across its categories. Where p_i is the proportion of attention given to a particular issue on the overall agenda, HHI is defined as

$$HHI = \sum p_{ix}^2.$$ (A.3)

Where x is a category and p is the proportion of activity falling in the category x, Renyi's entropy is defined as

$$REN_\alpha(x) = \frac{1}{1 - \alpha} \log \left(\sum_{i=1}^{n} p_i^\alpha \right).$$ (A.4)

Positive values of α bias the measure increasingly toward events with higher probability (i.e., occurrences in the center of the distribution). Negative values of α bias the measure increasingly toward lower probability events (i.e., occurrences in the tails of the distribution).

APPENDIX B

Statistical Models

This Appendix contains the full model results for most of the analyses presented in Chapters 5 and 6. Chapter 5 presents what is mostly descriptive inference in gauging the degree to which Congress is able to "tune" the information supply generated by bureaucracy through issue shuffling, issue bundling, and adjusting competition. Chapter 6 assesses the influence of bureaucracy on congressional agendas through problem monitoring, problem definition, and feedback.

B.I CONGRESSIONAL PROBLEM PRIORITIZATION

The presence of a trend in the data is a key concern in the descriptive analysis presented in Chapter 4. If a time series contains a trend, then breaking the series apart at any point in time will suggest statistical differences in the means of the series over time. Table B.1 contains the results of a Mann-Kendall test for trends in the SNRs of the issue series used in Chapter 5. Of the nineteen issues, a trend in the series is statistically detectable in only six issue series – agriculture, defense, housing, public lands & water, science & technology, and trade.

To examine whether the trends for these issues were problematic in assessing significant differences in the SNRs with regard to party control of Congress, I split these six issues in 1995 when party control switched from predominantly Democratic-controlled Congresses to predominantly Republican-controlled Congresses. I wanted to assess whether significant differences remained after controlling for the trends detected in these issue series. Table B.2 displays a Siegel-Tukey rank sum test with a continuity correction for these six issues.

After taking the first difference of each series, Table B.2 suggests that significant differences associated with party control of Congress remain for all but two of the issues – agriculture and trade. Interestingly, these are two issues that received enormous attention from the president during this period. The

TABLE B.1 *Mann-Kendall Test for Trends in Signal-to-Noise Ratios*[a]

Issue	τ	P-Value	Δ SNR[b]	P-Value
Agriculture	0.28	.00	−0.00	.97
Business & Finance	0.15	.12		
Civil Rights & Liberties	−0.09	.36		
Defense	0.21	.03	−0.01	.90
Education	−0.00	.98		
Energy	0.16	.09		
Environment	0.10	.29		
Foreign Affairs	−0.02	.86		
Government Operations	0.16	.09		
Health Care	0.09	.35		
Housing	0.34	.00	0.07	.50
Labor & Immigration	0.13	.19		
Law, Crime, & Family	0.11	.27		
Macroeconomics	0.08	.39		
Public Lands & Water	0.19	.05	0.08	.42
Science & Technology	0.48	.00	−0.05	.63
Social & Welfare	0.08	.38		
Trade	0.46	.00	0.04	.69
Transportation	−0.15	.11		

[a] Mann-Kendall tests for the presence of a trend in the SNRs for each issue over the period of the study. All values are rounded to two digits.
[b] Mann-Kendall τ for first difference of the series.

USDA was reorganized by the president, and its policy mission was reshaped through bipartisan efforts in Congress. The president also exerted considerable influence in the trade area with the introduction and approval of the North American Free Trade Agreement (NAFTA) during this time.

TABLE B.2 *Party Differences after Accounting for Trend*[a]

Issue[b]	Democratic Rank	Republican Rank	p-Value
Agriculture	42	75	.06
Defense	30	72	.00
Housing	31	76	.00
Public Lands & Water	19	75	.01
Science & Technology	15	74	.00
Trade	37	70	.07

[a] Siegel-Tukey rank sum test with continuity correction. The test compares the variances of SNRs for the issues associated with Democratic and Republican control of Congress. All values are rounded to two digits.
[b] Mann-Kendall tests for a trend showed support for the presence of a trend in this subset of issues. The tests in this table were conducted after differencing each issue series to remove the trend.

TABLE B.3 *Concentration of the Bureaucracy's Agenda and Concentration of the Congressional Agenda*

	Estimate[a]	St. Error
Bureaucracy's Concentration	10.91	1.71
Unified Democrat	0.01	0.03
Unified Republican	−0.06	0.03
Divided Government[b]	−3.65	0.16
HR Majority Median	0.03	0.04
Government Debt	−0.00	0.00
ϕ	5023	985
Pseudo R^2	.77	
Log Likelihood	218.2	

[a] Dependent variable is a Herfindahl-Hirschman index of congressional hearing sessions across the 19 topic categories. "Information supply" is measured as the Renyi entropy of the regulatory agenda across the same 19 topic categories. The model is a regression based on the beta distribution. All values rounded to two digits.

[b] Divided government is the intercept in the model and reference category. I opted for the conceptual label in the table.

B.2 BUREAUCRATIC PROBLEM SOLVING

Chapter 6 examines bureaucratic problem solving first by assessing the effects of issue fragmentation or, alternatively, concentration in the information supply on the congressional hearing agenda. Tables B.3, B.4, and B.5 present

TABLE B.4 *Information in the Bureaucracy's Agenda and Concentration of the Congressional Agenda*

	Estimate[a]	St. Error
Bureaucracy's Information	−.69	.11
Unified Democrat	.01	.03
Unified Republican	−.06	.03
Divided Government[b]	−0.25	0.37
HR Majority Median	.03	.04
Govt Debt	−.00	.00
ϕ	5042	989
Pseudo R^2	.77	
Log Likelihood	218.3	

[a] Dependent variable is a Herfindahl-Hirschman Index of congressional hearing sessions across the 19 topic categories. "Information supply" is measured as the Renyi entropy of the regulatory agenda across the same 19 topic categories. The model is a regression based on the beta distribution. All values rounded to two digits.

[b] Divided government is the intercept in the model and reference category. I opted for the conceptual label in the table.

TABLE B.5 *Information in the Bureaucracy's Agenda and*
Information in the Congressional Agenda

	Estimate[a]	St. Error
Bureaucracy's Information	.24	.04
Unified Democrat	−.00	.01
Unified Republican	.02	.01
Divided Government[b]	.54	.14
HR Majority Median	−0.01	0.02
Government Debt	.00	.00
AIC	111.24	

[a] Dependent variable is the Renyi entropy of congressional hearing sessions across the 19 topic categories. "Information supply" is measured as the Renyi entropy of the regulatory agenda across the same 19 topic categories. The model is a regression based on the gamma distribution. All values rounded to two digits.

[b] Divided government is the intercept in the model and reference category. I opted for the conceptual label in the table.

results from models based on beta regression (Ferrari and Cribari-Neto, 2004). In addition to the nature of the information supplied by bureaucracy on its rulemaking agenda, divided government and unified Republican control of government are the most prominent influences on the character of the agenda. Unified Democratic control showed no statistically detectable effect, nor did Congress's ideological composition or government debt. For concentration and the amount of information in the agenda, all the models performed reasonably well with no prominent red flags. For a discussion of influence of the bureaucratic agenda see Chapter 6.

Tables B.6 and B.7 show the results of quasi-Poisson regressions of congressional attention to public lands & water and to energy. The models assess the influence of information supplied by various bureaucracies active within each issue. In Table B.6, unified Republican government drives down attention to public lands & water. In Table B.7, divided government is associated with increased congressional attention to the issue of energy. See Chapter 6 for a full discussion of the influence of bureaucratic information supplied through regulations for the two issues and of bureaucratic influence on problem definition.

Table B.8 contains estimates for Beran's fractional exponent (1993) for each issue series in the rules and congressional hearing sessions. These estimates were used to difference the issue series for the fractional error-correction models (see Clarke and Lebo, 2003) presented in Chapter 6. Two features of the table are worth mentioning. First, the estimated memory for the issue series associated with bureaucratic rulemaking is much longer than for congressional issue attention. This is as expected given bureaucratic processes and the swiftness with which legislators may refocus their attention, especially through the

TABLE B.6 *Bureaucratic Problem Definition in Public Lands and Water*

	Estimate[a]	St. Error
Department of Interior Extraction Bureaus	0.45	0.12
Department of Interior Conservation Bureaus	0.29	0.13
Bureau of Indian Affairs & National Indian Gaming Commission	0.39	0.17
Forest Service & Natural Resources Conservation Service	0.18	0.08
Environmental Protection Agency	−0.15	0.10
Department of Defense	0.86	0.32
Unified Democrat	0.00	0.13
Unified Republican	−0.50	0.23
Divided Government[b]	1.01	1.02
HR Majority Median	0.35	0.30
Government Debt	−0.00	0.00
Dispersion Parameter	2.71	

[a] The dependent variable is a count of congressional hearing sessions on public lands & water. The model is a regression based on a quasi-Poisson distribution. All values rounded to two digits.

[b] Divided government is the intercept in the model and reference category. I opted for the conceptual label in the table.

hearing process. Second, there was a high degree of memory in almost all of the issue series for bureaucracy. For a complete discussion of feedback and the error-correction components of the models, see Chapter 6.

Although it is impractical to show the results for each of the 19 Fractional Error Correction Models in any orderly fashion, some examples illustrate the

TABLE B.7 *Bureaucratic Problem Definition in Energy*

	Estimate[a]	St. Error
Department of Energy	−0.40	0.19
Environmental Protection Agency	2.32	0.79
Department of Housing & Urban Development	2.22	0.80
Department of Agriculture	2.78	1.10
Department of Transportation	−0.30	0.14
Unified Democrat	0.32	0.22
Unified Republican	0.10	0.19
Divided Government[b]	4.04	0.29
HR Majority Median	0.11	0.34
Government Debt	0.00	0.00
Dispersion Parameter	2.26	

[a] The dependent variable is a count of congressional hearing sessions on energy. The model is a regression based on a quasi-Poisson distribution. All values rounded to two digits.

[b] Divided government is the intercept in the model and reference category. I opted for the conceptual label in the table.

TABLE B.8 *Beran's Fractional Exponent for the Bureaucracy and Congress Issue Series*

Issue	Bureaucracy[a]	Congress
Agriculture	0.74	0.47
Business & Finance	0.63	0.31
Civil Rights & Liberties	0.98	0.47
Defense	0.98	0.48
Education	1.02	0.08
Energy	1.07	0.61
Environment	0.75	0.51
Trade	1.10	0.73
Government Operations	0.99	0.40
Health Care	0.67	0.48
Housing & Community Development	0.98	0.40
Foreign Affairs	1.33	0.45
Labor & Immigration	0.84	0.28
Law, Crime, & Family	0.82	0.33
Macroeconomics	0.80	0.43
Public Lands & Water	1.17	0.08
Science & Technology	0.98	0.44
Social Welfare	0.88	0.45
Transportation	0.84	0.49

[a] Estimates of Beran's fractional exponent (Beran, 1993) for congressional hearing sessions and the SNRs of the bureaucracy within each of the issue areas. All values rounded to two digits.

properties and influences in these dynamic feedback models. Table B.9 displays the results for the issue of business & finance. The model includes controls for legislator ideology (here I use the DW-Nominate score for the majority party in the House of Representatives), party control of government, and congressional agenda uncertainty (measured using Renyi's entropy). Table B.9 suggests that, in addition to the long-run adjustment for the information supplied by bureaucracy in rulemaking, congressional ideology has both a statistical and substantive effect on the amount of attention given to business & finance. The effect is in the expected direction, with conservative Congresses decreasing attention to these issues.

Table B.10 displays results for the same model for the issue of the environment. In this model, divided government drives down attention to the environment in Congress. This might be expected given hotly contested partisan divisions on the issue. In addition, increased uncertainty measured by Renyi entropy is associated with increased attention to the environment. Given the nature of the series for the issue, this increased uncertainty is understandable in the context of issue dependencies. As the analysis over time would show, many other issues are increasingly tied to the environment in two ways. First,

TABLE B.9 *Feedback and Adjustment in Business and Finance*

	Estimate[a]	St. Error
Bureaucracy Δ_t SNR	54.92	45.58
Information Feedback$_{t-1}$	−0.34	0.14[c]
HR Ideology$_t$	−22.41	8.81[c]
Divided Government$_t$	119.00	73.98
Unified Democratic$_t$	5.22	10.16
Unified Republican$_t$	8.99	7.59
Congressional Agenda Uncertainty$_t$	−31.56	19.34
Adj R^2	0.14	
F	2.36	

[a] The dependent variable is the change in congressional hearing sessions. The model is an FECM. All values rounded to two digits.
[b] Divided government is the intercept in the model and reference category. I opted for the conceptual label in the table.
[c] $p \leq 0.05$.

partisan conflict, especially polarization (Theriault, 2008), has created issue dependencies and complementarities. Second, the increasing salience of climate change and global warming has led to issue spillover. Thus it is not too surprising that, as attention in Congress becomes much more fragmented across issues, the twin binders of partisan conflict and issue interdependence bring increased attention to the environment. This is a finding that tends to hold for other similar issues.

TABLE B.10 *Feedback and Adjustment in the Environment*

	Estimate[a]	St. Error
Bureaucracy Δ_t SNR	34.21	27.21
Information Feedback$_{t-1}$	−0.59	0.12[c]
HR Ideology$_t$	−13.32	8.18
Divided Government$_t$[b]	−147.65	72.31[c]
Unified Democratic$_t$	−1.69	9.06
Unified Republican$_t$	6.66	7.05
Congressional Agenda Uncertainty$_t$	38.23	18.90[c]
Adj R^2	0.32	
F	4.99	

[a] The dependent variable is the change in congressional hearing sessions. The model is an FECM. All values rounded to two digits.
[b] Divided government is the intercept in the model and reference category. I opted for the conceptual label in the table.
[c] $p \leq 0.05$.

References

Aberbach, Joel D. 1990. *Keeping a Watchful Eye: The Politics of Congressional Oversight*. Washington, DC: Brookings Institution.

Aberbach, Joel D., and Rockman, Bert A. 1988. Mandates or Mandarins? Control and Discretion in the Modern Administrative State. *Public Administration Review*, **48**(2), 606–612.

Aberbach, Joel D., and Rockman, Bert A. 2005. Civil Servants and Policymakings: Neutral or Responsive Competence. *Governance*, **7**(4), 461–469.

Adler, E. Scott, and Wilkerson, John D. 2012. *Congress and the Politics of Problem Solving*. New York: Cambridge University Press.

Agricultural Export Controls. 1984. *Washington Post*, **October 8**, A2.

Alchian, Armen A., and Demsetz, Harold. 1972. Production, Information Costs, and Economic Organization. *American Economic Review*, **62**, 777–795.

Appelbaum, Binyamin, and Goldfarb, Zachary A. 2009. U.S. Weighs Single Agency to Regulate Banking Industry; Plan is Key Facet of Sweeping Overhaul. *Washington Post*, **May 28**, A01.

Arrow, Kenneth J. 1974. *The Limits of Organization*. New York: W. W. Norton.

Balla, Steven J. 1998. Administrative Procedures and Political Control of the Bureaucracy. *American Political Science Review*, **92**, 663–673.

Balla, Steven J., and Wright, John R. 2001. Interest Groups, Advisory Committees, and Congressional Control of the Bureaucracy. *American Journal of Political Science*, **45**, 799–812.

Banks, Jeffrey S., and Weingast, Barry R. 1992. The Political Control of Bureaucracies under Assymetric Information. *American Journal of Political Science*, **36**(2), 509–524.

Baumgartner, Frank R., and Jones, Bryan D. 1993. *Agendas and Instability in American Politics*. Chicago: University of Chicago Press.

Baumgartner, Frank R., Jones, Bryan D., and MacLeod, Michael C. 1998. Lessons from the Trenches: Ensuring Quality, Reliability, and Usability in the Creation of a New Data Source. *The Political Methodologist*, **8**(2), 1–10.

Bawn, Kathleen. 1997. Choosing Strategies to Control the Bureaucracy: Statutory Constraints, Oversight, and the Committee System. *Journal of Law, Economics, and Organization*, 13(1), 101–126.

Bendor, Jonathan. 1985. *Parallel Systems: Redundancy in Government*. Berkeley: University of California Press.

Beran, Jan. 1993. Fitting Long-Memory Models by Generalized Linear Regression. *Biometrika*, 80, 817–822.

Bertelli, Anthony M., and Lynn, Laurence E. 2006. *Madison's Managers: Public Administration and the Constitution*. Baltimore: Johns Hopkins University Press.

Bourne, Joel K. 2009. The End of Plenty: The Global Food Crisis. *National Geographic*, 2009(June), 26–59.

Brehm, John, and Gates, Scott. 1999. *Working, Shirking, and Sabotage: Bureaucratic Response to a Democratic Public*. Ann Arbor: University of Michigan Press.

Burstein, Paul. 1991. Policy Domains: Organization, Culture, and Policy Outcomes. *Annual Review of Sociology*, 17, 327–350.

Carpenter, Daniel P. 1996. Adaptive Signal Processing, Hierarchy, and Budgetary Control in Federal Regulation. *American Political Science Review*, 90(2), 283–302.

Carpenter, Daniel P. 2001. *The Forging of Bureaucratic Autonomy: Reputations, Networks, and Policy Innovation in Executive Agencies, 1862–1928*. Princeton: Princeton University Press.

Clarke, Harold D., and Lebo, Matthew J. 2003. Fractional (Co)Integration and Governing Party Support in Britain. *British Journal of Political Science*, 33, 283–301.

Clinton, Joshua D., Bertelli, Anthony, Grose, Christian R., Lewis, David E., and Nixon, David C. 2012. Separate Powers in the United States: The Ideology of Agencies, Presidents, and Congress. *American Journal of Political Science*, 2, 341–354.

Clinton, Joshua D., and Lewis, David E. 2008. Expert Opinion, Agency Characteristics, and Agency Preferences. *Political Analysis*, 16(1), 3–20.

Cobb, Roger W., and Elder, Charles D. 1972. *Participation in American Politics: The Dynamics of Agenda-Building*. Boston: Allyn and Bacon.

Coglianese, Cary. 1997. Assessing Consensus: The Promise and Performance of Negotiated Rulemaking. *Duke Law Journal*, 46(6), 1255–1349.

Collingwood, Loren, Jurka, Timothy, Boydstun, Amber E., Grossman, Emmiliano, and van Atteveldt, Wouter. 2013. RTextTools: A supervised learning package for text classification. *The R Journal*, 5(1), 6–13.

Comiskey, Michael, and Madhogarhia, Pawan. 2009. Unraveling the Financial Crisis of 2008. *PS: Political Science and Politics*, 42(2), 271–275.

Cooper, Michael. 2009. U.S. Infrastructure Is in Dire Straits, Report Says. *New York Times*, January 27.

Cox, James H. 2004. *Reviewing Delegation: An Analysis of the Congressional Reauthorization Process*. Westport, CT: Praeger.

CRS. 2008. *Congressional Review of Agency Rulemaking: An Update and Assessment of The Congressional Review Act after a Decade*. Tech. rept. Congressional Research Service.

Dery, David. 1984. *Problem Definitiion in Policy Analysis*. Lawrence: University of Kansas Press.

Deutsch, Karl W. 1966. *The Nerves of Government*. New York: Free Press.

Dodd, Lawrence C., and Schott, Richard L. 1986. *Congress and the Administrative State*. New York: Macmillan.

Downs, Anthony. 1967. *Inside Bureaucracy*. New York: Harper-Collins.

Downs, Anthony. 1972. Up and down with Ecology: The Issue Attention Cycle. *Public Interest*, Summer, 38–50.

Durant, Robert F. 2000. Whither the Neoadministrative State: Toward a Polity-Centered Theory of Administrative Reform. *Journal of Public Administration Research and Theory*, 10(1), 79–109.

Durant, Robert F., and Warber, Adam. 2001. Networking in the Shadow of Hierarchy: Public Policy, the Administrative Presidency, and the Neoadministrative State. *Presidential Studies Quarterly*, 221–244.

Easton, David. 1965. *A Systems Analysis of Political Life*. New York: Wiley.

Egan, Jack. 1973. USDA Held Aware of Grain Deal Size. *Washington Post*, July 21 (July 21), A2.

Egan, Patrick J. 2013. *Partisan Priorities: How Issue Ownership Drives and Distorts American Politics*. New York: Cambridge University Press.

Eisner, Marc Allen, Worsham, Jeff, and Ringquist, Evan J. 2000. *Contemporary Regulatory Policy*. Boulder: Lynne Rienner.

Elmore, Richard F. 1979. Backward Mapping: Implementation Research and Policy Decisions. *Political Science Quarterly*, 94(4), 601–616.

Epstein, David, and O'Halloran, Sharyn. 1999. *Delegating Powers: A Transaction Cost Politics Approach to Policy Making under Separate Powers*. New York: Cambridge University Press.

Feldman, Martha S., and March, James G. 1981. Information in Organizations as Signal and Symbol. *Administrative Sciences Quarterly*, 26(2), 171–186.

Felsenthal, Dan S. 1980. Applying the Redundancy Concept to Administrative Organizations. *Public Administration Review*, 40(3), 247–252.

Ferrari, Silvia P., and Cribari-Neto, Francisco. 2004. Beta Regression for Modelling Rates and Proportions. *Journal of Applied Statistics*, 31(7), 799–815.

Finer, Herbert. 1972. Administrative Responsibility in Democratic Government. In *Bureaucratic Power in National Politics*, ed. F. E. Rourke. Second edn. Boston: Little, Brown.

Fish Need Food, Too. 2008. *Boston Globe*, August 25, A14.

Friedrich, Carl J. 1972. Public Policy and the Nature of Administrative Responsibility. In *Bureaucratic Power in National Politics*, ed. F. E. Rourke. Second edn. Boston: Little, Brown.

Gailmard, Sean, and Patty, John W. 2012. *Learning while Governing: Information, Accountability, and Executive Branch Institutions*. Chicago: University of Chicago Press.

GAO. 1998, GAO/RECD-98-109R. *Status of the Department of Agriculture's Reorganization*. Tech. rept. Washington, DC: Government Accountability Office.

GAO. 2007 (October). *Financial Regulation: Industry Trends Continue to Challenge the Federal Regulatory Structure*. Report GAO-08-32. Washington, DC: Government Accountability Office.

GAO. 2010. *Offshore Oil and Gas Development: Additional Guidance Would Help Strengthen the Minerals Management Service's Assessment of Environmental Impacts in the North Aleutian Basin*. Tech. rept. GAO-10-276. Washington, DC: Government Accountability Office.

GAO. 2014 (July). *DRINKING WATER: EPA Program to Protect Underground Sources from Injection of Fluids Associated with Oil and Gas Production Needs*

Improvement. Tech. rept. GAO-14-555. Washington, DC: Government Accountability Office.

Golden, Marissa Martino. 2000. *What Motivates Bureaucrats? Politics and Administration during the Reagan Years*. New York: Columbia University Press.

Golden, Marissa Martino. 2003. All of the Above (but with Congress Rising): Who Sets the Rulemaking Agenda in Federal Agencies. Paper presented at the Annual Conference of the American Political Science Association, Philadelphia, August 28–31.

Gormley, Willliam T. 1989. *Taming the Bureaucracy: Muscles, Prayers, and Other Strategies*. Princeton: Princeton University Press.

Graber, Doris A. 2003. *The Power of Communication: Managing Information in Public Organizations*. Washington, DC: Congressional Quarterly Press.

Hamilton, Alexander. 1788. Federalist Paper 72. In *The Federalist Papers*, 1982 edn. New York: Bantam Books.

Heilprin, John. 2006. U.N.: Number of Dead Zones Rise. *Washington Dateline*, October 19.

Heimann, C. F. Larry. 1993. Understanding the Challenger Disaster: Organizational Structure and the Design of Reliable Systems. *American Political Science Review*, 87(2), 421–435.

Heimann, C. F. Larry. 1995. Different Paths to Success: A Theory of Organizational Decision Making and Administrative Reliability. *Journal of Public Administration Research and Theory*, 5(1), 45–71.

Hilgartner, Stephen, and Bosk, Charles L. 1988. The Rise and Fall of Social Problems: A Public Arenas Model. *American Journal of Sociology*, 94(1), 53–78.

Howlett, Michael, and Ramesh, M. 1998. Policy Subsystem Configurations and Policy Change: Operationalizing the Postpositivist Analysis of the Politics of the Policy Process. *Policy Studies Journal*, 26(3), 466–481.

Huber, Gregory A. 2007. *The Craft of Bureaucratic Neutrality: Interests and Influence in Governmental Regulation of Occupational Safety*. New York: Cambridge University Press.

Huber, John D., and Shipan, Charles R. 2002. *Deliberate Discretion? The Institutional Foundations of Bureaucratic Autonomy*. New York: Cambridge University Press.

Huber, John D., Shipan, Charles R., and Pfahler, Madelaine. 2001. Legislatures and Statutory Control of Bureaucracy. *American Journal of Political Science*, 45(2), 330–345.

Jacobs, Lawrence, and King, Desmond. 2009. America's Political Crisis: The Unsustainable State in a Time of Unraveling. *PS: Political Science and Politics*, 42(2), 277–285.

Jervis, Robert. 1997. *System Effects: Complexity in Political and Social Life*. Princeton: Princeton University Press.

Jones, Bryan D. 1994. *Reconceiving Decision-Making in Democratic Politics: Attention, Choice, and Public Policy*. Chicago: Chicago University Press.

Jones, Bryan D. 2001. *Politics and the Architecture of Choice: Bounded Rationality and Governance*. Chicago: Chicago University Press.

Jones, Bryan D., and Baumgartner, Frank R. 2005. *The Politics of Attention: How Government Prioritizes Problems*. Chicago: Chicago University Press.

Jones, Bryan D., Larsen-Price, Heather, and Wilkerson, John. 2009. Representation and American Governing Institutions. *Journal of Politics*, 71(1), 277–290.

Katzmann, Robert A. 1989. The American Legislative Process as a Signal. *Journal of Public Policy*, 9(3), 287–306.

Kaufman, Herbert. 1960. *The Forest Ranger: A Study in Administrative Behavior*. Baltimore: Johns Hopkins University Press.

Kaufman, Herbert. 2001. Major Players: Bureaucracies in American Government. *Public Administration Review*, 61(1), 18–42.

Kerwin, Cornelius M. 2003. *Rulemaking: How Government Agencies Write Law and Make Policy*. Washington, DC: Congressional Quarterly Press.

Kilpatrick, Carroll. 1972. Radio Speech: Corn Sale to Chinese Announced. *Washington Post*, October 28, A1, A13.

King, David C. 1997. *Turf Wars: How Congressional Committees Claim Jurisdiction*. Chicago: University of Chicago Press.

Kingdon, John W. 1981. *Congressmen's Voting Decisions*. Second edn. New York: Harper and Row.

Kingdon, John W. 1984. *Agendas, Alternatives, and Public Policies*. Boston: Little, Brown.

Kraft, Joseph. 1973. Scandal and Diplomacy. *Washington Post*, May 17, A27.

Krause, George A. 1994. Federal Reserve Policy Decision Making: Political and Bureaucratic Influences. *American Journal of Political Science*, 38(1), 124–144.

Krause, George A. 1996. The Institutional Dynamics of Policy Administration: Bureaucratic Influence over Securities Regulation. *American Journal of Political Science*, 40(4), 1083–1121.

Krause, George A. 1999. *A Two-Way Street*. Pittsburgh: University of Pittsburgh Press.

Labaton, Stephen. 2008a. Agency's '04 Rule Let Banks Pile Up Debt, and Risk. *New York Times*, October 3, A0, p. 1.

Labaton, Stephen. 2008b. S.E.C. Image Suffers in a String of Setbacks. *New York Times*, December 16. www.nytimes.com/2008/12/16/business/16secure.html (accessed December 17).

Landau, Martin. 1969. Redundancy, Rationality, and the Problem of Duplication and Overlap. *Public Administration Review*, 29(4), 346–358.

Lewis, David E. 2002. The Politics of Agency Termination: Confronting the Myth of Agency Immortality. *Journal of Politics*, 64(1), 89–107.

Lewis, David E. 2003. *Presidents and the Politics of Agency Design: Political Insulation in the United States Government Bureaucracy, 1946–1997*. Stanford: Stanford University Press.

Lewis, David E. 2008. *The Politics of Presidential Appointments: Political Control and Bureaucratic Performance*. Princeton: Princeton University Press.

Lindblom, Charles E. 1959. The Science of 'Muddling Through.' *Public Administration Review*, 19(2), 79–88.

Lipsky, Michael. 1980. *Street-Level Bureaucracy: Dilemmas of the Individual in Public Services*. New York: Russell Sage Foundation.

Lowi, Theodore J. 1969. *The End of Liberalism: The Second Republic of the United States*. New York: W. W. Norton.

Lubell, Mark. 2007. Familiarity Breeds Trust: Collective Action in a Policy Domain. *Journal of Politics*, 69(1), 237–250.

Lubell, Mark, and Scholz, John T. 2001. Cooperation, Reciprocity, and the Collective-Action Heuristic. *American Journal of Political Science*, 45, 160–178.

March, James G., and Olsen, Johan P. 1989. *Rediscovering Institutions: The Organizational Basis of Politics*. New York: Free Press.

March, James G., and Simon, Herbert A. 1958. *Organizations*. New York: John Wiley.

Marjit, Sugata. 2003. Montoring Success: On a Fundamental Principle of Financial Regulation. *Economic and Political Weekly*, 38(19), 1871–1873.

May, Peter J. 1991. Reconsidering Policy Design: Policies and Publics. *Journal of Public Policy*, 11(2), 187–206.

May, Peter J. 2010. Beyond Subsystems: Policy Regimes and Governance. *Policy Studies Journal*, 38(2), 303–327.

May, Peter J., Jochim, Ashley E., and Sapotichne, Joshua. 2011. Constructing Homeland Security: An Anemic Policy Regime. *Policy Studies Journal*, 39(2), 285–307.

May, Peter J., and Koski, Chris. 2013. Addressing Public Risks: Extreme Events and Critical Infrastructures. *Review of Policy Research*, 30(2), 139–159.

May, Peter J., Sapotichne, Joshua, and Workman, Samuel. 2006. Policy Coherence and Policy Domains. *Policy Studies Journal*, 34(3), 381–403.

May, Peter J., Sapotichne, Joshua, and Workman, Samuel. 2009a. Widespread Policy Disruption: Terrorism, Public Risks, and Homeland Security. *Policy Studies Journal*, 37(2), 171–194.

May, Peter J., Sapotichne, Joshua, and Workman, Samuel. 2009b. Widespread Policy Disruption and Interest Mobilization. *Policy Studies Journal*, 37(4), 793–815.

May, Peter J., and Workman, Samuel. 2009. The Paradox of Agency Issue Attention: The Bush Administration and the Undermining of Homeland Security. In *The George W. Bush Administration's Influence over Bureaucracy and Policy: Extraordinary Times, Extraordinary Powers?*, eds. Colin Provost and Paul Teske. New York: Palgrave.

May, Peter J., Workman, Samuel, and Jones, Bryan D. 2008. Organizing Attention: Responses of the Bureaucracy to Agenda Disruption. *Journal of Public Administration Research and Theory*, 18(4), 517–541.

Mayhew, David R. 1974. *Congress: The Electoral Connection*. New Haven: Yale University Press.

McAuliff, Michael. 2011. GAO Cuts: Tom Coburn Hammers Senate for Money-Losing Proposal. *The Huffington Post*, November 16.

McCool, Daniel. 1990. Subgovernments as Determinants of Political Viability. *Political Science Quarterly*, 105(2), 269–293.

McCool, Daniel. 1998. The Subsystem Family of Concepts: A Critique and Proposal. *Political Research Quarterly*, 51(2), 551–570.

McCubbins, Mathew D. 1985. The Legislative Design of Regulatory Structure. *American Journal of Political Science*, 29(4), 721–748.

McCubbins, Mathew D., Noll, Roger, and Weingast, Barry R. 1987. Administrative Procedures as Instruments of Political Control. *Journal of Law, Economics, and Organization*, 3, 243–277.

McCubbins, Mathew D., and Schwartz, Thomas. 1984. Congressional Oversight Overlooked: Police Patrols versus Fire Alarms. *American Journal of Political Science*, 28(1), 165–179.

Melnick, R. Shep. 1983. *Regulation and the Courts: The Case of the Clean Air Act*. Washington, DC: The Brookings Institution Press.

Miller, Gary J. 1992. *Managerial Dilemmas: The Political Economy of Hierarchy*. New York: Cambridge University Press.

Miller, Gary J. 2005. The Political Evolution of Principal-Agent Models. *Annual Review of Political Science*, 8, 203–225.

Miller, John H., and Page, Scott E. 2007. *Complex Adaptive Systems: An Introduction to Computational Models of Social Life*. Princeton: Princeton University Press.

Miller, Lisa L. 2007. The Representational Biases of Federalism: Scope and Bias in the Political Process. *Perspectives on Politics*, 5(2), 305–321.

Mitnick, Barry M. 1975. The Theory of Agency: The Policing Paradox and Regulatory Behavior. *Public Choice*, 24(1), 27–42.

Moe, Terry M. 1984. The New Economics of Organization. *American Journal of Political Science*, 28(4), 739–777.

Moe, Terry M. 1985. Control and Feedback in Economic Regulation: The Case of the NLRB. *American Political Science Review*, 79(4), 1094–1116.

Moe, Terry M. 1987. An Assessment of the Positive Theory of Congressional Dominance. *Legislative Studies Quarterly*, 12(4), 475–520.

Moe, Terry M. 1989. The Politics of Bureaucratic Structure. In *Can the Government Govern?*, eds. John E. Chubb and Paul E. Peterson. Washington, DC: Brookings Institution.

Mortensen, Peter Bjerre. 2013. Public Sector Reform and Blame Avoidance Effects. *Journal of Public Policy*, 33(2), 229–253.

Mosher, Frederick C. 1968. *Democracy and the Public Service*. New York: Oxford University Press.

Newell, Alan, and Simon, Herbert. 1972. *Human Problem Solving*. Englewood Cliffs, NJ: Prentice-Hall.

Niskanen, Willliam A. 1971. *Bureaucracy and Representative Government*. Chicago: Aldine, Atherton.

Olson, Mancur. 1965. *The Logic of Collective Action: Public Goods and the Theory of Groups*. Cambridge, MA: Harvard University Press.

Patty, John W. 2009. The Politics of Biased Information. *Journal of Politics*, 71(2), 385–397.

Petrocik, John R. 1996. Issue Ownership in Presidential Elections with a 1980 Case Study. *American Journal of Political Science*, 40(3), 825–850.

Petrocik, J. R., Benoit, W. L., and Hansen, G. J. 2003. Issue Ownership and Presidential Campaigning, 1952–2000. *Political Science Quarterly*, 599–626.

Poole, Keith T., and Rosenthal, Howard. 1997. *Congress: A Political-Economic History of roll call voting*. New York: Oxford University Press.

Redford, Emmette S. 1969. *Democracy in the Administrative State*. New York: Oxford University Press.

Renyi, Alfred. 1970. *Probability Theory*. New York: Elsevier.

Riker, William H. (ed). 1993. *Agenda Formation*. Ann Arbor: University of Michigan Press.

Robinson, Scott E. 2004. Punctuated Equilibrium, Bureaucratization, and Budgetary Changes in Schools. *Policy Studies Journal*, 32(1), 25–39.

Robinson, Scott E., Caver, Floun'say, Meier, Kenneth J., and O'Toole Jr., Lawrence J. 2007. Explaining Policy Punctuations: Bureaucratization and Budget Change. *American Journal of Political Science*, 51(1), 140–150.

Rochefort, David A., and Cobb, Roger W. (eds). 1994. *The Politics of Problem Definition: Shaping the Policy Agenda*. Lawrence: University of Kansas Press.

Rose, Richard. 1989. Signals for Steering Government: A Symposium of the Wissenschaftszentrum Berlin. *Journal of Public Policy*, 9(3), 233–240.

Rosenbloom, David H. 2001. Whose Bureaucracy Is This Anyway? Congress' 1946 Answer. *PS: Political Science and Politics*, 34(4), 773–777.

Rourke, Francis E. (ed). 1965. *Bureaucratic Power in National Politics*. Second edn. Boston: Little, Brown.

Rowan, Miranda, and Lerner, Allan. 1995. Organizational Redundancy, and the Privatization of Public Services. *Public Administration Review*, 55(2), 193–200.

Rudavelige, Andrew. 2005. *The New Imperial Presidency: Renewing Presidential Power after Watergate*. Ann Arbor: University of Michigan Press.

Sabatier, Paul A. 1986. Top-Down and Bottom-Up Approaches to Implementation Research: A Critical Analysis and Suggested Synthesis. *Journal of Public Policy*, 6(1), 21–48.

Sabatier, Paul A., and Jenkins-Smith, Hank C. (eds). 1993. *Policy Change and Learning: An Advocacy Coalition Approach*. Boulder: Westview Press.

Sabatier, Paul A., and Jenkins-Smith, Hank C. (eds). 1999. *Theories of the Policy Process*. Boulder: Westview Press.

Salisbury, Robert H. 1969. An Exchange Theory of Interest Groups. *Midwest Journal of Political Science*, 13, 1–32.

Schattschneider, E. E. 1960. *The Semi-Sovereign People*. New York: Holt, Rhinehart, and Winston.

Schlosberg, David, Zavestoski, Stephen, and Shulman, Stuart W. 2008. Democracy and E-Rulemaking: Web-Based Technologies, Participation, and the Potential for Deliberation. *Journal of Information Technology & Politics*, 4(1), 37–55.

Schneider, Mark, Scholz, John T., Lubell, Mark, Mindruta, Denisa, and Edwardsen, Matthew. 2003. Building Consensual Institutions: Networks and the National Estuary Program. *American Journal of Political Science*, 47, 143–158.

Shannon, Claude E., and Weaver, Warren. 1949. *The Mathematical Theory of Communication*. Chicago: University of Illinois Press.

Shapiro, Stuart. 2007. The Role of Procedural Controls on OSHA's Ergonomics Rulemaking. *Public Administration Review*, July/August, 688–701.

Sheingate, Adam D. 2001. *The Rise of the Agricultural Welfare State:*. Princeton: Princeton University Press.

Shepsle, Kenneth A. 1978. *The Giant Jigsaw Puzzle*. Chicago: University of Chicago Press.

Shepsle, Kenneth A. 1979. Institutional Arrangements and Equilibrium in Multidimensional Voting Models. *American Journal of Political Science*, 57, 27–59.

Shepsle, Kenneth A. 1992. Congress Is a 'They' Not an 'It': Legislative Intent as an Oxymoron. *International Review of Law and Economics*, 12, 239–256.

Shepsle, Kenneth A., and Weingast, Barry R. 1987. The Institutional Foundations of Committee Power. *American Political Science Review*, 81, 86–108.

Shipan, Charles R. 2004. Regulatory Regimes, Agency Actions, and the Conditional Nature of Congressional Influence. *American Political Science Review*, 98(3), 467–480.

Shulman, Stuart W. 2009. The Case against Mass E-mails: Perverse Incentives and Low Quality Public Participation in U.S. Federal Rulemaking. *Policy & Internet*, 1(1), 23–53.

Simon, Herbert A. 1947. *Administrative Behavior: A Study of Decision-Making Processes in Administrative Organizations.* New York: Free Press.

Simon, Herbert A. 1971. Designing Organizations for an Information-Rich World. In *Computers, Communication, and the Public Interest,* ed. Martin Greenberger. Baltimore: Johns Hopkins University Press.

Simon, Herbert A. 1979. *Models of Thought.* New Haven: Yale University Press.

Simon, Herbert. 1996. *The Sciences of the Artificial.* Third edn. Cambridge, MA: MIT Press.

Soroka, Stuart N., and Wlezien, Christopher. 2009. *Degrees of Democracy: Politics, Public Opinion, and Policy.* New York: Cambridge University Press.

Spence, David B. 1997a. Administrative Law and Agency Policy-Making: Rethinking the Positive Theory of Political Control. *Yale Journal of Regulation,* 14(2), 407–450.

Spence, David B. 1997b. Agency Policy Making and Political Control: Modeling away the Delegation Problem. *Journal of Public Administration Research and Theory,* 7(2), 199–219.

Stigler, George. 1961. The Economics of Information. *Journal of Political Economy,* 69(3), 213–225.

Stone, Deborah A. 1989. Causal Stories and the Formation of Policy Agendas. *Political Science Quarterly,* 102(4), 281–300.

Sulkin, Tracy. 2005. *Issue Politics in Congress.* New York: Cambridge University Press.

Sulkin, Tracy. 2011. *The Legislative Legacy of Congressional Campaigns.* New York: Cambridge University Press.

Theriault, Sean M. 2008. *Party Polarization in Congress.* New York: Cambridge University Press.

Ting, Michael M. 2003. A Strategic Theory of Bureaucratic Redundancy. *American Journal of Political Science,* 47(2), 274–292.

Wallach, Philip, and Abdun-Nabi, Alex. 2014. *The EPA's Carbon Plan Asks the Least from States That Pollute the Most. Washington Post,* July 16.

West, William F. 2005a. Administrative Rulemaking: An Old and Emerging Literature. *Public Administration Review,* 65(6), 655–668.

West, William F. 2005b. Neutral Competence and Political Responsiveness: An Uneasy Relationship. *Policy Studies Journal,* 33(2), 147–160.

West, William F., and Durant, Robert F. 2000. Merit, Management, and Neutral Competence: Lessons from the U.S. Merit Systems Protection Board, FY 1988–FY 1997. *Public Administration Review,* 60(2), 111–122.

Whitford, Andrew B. 2005. The Pursuit of Political Control by Multiple Prinicpals. *Journal of Politics,* 67(1), 29–49.

Whitford, A. B. 2007. Designing Markets: Why Competitive Bidding and Auctions in Government Often Fail to Deliver. *Policy Studies Journal,* 35(1), 61–85.

Whitford, Andrew B., and Yates, Jeff. 2009. *Presidential Rhetoric and the Public Agenda: Constructing the War on Drugs.* Baltimore: Johns Hopkins University Press.

Wildavsky, Aaron B. 1964. *The Politics of the Budgetary Process.* Boston: Little, Brown.

Williams, Walter. 1998. *Honest Numbers and Democracy: Policy Analysis in the White House, Congress, and the Federal Agencies.* Washington, DC: Georgetown University Press.

Wilson, James Q. 1989. *Bureaucracy: What Government Agencies Do and Why They Do It.* New York: Basic Books.

Wilson, Woodrow. 1887. The Study of Administration. *Political Science Quarterly*, 2(2), 481–506.

Wood, B. Dan. 1988. Principals, Bureaucrats, and Responsiveness in Clean Air Enforcements. *American Political Science Review*, 82(1), 213–234.

Wood, B. Dan, and Waterman, Richard W. 1994. *Bureaucratic Dynamics: The Role of Bureaucracy in a Democracy*. Boulder: Westview Press.

Workman, Samuel. 2014. Congressional Bureaucracy and the Administrative Presidency: Policy Analysis as a Product of Institutional Conflict. Paper presented at the Annual Meeting of the Western Political Science Association, Seattle, April 17–19.

Workman, Samuel, Jones, Bryan D., and Jochim, Ashley E. 2009. Information Processing and Policy Dynamics. *Policy Studies Journal*, 37(1), 75–92.

Workman, Samuel, and Shafran, JoBeth S. 2015. Communications Frameworks and the Supply of Information in Policy Subsystems. In *Policy Paradigms in Theory and Practice: Discources, Ideas and Anomalies in Public Policy*, eds. Michael Howlett and John Hogan. Palgrave Press.

A Worsening Food Crisis; The U.S. and its Allies Need to Act. 2008. *Washington Post*, April 20, B06.

Worsham, Jeffrey. 1997. *Other People's Money*. Boulder: Westview Press.

Worsham, Jeffrey. 1998. Wavering Equilibriums: Subsystem Dynamics and Agenda Control. *American Politics Quarterly*, 26(4), 485–512.

Yackee, Susan Webb. 2005. Sweet-Talking the Fourth Branch: The Influence of Interest Group Comments on Federal Agency Rulemaking. *Journal of Public Administration Research and Theory*, 16, 103–124.

Yackee, Susan Webb. 2006. Assessing Inter-Institutional Attention to and Influence on Government Regulations. *British Journal of Political Science*, 36, 723–744.

Yackee, Susan Webb. 2012. The Politics of Ex Parte Lobbying: Pre-Proposal Agenda Building and Blocking during Agency Rulemaking. *Journal of Public Administration Research and Theory*, 22, 373–393.

Zavestoski, Stephen, Shulman, Stuart W., and Schlosberg, David. 2006. Demoncracy and the Environment on the Internet: Electronic Citizen Participation in Regulatory Rulemaking. *Science, Technology, and Human Values*, 31(4), 383–408.

Author Index

Subject Index

CPSIA information can be obtained at www.ICGtesting.com
Printed in the USA
LVOW12*0133160415

434614LV00004B/4/P